LA FAYETTE

Portrait of the Marquis de La Fayette

From the painting by Samuel Breese Morse, N. A. Painted for the City in 1824

LA FAYETTE

By

HENRY DWIGHT SEDGWICK

Author of Cortés the Conqueror

August 31, 1785

*T*HE *noble, conspicuous and disinterested part
which this nobleman has acted on the American
theatre, deserves all the gratitude this country can
render him, and all the eulogy which the pen of a
faithful historian can bestow.* George Washington

The CHAUTAUQUA PRESS

Chautauqua   New York

1928

Printed in the United States of America

To

R. M. S and **F. M. S**

πᾶσι δ'ανθρώποις ἄρ' ἦν
ψυχὴ τέκν'

—EURIPIDES

PREFACE

La Fayette ran a career that is without parallel in the history of our Western World. His life divides itself into episodes. First, that of his adventurous youth in America; second, during the French Revolution, when for a time—I am but quoting what others have said—he was master of the fate of France; and, third, when, in the revolution of 1830, after a long eclipse, a second time he held that fate in his hands. And, besides this, fourscore years later his spirit rose from the grave and did more than any other Frenchman, living or dead, to bring America into the struggle that determined his country's fate.

And yet Nature had not given him ten talents; she bestowed upon him zeal, courage, energy, honesty, frankness, simplicity, perseverence, a flaming enthusiasm for what he deemed high causes, a disposition so graced with charm that his wife, his family, his friends adored him, and—a rare quality in ambitious men—a power of admiration, and what is perhaps rarer still, a hero to admire worthy of that admiration.

I have tried, as far as I could, to let him and his contemporaries speak for themselves, as I think that in this way La Fayette will appear what he really was, not a great man, but a great-hearted gentleman, a worthy countryman of Jeanne d'Arc.

I have endeavored to portray his character in its larger outlines, and therefore have passed lightly over long periods of his life. In an appendix I refer to my authorities. Perhaps an unsympathetic reader may protest that I am not impartial. To this I reply that no man is impartial; we are all swayed by a host of prejudices, by nationality, by natural tastes, by education, by the peculiar circumstances of our interests. Nevertheless I did not start upon the book with any conscious partiality. I believe the duty of a biographer to be that of a juror: he should listen without bias to all the evidence, and make up his mind solely according to that evidence. This duty I have striven to perform.

H. D. S.

CONTENTS

CHAPTER		PAGE
I	Boyhood	1
II	Off to America	13
III	From Charleston to Brandywine	29
IV	A Full Major-General	45
V	The Irruption into Canada	57
VI	Barren Hill and Monmouth	68
VII	The Expedition against Newport	81
VIII	Autumn, 1778	93
IX	Home and Return, 1779-1780	105
X	The Virginia Campaign	116
XI	Yorktown	126
XII	Philanthropy	135
XIII	The Assembly of Notables	147
XIV	The States-General	164
XV	La Fayette in Power	176
XVI	October 5-6, 1789	187
XVII	Duc d'Orléans, Mounier, Bouillé	201
XVIII	La Fayette and Mirabeau	209
XIX	The Via Media, 1789-1790	220
XX	Between Scylla and Charybdis	228
XXI	The Fete of Federation and the Mutiny at Nancy	238
XXII	June 20 and July 17, 1791	250
XXIII	Back in Chavaniac	264
XXIV	On the Belgian Frontier	274
XXV	La Fayette Defies the Jacobins	285
XXVI	Flight	296
XXVII	Arrest	310
XXVIII	Imprisonment	319
XXIX	From the Guillotine to Olmutz	329

CONTENTS—*Continued*

CHAPTER		PAGE
XXX	RELEASE	343
XXXI	EXILE	356
XXXII	UNCERTAINTY	363
XXXIII	DEATH OF MADAME DE LA FAYETTE	371
XXXIV	THE RESTORATION	380
XXXV	VISIT TO AMERICA	390
XXXVI	THE REVOLUTION OF 1830	403
XXXVII	EPILOGUE	411
	AUTHORITIES	421
	INDEX	427

LIST OF ILLUSTRATIONS

The Marquis de La Fayette . . . . . . *Frontispiece*

Facing page

La Fayette as a child 16
Plan of the Battle of Brandywine 17
Madame de La Fayette with her son 58
Wounding of La Fayette at the battle of Brandywine . 59
La Fayette about twenty years old 98
Madame de La Fayette, La Fayette's wife 99
The Surrender of Lord Cornwallis' Army 132
Reunion of the generals of the American and French
    armies after the capitulation of Yorktown 133
Château Chavaniac 168
Danton 169
The Marquis de La Fayette, Commanding General of the
    National Guard 212
Mirabeau 213
Marat dying 254
Robespierre 255
Caricature of the Constitution of France 292
Caricature of the minister, solemn director of the per-
    formance 293
La Fayette a short time before his death 340
Napoleon crossing the Alps 341
La Grange 382
Bust of La Fayette at Richmond, Virginia 383

LA FAYETTE

LA FAYETTE

CHAPTER I

BOYHOOD

THE ancient province of Auvergne, now divided into departments, lies at the center of southernFrance. It takes its name from the tribe of the Averni, famous in Cæsar's *De Bello Gallico*, because their leader, Vercingetorix, stirred up the Gallic tribes roundabout to make a last stand against the conquering Romans. It is for the most part a mountainous land, with odd conical hills scattered about, but there is also a long rich plain, through which the River Allier flows on its northward way to join the upper waters of the Loire. Near the southern extremity of this plain, on the edge of the Monts du Velay, is situated the hamlet of Chavaniac. The houses of this hamlet are huddled together along a little winding street that leads to the dignified parish church in which, the day after his birth, the subject of this biography was baptized and given the names Marie-Joseph-Paul-Yves-Roch-Gilbert du Motier. A few hundred yards to the west of the hamlet, the Château de Chavaniac, once a *maison forte* built, they say, in the fourteenth century, stands out on the slope that commands the valley. Its long flat front, two stories high, with circular towers on either

1

end, faces northward, while at the back, connected by intermediate buildings, is the great keep. From the château the upland sinks gently to the plain, which stretches, soft and smooth, helping create a sort of Virgilian landscape, toward the violet rim of mountains on the northern horizon. In the château, (according to an unjustified tradition, in a chamber of the western turret) La Fayette was born on the sixth day of September, 1757.

His family was of the old noblesse, with a long record of patriotic service in war. In the thirteenth century a seigneur de La Fayette was a crusader; in the fourteenth, another seigneur de La Fayette was killed on the disastrous field of Poitiers; in the fifteenth a third was created Marshal of France, and he also possesses a prouder title, "companion in arms to Joan of Arc."

But as to La Fayette's genealogy and boyhood, I had best quote what he says in an autobiographical letter, although written hastily and carelessly:

"You ask me, dear Lady, some details about my family, my birthplace, and of my first years. Between you and me, a genealogy ought to be short. I can't tell you whether I am a Gaul or a Frank; I rather think a Gaul because very few Franks established themselves in the mountains of Auvergne. I like Vercingetorix defending our mountains better than Clovis and his successors. My family used to possess Auvergnat charters and title deeds about as old as the custom of using them; they were all burned, properly enough, and the counter-revolution will not make them rise again from their ashes. I have a recollection that the elder branch of my family was extinguished in that of

La Tremoille. . . . The younger branch never left the province, except to make war; it never figured at court. It was reckoned that so great a proportion of its men were killed, from father to son, on the field of battle, that it became a sort of proverb in our province. Nevertheless, my grandfather had received such a number of wounds that he retired before he was killed. He lived on an estate between the towns of Brioude and le Puy, where one of the châteaux, perched on a mountain, had been built in 1400 by the Maréchal de La Fayette. He married his neighbor Mlle. de Chavaniac, who had inherited the place where I was born; she was only twelve years old. They had a dozen children. My oldest uncle . . . one of the handsomest and most attractive young men, they say, ever seen . . . was at eighteen a captain of dragoons in the Italian wars. . . . He was killed. . . . My father went to Paris. There he married Mlle. de la Rivière, who at that time had only a *dot* proportioned to my father's fortune, of about a thousand livres of income. But as my mother's two brothers died one after the other, I found myself heir to the whole La Rivière fortune. My father, whom I never knew for I was only two years old when he died, was beloved and esteemed by everybody who knew him. It would seem that his personality was very distinguished and his disposition most kindly. He was killed at Minden [1759], colonel in the Grenadiers of France. . . . The Prince of Chimay, an intimate friend of my father, was killed at the head of the first battalion. My father, who was next in rank, took his place and was carried off by a cannon ball fired from an English battery. General Phillips was there then as an artillery officer. By an odd chance, twenty-two years later, we were firing two pieces of cannon at the English quarters at Petersburg, on the Appomattox in Virginia, and a ball passed through the house where General Phillips lay ill. He died immediately.

"My family was composed of my grandmother, a woman of the highest deserts, respected throughout the province; people came from twenty leagues about to consult her on anything that concerned their families. Her good head, her lofty soul, and her influence in the province were very remarkable. She had two daughters, of whom one, who had married M. de Chavaniac of the neighboring province (le Gevaudan), came to live altogether with my mother after her husband's death; it was she that lived to a great age. I lost her a few years after my return to France. Up to her death she enjoyed great consideration. The other daughter could not bring herself to leave her family, and so did not marry. She bore the name of Mlle. Dumottier. It was she that took charge of my earliest education. She was a woman of extraordinary merit. My aunt de Chavaniac had a daughter older than I by a year. Never did brother and sister love one another more dearly than we did. She married sometime after I did and died in childbed while I was in America. That was one of the greatest sorrows of my life.

"My mother was a woman of quick mind. She lived in Paris, at her father's house, the Marquis de la Rivière, next door to her grandfather of the same name. Her grandmother de la Rivière, one of the handsomest women of her time, was no longer alive. Although my mother loved me dearly, the thought of taking me away from my grandmother La Fayette never entered her head, so greatly was her mother-in-law venerated. She used to come and stay with us for several months, and then go back to her father's. I was brought up in that fashion until I was eleven years old.

"When I was five, I was given a tutor, an abbé, a very intelligent man. At seven it was necessary to change for another tutor, an excellent person. But I believe that the real education lies in the family sentiment that surrounds the child, and never was a boy better off in this respect than I. It was natural that in a family that always dwelt on its memories and losses, and adored my father's memory, I should hear a great deal of war and glory. That was no doubt the reason why, when I was eight, I had so keen a desire to meet a hyena that had escaped into the mountains. I don't think that I should have been afraid of it; I won't be sure, but I was furious that, by mistake, they gave my name to a fellow who, they said, did not succeed in killing the beast because he was afraid of it. I wrote to the newspaper a letter that my relatives had the good sense not to send.

"When I was eleven, my mother at last got permission to take me to Paris. It was a great sorrow to leave my grandmother, my two aunts, and my cousin whom I adored. I had no feeling whatever of curiosity to see the capital. I remember being astonished on my way there because everybody did not take their hats off to me, as they used to do at Chavaniac to the young lord of the village.

"When I got to Paris I was presented to my two grandfathers. The first, who had a charming face and had just given up the command of the second company of Musketeers, was a man of the world. He died during my first campaigns in America. The other, the

Marquis de la Rivière, was an old Breton gentleman, well educated, wholly absorbed in the affairs of his province. He had been involved in the conspiracy of the Breton noblesse against the Regent, and, to save his head, had been obliged to fly to Spain. Some untoward accidents got him into trouble; he was even arrested by mistake for another man. These circumstances had prevented him from going into the army. He used to spend a large part of the year in his old château of Kéroflois. He was very rich; and people thought him miserly, as he lived in great parsimony, and (as they supposed) hardly giving away anything; but after his death it was discovered that he had bestowed very considerable alms.

"When I was thirteen, I lost my mother. Her father, who under a cold exterior had a tender heart, died of grief a few weeks later. I had expected to have, like my father, twenty-five thousand livres income, but found myself, at sixteen, with one hundred and twenty thousand. My tutor was more alive to this inheritance than I, for I had no thought but of sorrow for my mother and had never felt any want o money.

"On my arrival, I was put at school in the collège du Plessis. My grandfather would not believe that I could enter in the fourth form, which however did not exact great ability. At the college I learned a good deal of Latin; but I was taught no Greek for which I am sorry. I stayed there four years. My literary courses were pretty good. I took 'college prizes,' but not 'university prizes,' because there the boys ran into competition with young men who had repeated their classes two or three times. Nevertheless the reason I lost one prize was because it is impossible for me to copy exactly what I have written. I had received compliments from everybody on my certain triumph, and I was greatly taken aback not even to get a 'mention.' They had counted as a fault each word of a sentence omitted in my Latin translation.

"I was crazy to wear a uniform. At thirteen I was entered in the company of Musketeers, that my grandfather had commanded. I had the honor to take part in reviews before the King, and to ride to Versailles in full uniform to hear him, as he went by, tell me that he had no orders to give, and to come back and report this information to the commandant of Musketeers, the same that he received three hundred and sixty-five times a year. I thought all that delightful, all the more because in order to take part in a review, it was necessary to attend drill with my companions.

"I can say that I was much liked at college. I had acquired, also, a certain ascendency over my companions, and as soon as I appeared at court, I was surrounded by young friends, most of them bigger than I, who were glad to give themselves the airs of disciples; they would have defended me to desperation, if necessary. Once I wanted to raise a riot to prevent one of my companions from being unjustly punished, but I was not as well supported as I had hoped. As for me, I had made up my mind that I did not deserve any punishment, and none was meted out, but I think that I should have defended myself well with my sword, for according to the admirable customs of that time, boys when they went out to dinner wore swords, which went very well with their embroidered coats and their hair all garnished with powder and pomade.

"Once I was bidden write a composition on a perfect horse, who became obedient at the mere sight of his rider's whip; I described a perfect horse as throwing his master off at the sight of the whip. My literature teacher, M. Binet, a sensible man, smiled instead of getting angry. He has since reminded me of the anecdote. Twice I went to pass my vacation in Auvergne. I was there again when I had attained my fourteenth year, and we learned there that my grandfather had arranged my marriage with Mlle. de Noailles, the second daughter of the Duc d'Ayen, then twelve years old. I went to live at the Luxembourg where my grandfather lived, and I was taken into the family of his second son-in-law M. de Luzignem, who had lost his wife. But she was soon replaced, so far as I was concerned, by his second wife, toward whom I have kept a most tender and affectionate gratitude. My tutor stayed with me."

The Noailles family, to which the Duc d'Ayen belonged, was a very eminent family in the aristocratic world, and enjoyed prodigal proofs of royal favor, drawing two million francs, it is said, from the King's treasury. The Duke himself was an officer in the King's body-guard, a self-willed, cultivated, scholarly man, fond of gay society and with amiable, attractive traits. It had been decided that his eldest daughter, Louise, should marry her cousin, the Vicomte de Noailles, and that Adrienne, the second daughter, should marry La Fayette. The father approved the match heartily. But Madame la Duchesse d'Ayen, in spite of her place in the world of fashion, was not worldly-minded. She was a most devout Christian, and had brought up her little daughters on the *Catechism of the Council of Trent,* the *Exposition of Christian Doctrine* and the *Cathechism of Montpellier* which they learned by heart. Her habit was to take her daughters to her room after dinner, and there with her snuff-box, her knitting needles and her books, talk to them of poetry and things religious. All the daughters, certainly Adrienne, always bore the clear-cut impression of this strict piety. The mother did not feel sure that it would be prudent to give her tender, serious, passionate, little girl to a young man who was still a mere boy, with no near relations to guide him, and she feared his large fortune of which he already had control. These considerations outweighed the good opinions of him that she heard on every side, and she refused to consent. Her husband was very angry, and let the household know it. After a few months the Duchess gave way, and Adrienne, who was not yet thirteen, although she did not know the cause of the quarrel, always remembered her poignant joy at beholding the reconciliation between her father and mother. The Duchess, however, had exacted conditions: the marriage should be postponed for a year and a half, and then the young couple should live with them in the Hôtel de Noailles in Paris, and in the meantime La Fayette should continue his education.

The elder sister was married on May 12, 1773, and Adrienne was then told for the first time that she was to marry young La Fayette. He was then a tall, gawky boy with red hair, long nose and retreating forehead, reserved, shy, a bad dancer and a poor rider, but brave and generous. Even then he was beset by a burning ambition to distinguish himself, to obtain what the French call *gloire,* which is best translated into English, perhaps, by the word *honor,* but *gloire* is more richly hued, more fancifully conceived, and more amorously pursued. In his *Mémoires* he says that his earliest recollection was of an enthusiasm *pour les anecdotes glorieuses,* and of a purpose to go all over the world in pursuit of fame.

It was at or about this time that he attended the Academy of Versailles, where young noblemen prepared themselves to become officers. There he made familiar acquaintance with the Dauphin's younger brother, the Comte d'Artois, just his age, who was a great friend and playmate of the Dauphin's young wife, Marie Antoinette. They practised gymnastic exercises, and learned to ride together. Long afterward the royal prince spoke of La Fayette as clumsy and awkward, but agreeable, amiable and amusing. According to other testimony, as he grew from boyhood into a young man, his cold and reticent manners made him appear timid and embarrassed, but underneath this exterior his intimates could discern an active mind, a resolute character and a passionate spirit.

La Fayette and Adrienne were married on the eleventh day of April, 1774, in the chapel of the Hôtel de Noailles. The hôtel stood in rue Saint-Honoré, opposite the Tuileries, about where the rue d'Alger now runs into the rue de Rivoli. John Adams, who went there later, says that the house, gardens, promenades, pictures and furniture were very magnificent. Among those present at the wedding who come into his later history, were the Marquis de Bouillé, then a brigadier-general, the Duc de Mouchy,—let me give him his full title, Philippe de Noailles, Maréchal, Duc de Mouchy, Grand d' Espagne de la première classe, Chevalier des ordres du Roi et de la Toison d'or, Grand croix de l'ordre de Malte, Lieutenant-Général de Guienne— and the Comte de Tessé. The young couple at once took up their residence with her parents. Within a month Louis XV died, and his grandson, the Dauphin, became Louis XVI. The Court turned over a new leaf, Madame du Barry was sent away, and the gay, ignorant, spoiled, laughter-loving, unintellectual Marie Antoinette romped with a merry company at the Petit Trianon and in the Gardens of Versailles. La Fayette, thanks to the Court influence of his father-in-law, was given a company in the regiment of the Noailles dragoons—it being the custom in those days for a great family to have a proprietary right in a regiment, as the Dillons had, for instance—but on the condition that he should not take command until he was eighteen. Such a military system helps one to understand why the French armies under the Republic and under the Empire, officered according to merit, triumphed over the armies of Europe that were still officered by young aristocrats. The Noailles dragoons were stationed at Metz, where La Fayette joined them; but he was far from staying there continuously. While living in Paris, the young couple—I presume in obedience to the wishes of the Duc d'Ayen, for neither La Fayette nor his wife, whose interests were centered in her husband, her family and her religion, cared much for social pleasures—frequented the Court at Versailles, in company with other young people of the aristocracy, the Ségurs, the Coignys, the Dillons, the Guéménés and such like. The Duchesse d'Ayen, probably in part out of deference to her husband's wishes, and also perhaps with an eye to La Fayette's future, for she had already become very fond of him, extended the hospitalities of the Hôtel de Noailles to his friends and to those of her other son-in-law, her elder daughter's husband, the Vicomte de Noailles, who was a charming person with many graces and shone in a drawing-room.

The only anecdote of those days, apart from vague stories of liberal opinions freely expressed at a tavern, *l' Épée de bois,* is that La Fayette tried to emulate the social successes of his brother-in-law, who among other valued qualities possessed a strong head and could drink as hard as an Englishman. On one occasion, having done his best, which was but mediocre, at the bottle, he was carried off and put into his carriage: "Tell Noailles," he was clear enough to say, "tell Noailles, how jolly well I have drunk."

It seems that at about this time he was rude to the Comte de Provence, the King's next brother, afterward Louis XVIII. The distinguished old Maréchal de Noailles, his wife's grandfather, wished to obtain a place for him in the Comte's household; but La Fayette, having no inclination to any such position, said something blunt on purpose that caused the Prince to refuse the favor. For this reason, and also because he was aware that his taciturnity and awkward manners often created an unfavorable impression, he was glad to rejoin his regiment at Metz, which he did in the summer of 1775, a month or two before his eighteenth birthday. It was then that an incident occurred that was destined to be of dominating consequence in his life.

CHAPTER II

Both from reading and from conversation, La Fayette must have been acquainted with the doctrines current in Paris concerning the dilapidation of old things and the need of new, acquainted with the writings of Voltaire, Rousseau, Diderot and their fellows, who questioned, criticized and undermined the social, political and ecclesiastical fabric built by past centuries, and so he must have been familiar with the theories that men, unhampered by old decrepitude, by antique customs and beliefs, would show themselves innocent, virtuous and capable, and build up a new society in which all men should be happy. Something of this must have inspired his ambition with the hope that he, too, might become a worker for this golden age. Another motive was also at work. French officers did not like England and the English. For hundreds of years, from generation to generation, England had been a traditional enemy, and the memory of the Seven Years' War (1756-1763) was still fresh and galling. Before that war France and England had been rivals for dominion round the world. France had held Canada and a promising place in the Antilles and in India. But in that ill-conducted, mismanaged war, in which La Fayette's father had lost his life, the French armies had been beaten on land, and the French

13

navies had been beaten on sea. Great Britain had become a mighty empire, and France had been reduced
to a rank of but little more account than Spain.

La Fayette, then, full of a vague and passionate
animosity against *Albion perfide,* and of romantic enthusiasm for a regenerated world, in which nature
should supplant fashion, justice prevail, and men, free
and equal, walk erect like Plutarch's heroes in simple
dignity, was as I have said, with his regiment at Metz,
awaiting the right to command his company that
should fall due on the sixth of September. It chanced
that in the beginning of August the Duke of Gloucester,
brother to George III and at that time out of royal
favor because of his marriage with the natural daughter of Horace Walpole's brother, and therefore referred to in Walpole's letters as "my sweet nephew,"
was traveling on the continent incognito and came
to Metz. The Comte de Broglie, Governor of the
city, gave a banquet in his honor and invited the officers, including La Fayette, to meet his Royal Highness. The Duke, owing to his quarrel with his brother,
had strong sympathies with the American rebels. He
talked of the latest news he had. Since the battle of
Lexington the colonists had cast out the royal gover-
nors, Ethan Allen had captured Fort Ticonderoga,
Congress had met in Philadelphia, a continental army
had been formed, Schuyler, Charles Lee, Putnam and
Ward, had been named major-generals, troops were
marching from the neighboring colonies into Massachusetts to drive the British from Boston, and Congress had appointed a colonel of Virginian troops,
George Washington, celebrated for bravery and skill
in the wars against the French and Indians, commander-in-chief. All this was new to La Fayette; he

became so deeply interested that, though perhaps the youngest present, he ventured to ask questions. Here was a people fighting for their liberty; in the Parisian salons they talked of liberty, but there, across the Atlantic, men were fighting for it, confederated colonists confronted the strongest power in Europe. The idea went to his head, and as he told Jared Sparks long years afterwards, before he had left the table his imagination had leaped to the thought that he would go to America, and offer his services to the Americans. Whenever in later years he thought of this struggle his sympathies flashed and flared up again: "Never had so fair a cause come to the attention of mankind." Walpole's "sweet nephew" was probably pleased to have so rapt a listener.

La Fayette, full of high enthusiasm, and, as he says, "given over from youth to aspiration for liberty," could see that the freedom of America meant the safety of France, but from his experience of the Court of Versailles he thought himself the first man awake to the interest that France should take in the rebellion of the Thirteen Colonies, and had no notion that there were older heads who perceived this still more clearly than he. He did not suspect that the Comte de Vergennes, the Minister of Foreign Affairs, was making secret arrangements to send a spy, Monsieur Bonvouloir, to America, who should learn all he could concerning the state of popular feeling there and what was going on; and also that the same minister, on the very day before the banquet given to the Duke of Gloucester, had sent instructions to the French Ambassador at Madrid to lay before the Spanish Government plans for joint action against England. In fact, the Minister of Foreign Affairs had been considering with great care for some time what France had better do to bring about the severance of England's colonies from the mother country, and had made up his mind that war was necessary; at the same time he was blandly protesting to the English Government that his Majesty, Louis XVI, would never do so wrong a thing as to encourage the American rebels. There was no doubt as to French interests. La Fayette, looking back in later years, stated them very clearly: "The destiny of France was in the balance as well as that of England . . . if England could retain those Thirteen Colonies in her empire, there would be an end to our West Indies, to our possessions in Africa and Asia, to our maritime commerce, and consequently to our navy, in short to our political existence."

In complete ignorance of all this, La Fayette went back to Paris to make further inquiries and consider what he should do. The first thing he did was to swear his intimate friends, the Comte de Ségur and the Vicomte de Noailles, to secrecy, then he confided to them his purpose and asked them to join him. They jumped at the idea, but as they had no money of their own they could do nothing definite until they should be assured of places and pay in the American army, whereas La Fayette had now an income of one hundred forty thousand livres and, therefore, was quite independent of pecuniary assistance.

But there were other obstacles, however, to his going. His girl wife was to have a baby in December, and his father-in-law, with his worldly ambition for his advancement at the French Court, would scarcely wish him to start off on a wild goose chase for liberty three thousand miles away; so La Fayette was careful to give them no inkling of his plans. Instead, he con-

La Fayette as a child

From *France and New England*. Photograph by Giraudon, **Paris**

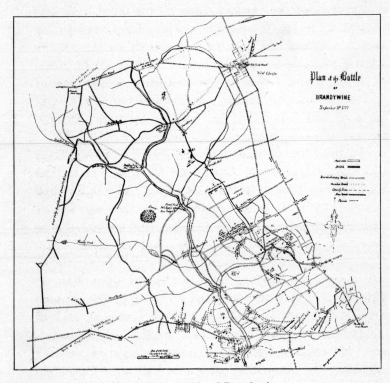

Plan of the Battle of Brandywine

sulted the Comte de Broglie, who expressed himself very clearly: The plan was chimerical, full of hazards of all sorts, barren of any likelihood of success, and had better be dropped forthwith. La Fayette reiterated that he had made up his mind to go and begged the Comte to keep his secret. The Comte promised but added: "I saw your uncle die in the Italian wars, I was present at your father's death at the battle of Minden, and I will not be accessory to the ruin of the one remaining branch of the family," and he put forth all his powers of persuasion to divert the enthusiastic young man from his purpose, but in vain.

An important consequence followed, however, from this disclosure to the Comte de Broglie. Baron de Kalb was by birth a German peasant. As a lad he had enlisted in a German regiment in the service of France; he had risen to be a major, had served during the Seven Years' War under the Comte de Broglie and attained the rank of lieutenant-colonel. His title of baron appears to have been conferred upon him by himself, in order to facilitate his rise in the French army. As early as 1769 the Duc de Choiseul, at that time prime minister, and already on the alert to ascertain to what extent the British stamp taxes had alienated the American colonists, had sent Baron de Kalb on the very same errand that Vergennes had recently sent Monsieur Bonvouloir.

Baron de Kalb had stayed in America a year or two, and after his return had gone to Metz, to his old commander the Comte de Broglie, but now that war had broken out in America he proposed to go back there and seek his fortune. He seems to have awakened in the Comte de Broglie bright dreams of glory and gain in America, and to have encouraged him in the notion that a man of his position and experience in war would be of priceless service to the undisciplined levies of farmers—"How can he get wisdom that holdeth the plough; that driveth oxen; and is occupied in their labours; whose talk is of bullocks?"—of huntsmen, village lawyers and men of mechanical occupations, who were rushing incontinently into war with a great military monarchy. The Comte was ready to be their general-in-chief, provided that they would put him in charge of foreign relations, pay him a large salary, in short grant to him, as Holland had done to the Princes of Orange, a sort of stadtholdership. Baron de Kalb, while pushing his own career as a soldier of fortune, was to see if any door stood open to such readiness for service. This suggestion was not as preposterous as it looks to us, who know the abilities of the American leaders as well as the upshot of the revolution, for the Comte de Broglie would probably have taken with him a number of trained officers, and also might have secured the French alliance. Nothing of all this, of course, was told to La Fayette, but Broglie gave him an introduction to Baron de Kalb.

It was now the summer of 1776. The situation in America was still more stimulating, for the colonies had declared themselves free and independent, and an official agent, Silas Deane, had come to Paris to procure arms and ammunition, enlist volunteers, and urge the French Government to recognize the young nation. La Fayette's first step was to obtain semi-retirement from the army (June eleventh), so that he should be free to leave the country without becoming a deserter. Then he and Baron de Kalb went to see Silas Deane. The whole situation was hedged about with difficulties. Mr. Deane, beset by all sorts of soldiers of fortune and adventurers, swashbucklers, scamps, debtors, ne'er-do-weels, who wished for positions in the American army, was confronted with the task, to which he was not wholly adequate, of selecting those that would prove useful, without giving offense to those rejected or causing British spies to think that the French Government had knowledge of what he was doing. The Comte de Vergennes for his part, knowing very well what was going on, and eager to give and permit whatever help could escape detection or plausibly be denied, was confronted by an indignant British Ambassador and worse still by an empty treasury, a vast debt, and an ever increasing difficulty of raising money by taxation or by borrowing. The French monarchy, as events were to prove, had to choose between the alternatives of humble obeisance to the British Empire or bankruptcy and revolution at home. Vergennes practised such duplicity as was possible; at the front door he reiterated his protestations of good faith to the British Ambassador, while at the back door he encouraged Beaumarchais, the brilliant author of the *Barbier de Séville*, to carry on a traffic in arms and ammunition with the American insurgents, and so forth.

Such was the juncture when La Fayette and Baron de Kalb knocked on Mr. Deane's door. La Fayette says: "When I presented to Mr. Deane a face hardly nineteen years old, I said more concerning my zeal than concerning my experience, and made the most of the little stir that my departure would cause." Mr. Deane was persuaded, and on November 6, 1776, La Fayette, the Comte de Ségur and the Vicomte de Noailles were all accepted for positions in the American army. Baron de Kalb, having just obtained by influence of the Comte de Broglie a leave of absence for two years, also received the promise of a commission; he and La Fayette were to be major-generals. The Comte de Ségur and the Vicomte de Noailles, as I have said, were not their own masters, and when their project came to the ears of their families they were forbidden to go. Noailles, hoping to override his family, applied to the War Office for leave to serve as a French officer in the American army; the Prime Minister, Monsieur de Maurepas replied, untruthfully, that he was not aware of French officers entering into the service of the English colonies, that such a step would be an act of hostility to a friendly nation and could not be allowed. In spite of this La Fayette's secret was kept, as he says, by a miracle from family, friends, the ministry, French spies and English spies, and on December seventh he signed an agreement to enter the service of the United States and depart whenever Mr. Deane should say, reserving for himself the right to return to France if his family or his King should recall him.

Then came the question how to get to America. He and Baron de Kalb went together to the Comte de Broglie. But by this time the news from America was very bad: Washington had been defeated, the British were in possession of New York City, and advancing at their pleasure in New Jersey, while an invasion of Canada had been disastrous. Matters looked so black that the American envoys (for Doctor Franklin and Arthur Lee having arrived, there were now three) felt it their duty to discourage La Fayette from going; they said that their credit was exhausted and that they could not possibly charter a ship. La Fayette went to

Deane, thanked him and said: "So far, Sir, you have only seen my zeal, perhaps that zeal may now become of use. I am going to buy a ship to carry your officers. We must put on a brave face. I like to share your fortunes in the hour of danger." Through an officer from Haiti, the brother of the Comte de Broglie's secretary, who had come to purchase uniforms at Bordeaux for his regiment, La Fayette bought a ship, the *Victoire,* Captain le Boursier, upon the condition that she was to be delivered at Bordeaux by the middle of March.

In the meantime until the ship should be ready, in order to lull suspicion to sleep, La Fayette accompanied a friend to London to visit his uncle, the Marquis de Noailles, who was then ambassador to the Court of Saint James. He enjoyed himself, for the English policy was to pretend that the English and French Courts were on excellent terms, and to encourage hospitality to young French gentlemen of quality. He was presented to the King, met a number of distinguished people, and accepted various invitations; nevertheless, as he always remembered with satisfaction, scruples of propriety prevented him from visiting the seaports and observing the embarkations of troops for America. From London he wrote a letter to his father-in-law, the Duc d'Ayen, telling of his plan, but the letter was to be held back and not delivered until he should be safely on board his ship at Bordeaux.

"London, March 9, 1777
"Dear Papa:
"You will be amazed at what I am going to tell you, and not to consult you has cost me more than I can

say. My respect, my fondness for you, my trust in you will warrant that. But I had pledged my word, and you would lose your esteem for me, if I were not to keep it.

"I have found the rarest chance to distinguish myself and to learn my profession. I am a general officer in the army of the United States of America. My zeal for their cause and my frankness have won their confidence. On my side I have done what I could for them, and some day their interests will be dearer to me than my own. So, dear Papa, for the present I am in London waiting news of my friends. As soon as I shall receive it, I shall leave here, and without stopping in Paris I shall go aboard a ship that I have loaded, and that belongs to me. . . . I am perfectly delighted to have found so good an opportunity to do something and to learn something. I am well aware of the enormous sacrifices I am making, and that I shall suffer more than anybody at leaving my family, my friends, and my dear Papa, because I love them more fondly than anybody ever loved. But the voyage is not long. Men take longer voyages all the time merely for pleasure, and besides I hope to come back more worthy in the eyes of all who will be so kind as to miss me. Good bye, dear Papa, I hope to see you soon. Keep your affection for me; I want very much to deserve it, and I do deserve it now by the affection I feel for you, and by the respect that a devoted son will entertain for you all his life."

At the end of three weeks he went back secretly to Paris, and stayed with Baron de Kalb at Chaillot, a quarter then on the outskirts of the city. He avoided his family and all acquaintances, but one morning at seven o'clock he burst into the Comte de Ségur's bedroom, shut the door tight, and taking a seat by the bedside said: "I am off for America." Ségur inquired what preparations he had made. La Fayette told him the arrangements and who were to go. Then he also went and told the Vicomte de Noailles, his brother-in-law.

What he had done was this: He had called on Silas Deane with Baron de Kalb, and the three had executed their final agreements. The contracts are dated December 7, 1776, but the commentators think that they were not really executed till February or March, 1777. The list of officers to go, headed by Monsieur de La Fayette, with the rank of major-general, and Baron de Kalb, also a major-general, includes two colonels, two lieutenant-colonels, two majors, two captains and two lieutenants. Deane also signed a paper concerning La Fayette, that terminates as follows: "His high birth, his alliances, the great dignities which his family hold at this Court, his considerable estates in this realm, his personal merit, his reputation, his disinterestedness, and, above all, his zeal for the liberty of our provinces, are such as have only been able to engage me to promise him the rank of major-general in the name of the United States." With that everything was done except to get aboard the ship, which was not yet ready.

It may seem a little unkind in La Fayette to have left his girl wife of seventeen (with one baby born and a second on its cradle-ward way) whom he had not seen since leaving for England, but to see her meant to be stopped, and all his love of liberty, his passion for glory, his desire to win a reputation for her sake as well as his own, and prove to the Noailles family and the young gallants of Versailles that the awkward, clumsy, red-haired boy possessed qualities of no mean order, lay heavy in the opposite balance. Madame de La Fayette leaves much unsaid when she wrote long afterwards: "I was going to have a baby and I loved him dearly," but Jared Sparks says, and he had it from La Fayette, that "his wife did not join in the outcry, but approved of his enterprise from the beginning and threw no obstacles in his way." As she knew nothing of her husband's going till he had gone, the statement of Jared Sparks can mean no more than that when she heard of what he had done she approved of it. As it turned out, it was his duty to go. Great issues weighed against transitory sorrows. On March sixteenth, he and the Baron de Kalb started for Bordeaux where they were to meet the other officers.

It seems that the Duc d'Ayen was informed of his son-in-law's movements by the British Ambassador, who did not give implicit faith to the protestations of Monsieur de Maurepas and the Comte de Vergennes. The Duke and all the family were very angry except the Duchess; for though she cared little for fame or for ambition, she knew that La Fayette felt real grief at leaving his wife, to whom she was obliged to break the news, and she had complete confidence in his character, and from the start judged his behavior (as his wife said afterward) as all the world came to judge it when he returned.

The Duke rushed at once to the Ministers, who must have been annoyed. They were glad to have young officers go to help the rebels, so long as they went unobserved, but they were most reluctant to have England know that they knew of such goings; they were not ready for war, their ships were not equipped, nor manned, and the military situation in America was far from satisfactory. There was nothing for them to do, therefore, but to be shocked by the Duke's information and to dispatch orders forbidding La Fayette to sail.

Others were annoyed, too; Mr. Deane was apprehensive lest he should get into trouble for his share in the matter, the Marquis de Noailles also feared that he might be held responsible, and the King was displeased for he did not think it very good form to help rebels. So for the sake of appeasing the English Ambassador, whether of his own volition or at his Ministers' suggestion, the King issued an order forbidding any of his officers to take service in the English colonies, naming in particular the Marquis de La Fayette. When the news got about Paris, everybody else applauded the bold and chivalric youth who was starting out like a knight of old in quest of glorious adventures. Madame du Deffand in a letter to Horace Walpole dated March 31, 1777, having spoken of people going away, says: "Of all departures just now the most singular and astonishing is that of M. de La Fayette, whom you may have seen the day that you dined at our Ambassador's. He is not twenty yet. He has recently left for America, and takes eight or ten of his friends with him. He told no one of his plans except the Vicomte de Noailles, and to him under the greatest secrecy. He has bought a ship, fitted it out, and has gone aboard at Bordeaux. As soon as his relatives heard of it they sent men racing after him to stop him and bring him back, but they arrived too late, he had already gone aboard three hours before. He had made an agreement, they say, with a man named Hill who lives with Franklin; he will have the title or rank of major-general, with permission to return to France in case we are at war or if domestic affairs make his return necessary. It is folly, no doubt, but it does not dishonor him, on the contrary, it manifests his courage and desire for glory. He is more praised than blamed, but his wife, who is gone four months with child, his father-in-law, his mother-in-law, and all the family feel dreadfully about it."

In order the better to conceal his purposes, La Fayette, upon arriving at Bordeaux, paid a visit to his wife's great-uncle, the Maréchal de Mouchy, who commanded the troops in Guyenne. He then entered his name on the ship's register as Gilbert du Motier, Chevalier de Chavaniac, and on the night of March twenty-fifth, went down to the dock. But he and the Baron had barely got into a wherry to join the ships at Pauillac (an anchorage some thirty miles down the Gironde from Bordeaux), when a letter was handed him written by his friend the Vicomte de Coigny to say that the King had issued orders to forbid his departure. He asked the Baron what he had better do, and the Baron advised him to submit and keep on good terms with his family. La Fayette decided to learn what the orders said, but first to get out of French jurisdiction. They went aboard the *Victoire,* hoisted sail and after a seasick passage, anchored off the Spanish coast at the little port of Los Pasajes, near San Sebastian. There they waited for the letters from Paris.

La Fayette, it seems, had flattered himself that the Duc d'Ayen would approve of what he was doing, but the letters that came he describes as "terrible"; and the orders from the King commanded him to betake himself directly to Marseilles and accompany his father-in-law from there on travels in Italy. La Fayette, greatly troubled by thoughts of his wife, the anger of her family and the displeasure of the government, set off at once by land back to Bordeaux, hopefully bidding Baron de Kalb wait for him; but the Baron did not expect to see him again. At Bordeaux he declared to the commandant that the responsibility of the whole affair was his and his alone; he wrote to Monsieur de Maurepas and to the Duc d'Ayen arguing his right to proceed, and justified himself in letters to his friends to whom he said, with reference to the accusation that he was violating his oath of allegiance, that when the Ministers should be faithful to their pledges to the people, they might talk with better grace of his violating his oath.

At one time he thought of going to Marseilles to try to talk his father-in-law round, but while he was hesitating and uncertain he heard that the royal order had been procured by the Duc d'Ayen, and that outside his relatives everybody else sided with him, and that the Ministers had said they would not have done anything had it not been for the Duke, so he cut the Gordian knot. He wrote to Monsieur de Maurepas that, as he had received no answer to his petition, he assumed that silence meant consent.

Telling the commandant that he would proceed to Marseilles, he set off in a carriage with a friend who likewise wished to serve in America. The carriage had hardly got out of sight of Bordeaux, when La Fayette changed his clothes, disguised himself as a courier, mounted a horse, and rode ahead on the road that led, not to Marseilles, but to Bayonne. There they changed horses and proceeded to Saint Jean de Luz. While changing horses again, the daughter of the man that kept the post-house, who had seen him but a few days before when he passed through on his way from San Sebastian to Bordeaux, recognized him. La Fayette made a sign to her which she understood, and when but a short time later, pursuers came up and gave a description of him, she said that a carriage had passed by but that there was no such person in it as they described. This threw the pursuit off the scent long enough to enable La Fayette to reach Los Pasajes and go aboard his ship (April seventeenth). Three days later they hoisted sail for America.

CHAPTER III

THE voyage lasted eight weeks. La Fayette was a bad sailor, but after he had got on his sea legs he set about learning English and reading books on the art of war. Sundry incidents colored the days. A privateer bore down on them, but it proved to be American, then two English frigates appeared, but the winds baffled them; also, the captain wished to put in at the Windward Islands in order to sell his cargo, but La Fayette, fearing that there might be a *lettre de cachet* awaiting him there, as in fact there was, bought him out, and the ship headed for the mainland. He wrote to his wife:

"On board *La Victoire,* May 30th, 1777
"My dear Heart;
"I write far from you, and to this cruel separation is added the still worse uncertainty as to when I shall get news of you. But I hope to hear soon; among all the motives that make me eager to land, none makes me so impatient as that. How many fears and worries must I add to my grief, already so sharp, at leaving all that is most dear to me! How did you take my going? Did you love me less? Have you forgiven me? . . . Your regrets, those of my friends, Henriette [the baby] all rise before my mind in a heart-

29

breaking manner; and then I see no excuse for myself. If you only knew what I have suffered, what sad, sad days I have passed in quitting all that I love in the world! . . . If I only hear that you are well, that you love me still, that my friends do, too, my philosophy will be proof against all the rest. . . . I shan't send you a diary of the voyage; days follow each other, and are all alike; always sky and sea, and the next day, just the same. . . . Let us talk of more interesting things; of you, of our Henriette, of her brother or sister. Henriette is so sweet, that she makes one want a girl. Whichever it is, I shall welcome it with the liveliest delight. Don't leave a moment to make me happy by news of the birth. . . .

"June 7th. I am still on this dull stretch, it's the most boring thing possible. For comfort I think of you, of my friends. I am thinking of the pleasure of seeing you again. How wonderful when I come home, to take you in my arms all unexpectedly. Perhaps you will be with your children. . . .

"June 13, At Major Hugers: Here I am, dear Heart, in excellent health, at the house of an American officer. . . . I go to-night to Charleston. . . . Goodbye, my Heart. From Charleston I shall go by land to Philadelphia, to the army. Is it true that you will love me forever?"

By good luck his vessel had not met any of the British ships patrolling the coast, and had anchored in Winyan Bay, near Georgetown, in South Carolina. La Fayette, Baron de Kalb and some others got into a little boat and rowed up the river to a house that showed lights. Dogs began to bark; the inmates were frightened, thinking that it might be a marauding party of the enemy. Baron de Kalb, who spoke English, explained who they were. They received a hearty welcome. La Fayette was delighted by his first experience of America, by the kindness of the people, and by many strange objects, by the mosquito netting round his bed, by the negro servants, and so forth. "The manners of the people here are simple, honest, and in every way worthy of a country where the noble name of liberty resounds on all sides."

They left Major Huger's the next day for Charleston, where they were presented to the American officers. In a letter to his wife, dated June nineteenth, he writes: "Everybody here with whom I have made acquaintance has covered me with civilities . . . my own personal reception has been as agreeable as possible on all hands. . . . From the pleasant time I am having in this country, from the sympathy that puts me at my ease with the people as if I had known them for twenty years, and the likeness between their way of thinking and mine and from my love for glory and liberty, it might be thought that I am very happy; but you are away, dear Heart, my friends are away, and there is no happiness for me far from you and them. I ask you if you always love me, but I ask the question of myself far oftener, and my heart always answers, Yes. I trust that it does not deceive me. I await news of you with inexpressible impatience. Kiss Henriette; can I say, my Heart, kiss our children? Those poor children have a vagabond father, but a good fellow at bottom, and a good father, who loves his family very much, and a good husband, too, for he loves his wife with all his heart."

At Charleston he bought horses and light carriages for himself and his companions, and they started off northward. The journey to Philadelphia was nine hundred miles, and they must have traveled well, for they left Charleston on June twenty-fifth, and arrived at their destination on July twenty-seventh. Their road ran by Raleigh in North Carolina, and on to Petersburg in Virginia, where La Fayette wrote another letter to his wife:

"Petersburg, July 17, 1777

"Dear Heart:

. . . I am now in the beautiful country of Virginia eight days' journey from Philadelphia. All hardships are over, and I fear that those of war will be very slight, if it is true that General Howe has left New York to go I don't know where. . . . You will have heard about the beginning of my journey. You know in how smart a fashion I started out in a carriage, and now you must know that we are all on horseback after having smashed up the carriages (according to my praiseworthy way of doing), and I expect to write you in a few days that we arrived on foot. It is fatiguing, but though several of my companions have suffered a good deal, I haven't even noticed it. . . . I can hardly bear to think of the baby being born, dear Heart, and yet I think of it every minute, and I tremble and feel horribly afraid. In truth I am very unhappy to be so far away; even if you did not love me, you would be sorry for me, but you love me and we shall always be happy in one another. . . .

"The farther north I go, the more I like this country and its inhabitants. There is no kindness or courtesy that I do not receive, though many people hardly know who I am. But I will write you all about this from Philadelphia. I have only time to beg you, dear Heart, not to forget an unhappy man who has paid dear for the wrong-doing of leaving you, and who has never felt so strongly how much he loves you."

They arrived in Philadelphia, as I have said, on July twenty-seventh. The journey had been harder than he admitted to his wife. One of his companions wrote that it was as hard as any campaign in Europe, but that they were encouraged by the welcome from the public along their way, and adds: "The enthusiasm of La Fayette would have kept all the rest of us going if any of us had been less inclined to danger than he." They presented their letters, together with Mr. Deane's agreement, to Congress. Unluckily they had been preceded by a lot of adventurers. Mr. Deane (in Horatio's phrase) "had shark'd up a list of landless resolutes," and these foreigners, mere self-seekers, many of them without knowledge of military affairs, without capacity or character, had received commissions from Congress, and, as Washington said, "the error of these appointments is now manifest." In consequence Congress had become very diffident as to accepting more volunteers. One of their members, Mr. Lovell, who spoke French, was delegated to express this sentiment in plain terms. The reception was "more like a dismissal than a welcome."

A companion of La Fayette tells of this interview. "Mr. Lovell talked with us in the street, where he left us, after having treated us, in excellent French, like a set of adventurers. He ended his speech by saying, 'Gentlemen, have you any authority from Mr. Deane? We authorized him to send us four French engineers; but instead of that, he has sent us Mr. du Coudray and some men who pretend to be engineers but are not, and some artillerists who have never seen service. We then instructed Mr. Franklin to send us four engineers, and they have come. It seems that French officers have a great fancy to enter our service without being invited. It is true we were in need of officers last year, but now we have experienced men and plenty of them.' This was our first reception by the Congress.''

Then La Fayette, who possessed prudence and tact as well as enthusiasm and courage, wrote a petition and said: ''After the sacrifices I have made I have the right to insist upon two favors: (1) to serve at my own cost, and (2) to begin my service as a volunteer.'' Mr. Lovell and whatever other Congressmen made La Fayette's acquaintance, like everybody else, were evidently most favorably impressed by his good breeding, his charm, his enthusiasm and his good sense. The consequence was that on July thirty-first, Congress passed the following resolution:

''Whereas the Marquis de La Fayette, out of his great zeal to the cause of liberty, in which the United States are engaged, has left his family and connections, and at his own expense come over to offer his service to the United States, without pension or particular allowance, and is anxious to risk his life in our cause:

''Resolved that his service be accepted, and that, in consideration of his zeal, his illustrious family, and connections, he have the rank and commission of major-general in the army of the United States.''

La Fayette, who was not yet twenty years old, wrote his thanks to the President of Congress (John Hancock) and said: ''The feelings of my heart, long before it became my duty, engaged me in the love of the American cause. I not only considered it as the cause of Honor, Virtue, and universal Happiness, but felt myself impressed with the warmest affection for a nation who exhibited by their resistance so fine an example of Justice and Courage to the Universe. I shall neglect nothing on my part to justify the confidence which Congress of the United States has been pleased to repose in me as my highest ambition has ever been to do everything only for the best of the cause in which I am engaged. I wish to serve near the person of General Washington till such time as he may think proper to entrust me with a division of the Army.

"It is now as an American that I'll mention every day to Congress the officers who came over with me, whose interests are for me as my own, and the consideration which they deserve by their merits, their ranks, their state and reputation in France.

"I am, Sir, with the sentiments which every good American owes to you,

"Your most obedient servant
"the MARQUIS DE LA FAYETTE."

A little later, on or about August first, he made the acquaintance of General Washington, who had come to Philadelphia. The military situation was not good. Fort Ticonderoga, at the lower end of Lake Champlain, had been captured by General Burgoyne, and the two Howes, general and admiral, had left New York to make some great attack, but nobody knew where. Their fleet has been sighted off the mouth of the Delaware, and therefore Washington had marched from New Jersey to protect Philadelphia. A dinner was given in the General's honor, and on this occasion

La Fayette was presented to him. Long years afterward La Fayette recounts how he recognized Washington at once by the majesty of his face and figure, and by his high-bred and kindly manners. Washington, too, seems to have taken a marked liking to this enthusiastic young man, not half his own age. He took him aside, complimented him on the noble spirit he had shown and on the sacrifices he had made in the American cause, bade him look upon the quarters of the Commander-in-Chief as his home, and himself as one of the Commander's family, and added that as he was now an American soldier he would doubtless contrive to accommodate himself to that character, and submit with good grace to the customs, manners and privations of a republican army.

About a week later La Fayette joined Washington's camp as a volunteer, where he found a ragged army, clothed in all kinds of garments, poorly armed and very ignorant of drill and tactics. "We shall be embarrassed," Washington said, "to be seen by an officer who has just come from French troops." "I have come," La Fayette answered, "to learn and not to teach." And such seems to have been his attitude, due no doubt both to his own good sense and to his immense admiration for the character and abilities of Washington.

Of course he was itching for a definite place in the army, and to take actual command of troops, and, naturally enough, his rank of major-general and the flattering words of General Washington, had given him the notion that he was to receive an active command, and he did not conceal his readiness to receive it at once. This was a little awkward for Washington, as you will see by this letter.

GEORGE WASHINGTON TO BENJAMIN HARRISON

"Neshaminy Bridge (Bucks County, Pa.)
Aug. 19, 1777

"Dear Sir:

"If I did not misunderstand what you or some other member of Congress said to me, respecting the appointment of the Marquis de La Fayette, he has misconceived the design of his appointment, or Congress did not understand the extent of his views; for certain it is, that I understood him, that he does not conceive his commission is merely honorary, but given with a view to command a division of this army. It is true he has said that he is young and inexperienced, but at the same time has always accompanied it with a hint, that, so soon as I shall think him fit for the command of a division, he shall be ready to enter upon the duties of it, and in the meantime has offered his service for a smaller command. . . . What the designs of Congress respecting this gentleman were, and what line of conduct I am to pursue to comply with their design and his expectations, I know not, and beg to be instructed. If Congress meant that this rank should be unaccompanied by command, I wish it had been sufficiently explained to him. If, on the other hand, it was intended to invest him with all the powers of a major-general, why have I been led into a contrary belief, and left in the dark with respect to my own conduct toward him? . . . Let me beseech you then, my good Sir, to give me the sentiments of Congress on this matter, that I may endeavor so far as it is in my power, to comply with them. . . . The Marquis is now in Philadelphia but expected up this day or tomorrow."

The matter was left to Washington's discretion and by the end of the campaign settled itself; in the meantime, La Fayette acted as volunteer, and in his capacity of major-general, took part in councils of war. The two Howes were still out at sea, and nobody knew what their destination might be; some thought that they would sail southward and attack Charleston, others that they would sail northward and up the Hudson River; and others had no theory. Washington was on tenterhooks. At last, word came that the British fleet was seen sailing up Chesapeake Bay. On this news, Washington marched his army southward, through Philadelphia, with La Fayette riding by his side, toward the Maryland border in order to take the best position to defend the city, which was highly important to the American cause both for its size and because Congress was sitting there.

Sir William Howe, having sailed up Chesapeake Bay, continued on up Elk River, and disembarked his army of eighteen thousand men in the northeast corner of Maryland near what is now Elkton, close to the Delaware border, and scarce fifty miles from Philadelphia. Washington with some fifteen thousand men, many of whom were still as ill provided with clothes, arms and ammunition as when La Fayette first saw them, came in between, in hope to bar their way. He took a position (September ninth) on hilly ground to the east of the Brandywine, a small stream that runs southeasterly from Pennsylvania into the Delaware River. The Brandywine was shallow at that season of the year, and fordable in several places. The country was well wooded, with many roads intersecting one another and leading to the fords. Washington's headquarters were a mile east of Chadd's Ford, and La

Fayette lodged in a little cottage near by that is still standing.

On the morning of the eleventh of September, the English army advanced toward Chadd's Ford from the west, in two columns, led respectively by Lord Cornwallis and General Knyphausen. Washington was prepared to meet them at this ford and assigned his divisions to their places accordingly. But General Howe made merely a feint of attacking at this point; he sent General Knyphausen there with five thousand men and bade him open a cannonade, while he and Lord Cornwallis, taking advantage of the woods, swung off to the left with thirteen thousand men, crossed the Brandywine at higher fords and swept down on the rear of the American right wing. Not till midday was this maneuver perceived, and then contradictory reports came in, but by two o'clock the main British army was in full view. General Sullivan was dispatched at once to occupy some high ground on the right and make a stand against Howe and Cornwallis who, it was obvious, would soon reach that point. La Fayette begged for permission to follow, and so went into action for the first time. He tells a little about what happened in a letter to his wife:

"September 12, 1777, Philadelphia.
"Dear Heart:
"I write two words by some French officers that are going back to France. I will begin by saying that I am very well, because I must finish by saying that yesterday we had a real fight, and that we did not get the best of it. Our Americans, after standing firm for some little time, were at last put to rout; while I was trying to rally them, *messieurs les Anglais* favored

me with a gunshot that wounded me slightly in the leg, but it is nothing, dear Heart, for the ball didn't touch bone or nerve, and I got off with nothing worse than to be on my back for a time, but that vexes me greatly. This affair, I am afraid, will have bad consequences for America. We must try to make up for it, if we can.''

The defeat, in reality, was nearly a rout. After Howe and Cornwallis had turned the American flank, Knyphausen forced a crossing at Chadd's Ford, and in spite of Washington's endeavors the American army was caught between the two divisions of the British army, and obliged to retreat as best it could. In places there was a stampede, fugitives fled head-long, men, wagons, cannon, horses dashing with carts, all hurrying helter-skelter on the road toward Philadelphia.

La Fayette's later account of his own share in the battle, which he tells in the third person, is this. He found himself at the American center, where General Conway and General Sterling were facing Cornwallis, their wings gave way and the British concentrated their fire on the center. ''The confusion became very great, and while rallying the troops La Fayette had his leg pierced by a ball. At this juncture, all the line that still held gave way. La Fayette owes it to his aide-de-camp, Gimat, that he had the luck to get on horseback again. General Washington came up with fresh troops; La Fayette was going to join him when loss of blood forced him to stop in order to bandage the wound; he just missed being captured, whilst fugitives, cannon, wagons dashed pell-mell along the Chester road. What remained of daylight was used by the General to delay the enemy. Some regiments behaved well, but the rout became complete. During this time Chadd's Ford had been carried, our cannon taken, and the Chester Road became the line of retreat for the whole army. In the midst of this horrible confusion and the darkness of night, it was impossible to recognize one another; but at Chester, twelve miles from the battlefield, there was a bridge that had to be crossed. La Fayette busied himself with stopping the fugitives at this spot; order was a little reestablished, the Commander-in-Chief and the generals arrived, and La Fayette had time to have his wound dressed."

He was carried by water to Philadelphia and from there, for the British would soon be marching in, again by water to Bristol. Here Henry Laurens, who had left Philadelphia in his carriage, placidly smoking his pipe, while the other members of Congress fled precipitately, picked up La Fayette and drove him on to Bethlehem, a Moravian settlement, "where the gentle religion of this large family of brothers, their community in property, education and all general concerns made a marked contrast with the scenes of carnage and the turmoil of civil war." They, too, an undemonstrative people, found him a very intelligent and pleasant young man. Here he stayed in bed for six weeks, suffering more from inaction than from his wound, and occupying himself with various plans to attack England; one was that the French Governor of the Windward Islands should make a raid on the British West Indies; another that the Comte de Vergennes should stir up rebellions in India; and so on.

TO HIS WIFE:

"October 1, 1777

"Dear Heart:

". . . Let me tell you about my wound; it is a mere flesh wound, and does not touch bone or nerve. The surgeons are amazed at its healing so quickly. They fall into an ecstasy at every dressing, and say that it is the loveliest thing in the world. For my part, I think that it is ugly, a nuisance, and painful enough; but it is all a matter of taste. . . . There, dear Heart, is the story of what I pompously call my wound in order to give myself airs and make myself interesting. . . . Be easy about it; all the doctors in America are ready to take care of me. I have a friend who has spoken to them in such a way that I shall be well cared for; it is General Washington. This splendid man whose talents and virtues I admire, whom I venerate the more, the better I know him, has become my intimate friend. His affectionate interest in me has won my heart. I am at home in his quarters, we live like two united brothers, in reciprocal intimacy and confidence. His friendship makes me as happy as I can be in this country. When he sent his first surgeon, he bade him take care of me as if I were his own son, because he loved me as such. When he learned that I wished to go back to the army too soon, he wrote me a letter full of affection to make me promise to get well and strong. I tell you all these details, dear Heart, in order that you may be easy as to the care they take of me. [He then speaks of the misunderstandings and bickerings among the foreign officers.] For my part, in the midst of disputes and discussions, common in all armies, especially where there are foreign officers, I being of an easy disposition am lucky enough to be liked by everybody, foreigners or Americans. I like them all. I hope to deserve their good opinion, and we are naturally well content with one another. I am at present in the solitude of Bethlehem. . . . This establishment is really touching and very interesting; they have a sweet and quiet life. We will talk about it when I come home. I expect to bore all those I love, you first of course, with tales of my travels, for you know what a chatterbox I am. . . . Adieu, adieu, dear Heart, love me always, I love you so dearly."

La Fayette did not deceive himself as to his popularity. Stiff old Baron de Kalb, who disliked the French officers, says: "La Fayette is the only exception; I always meet him with the same cordiality and the same pleasure." General Nathanael Greene, a man of thirty-four, says: "He is one of the sweetest tempered young gentlemen"; and Patrick Henry wrote to Washington: "I beg to be presented to him in the most acceptable manner. I greatly revere his person and his amiable character."

"Camp near Whitemarsh, October 29, 1777
"Dear Heart:
"M. de Valport will give you a long account of me; but I, I want to tell you how much I love you. I get too much pleasure from this sentiment, not to say it over a thousand times, if I could. I have no resource, dear Heart, but to write and write again without hope that my letters will reach you, and to try to console myself by the pleasure of talking to you about the grief, the mortal woe, of not receiving a word

from France. It is not possible to tell you to what degree my heart is disquieted, often torn. . . . Oh! do you pity me, do you realize how much I suffer? If I only knew what you are doing, where you are. . . . I wait for letters with an eagerness that nothing can distract. Don't neglect any opportunity to write to me, dear Heart, if my happiness still concerns you. Tell me again that you love me; the less I deserve your love, the more you assure me of it comforts me. . . . I have received four idiotic lines from the Maréchal de Mouchy; he doesn't say a word of you. . . . It is a terrible thing to be reduced to mere writing when a man loves as I love you, and shall till my last breath.''

As a result of the victory at Brandywine, the British occupied Philadelphia.

CHAPTER IV

A FULL MAJOR-GENERAL

LA FAYETTE's wound, not being dangerous, was a wonderful bit of good luck. He was now initiated into the inner circle of lovers of liberty, he was brother by ties of blood to all the soldiers in the American army, and his place in their esteem and their hearts was solidly established. In one of his letters to his wife, he says: "I count on my star," and his star had justified his trust, twinkling in the sky of fame. By the time that news of the battle reached Amsterdam, rumor said that he had commanded an army, captured six hundred British soldiers, and after an obstinate and bloody battle, put the rest to rout; no doubt rumor had read one of the day-dreams passing through his head and had repeated it too heedlessly.

While he was lying in bed among the kind Moravians, dreaming day-dreams and devising plans for overthrowing the British Empire ("light ideas that I dare lay down faster than I think"), Washington had fought the battle of Germantown (October 4, 1777), and had gone into camp at Whitemarsh a dozen miles north of Philadelphia; his primary object was to maintain the American forts along the Delaware, and so prevent the British ships from bringing supplies to their troops in the city. Here La Fayette rejoined the army, though his wound was not fully healed, conscious of the dignity of having been under fire, and more eager than ever with all the eagerness of twenty, that his honorary rank as major-general should acquire a real significance. How desirous he was may be gathered from this further letter of General Washington addressed to the President of Congress:

"Headquarters near Whitemarsh
"November 1, 1777

"Sir:

". . . I would take the liberty to mention that I feel myself in a delicate situation with respect to the Marquis de La Fayette. He is extremely solicitous of having a command equal to his rank, and professes very different ideas as to the purposes of his appointment, from those Congress mentioned to me. He certainly did not understand them. I do not know in what light they will view the matter, but it appears to me, from a consideration of his illustrious and important connections, the attachment which he has manifested for our cause, and the consequences which his return in disgust might produce, that it will be advisable to gratify him in his wishes; and the more so, as several gentlemen from France, who came over under some assurances, have gone back disappointed in their expectation. His conduct with respect to them stands in a favorable point of view, he having interested himself to remove their uneasiness, and urged the impropriety of their making any unfavorable representations upon their arrival at home; and in all his letters he has placed our affairs in the best situation he could. Besides he is sensible, discreet in his manners, has made great proficiency in our language, and, from the disposition he discovered at the battle of

Brandywine, possesses a large share of bravery and military ardor.''

Congress did not act precipitately; but Washington gave La Fayette a chance to prove his mettle. Lord Cornwallis had crossed over into New Jersey, in order to attack one of the American forts on the farther side of the Delaware. General Greene was sent to hinder him, and La Fayette, serving under him, was given a command of three or four hundred men and ordered to make a reconnaissance. In doing this La Fayette came upon an outpost of Hessians of about the same numbers. He attacked and they retreated; he pressed on, but not imprudently, until Lord Cornwallis came up with his army, and then he withdrew. General Greene sent word of the affair next day to Washington:

''The Marquis, with about four hundred militia and the rifle corps, attacked the enemy's picket last evening, killed about twenty, wounded as many more, and took about twenty prisoners. The Marquis is charmed with the spirited behavior of the militia and rifle corps; they drove the enemy about half a mile, and kept the ground until dark. The enemy's picket consisted of about three hundred, and were reinforced during the skirmish.''

La Fayette also wrote an account of the skirmish to Washington:

''Haddonfield, November 26, 1777
''Dear General:
''. . . After having spent the most part of the day in making myself well acquainted with the cer-

tainty of the enemy's motions, I came pretty late into the Gloucester road between the two creeks. I had ten light-horse, almost one hundred and fifty riflemen, and two pickets of militia. Colonel Armand, Colonel Laumoy, and the Chevaliers Duplessis and Gimat were the Frenchmen with me. A scout of my men under Duplessis went to ascertain how near to Gloucester were the enemy's first pickets, and they found at the distance of two miles and a half from that place a strong post of three hundred and fifty Hessians, with field-pieces, and they engaged immediately. As my little reconnoitering party were all in fine spirits, I supported them. We pushed the Hessians more than half a mile from the place where their main body had been, and we made them run very fast. British reinforcements came twice to them, but, very far from recovering their ground, they always retreated. The darkness of night prevented us from pursuing our advantage. After standing on the ground we had gained, I ordered them to return very slowly to Haddonfield. . . . I take the greatest pleasure in letting you know that the conduct of our soldiers was above all praise. I never saw men so merry, so spirited, and so desirous to go on to the enemy, whatever force they might have, as that small party in this little fight."

He says that he lost but one man killed and six wounded, and apologizes for so long an account of so little an affair.

Washington wrote to Congress suggesting La Fayette's appointment to active command, and accordingly, Congress voted that it would be highly agreeable to them for him to appoint the Marquis de La Fayette to the command of a division in the

Continental army. And three days later it was proclaimed in a public order that he was to take command
of a division. He was then twenty years and two
months old. As Washington's letters show, political
considerations were an essential factor but these
would hardly have procured for La Fayette the command of a division had they not been seconded and
supported by his character, his good judgment, his
success in dealing with American soldiers and his
ability to handle troops. The real value of it was that
this reward was approved by the man best fitted to
judge, General Washington.

Fighting, however, was over for the season, and
the army went into winter quarters at Valley Forge
on the Schuylkill some twenty miles from Philadelphia.
A few days before they moved La Fayette wrote a
long letter to his father-in-law, the Duc d'Ayen, a
part of which I will quote. No letter could better express respect for an older man, together with a desire
to be on affectionate terms. In the first part he asks
after matters at home, and recounts the situation in
America, and the doings of the American army. A
letter could hardly have been written with greater skill
to interest the Duke in the American cause, to persuade him that La Fayette had been right to come, and
to show himself in a most deferential and affectionate
attitude.

"Camp in Pennsylvania, December 16, 1777
". . . Our General is verily made on purpose for
this revolution that could not be successful without
him. I see him at closer range than anybody and I
see that he is worthy of the admiration of his country.
His kindness to me, and his complete confidence in me

as to all matters military and political, great and little, that concern him, put me in a position to judge all that he has to do, and conciliate and overcome. Every day I admire more and more the beauty of his character and of his soul. . . . His name will be revered forever by all lovers of liberty and of mankind. . . . There are many interesting things that I can't write, but will tell you some day, on which I ask you to suspend your judgment, that will double your esteem for him. . . .

". . . After having bored you with public matters, you cannot get out of being bored with mine. It would be impossible to be better off in a foreign country than I am here. I must congratulate myself, and I have reason to be more and more satisfied day by day by the behavior of Congress toward me, although my military duties have left me time to make acquaintance with but few members. Those that I do know cover me with politeness. The new president, M. Laurens, one of the most estimable men in America, is a particular friend. As for the army, I have the luck to be on the best terms with everybody; they never lose an opportunity to prove this. The summer has passed without my having command of a division, as, you know, I had hoped; I have been all this time at General Washington's just as if I had been at the house of a friend of twenty years standing. Since I came back from New Jersey, he has told me to choose from several brigades the division that would best suit me. I have taken one composed entirely of Virginians. It is weak at present, just as all the army is, and it is almost naked, but I am given to hope that there will be cloth, out of which I shall have garments made, and recruits, of whom I must make soldiers, both at the same time; unluckily, one job is harder than the other, even for cleverer men than me. My duties, supposing that I have learned enough to perform them properly, will help my military education. A major-general does the work of a lieutenant-general and of a quarter-master in their most important duties, and I should have scope both for capacity and for experience, if Providence and my baptismal certificate had given me a chance to boast of such. I read, I study, I examine, I listen, I think, and out of it all I try to come to a conclusion into which I pack as much commonsense as I can. I shall not talk very much for fear of talking foolishly; still less, shall I run risks, for fear of doing something foolish; for I have no mind to abuse the confidence that they condescend to show me. Such is the line of conduct that I have followed up to now and mean to follow. But when I get some ideas that seem to me, after a little shaping, to be feasible, I submit them at once to a good judge who is kind enough to make me believe that he likes them. On the other hand, when I feel in my bones that an opportunity is favorable, I shall not refuse to run a risk, but I do not think that the lustre of success ought to make me risk the safety of an army (or any of its divisions) that is not prepared for an offensive. If I dared venture a general principle with some warrant of not talking nonsense, I should say that whatever our forces may be, we must stay purely on the defensive, excepting just at the very moment that we are forced into action, because I think that I have perceived that the English troops would be more taken aback then by a sudden charge than by steady resistance.

"This letter will be delivered to you by the distinguished [John] Adams, whose name you surely are acquainted with. . . . He wished me to give him introductions in France, especially to you. . . . I fancy that you will not object to talk to a man of such well known deserts. He has the most lively wish to win the good opinion of our people."

The winter of 1777-1778 at Valley Forge, besides the hardships of destitution, was rendered harder by intrigues against General Washington. A plan had been concocted in the interest of General Gates, whose success over Burgoyne at Saratoga had swelled his reputation to an undeserved bigness, and who had been appointed president of a new Board of War, to oust Washington as commander-in-chief. Among others concerned in the plot was Conway, by whose side La Fayette had fought at Brandywine, and who, to the dissatisfaction of Washington and many of the American officers, had recently been made a major-general.

La Fayette, like everybody else, had applauded Gates's victory over Burgoyne and admired him for it, and he judged Conway, as he was, a bold and capable officer, but disclosures made to him concerning the cabal, shocked and alarmed him; he tried to see Washington, and failing, wrote a long, affectionate, apprehensive letter, telling of the dissensions and intrigues in Congress and out: "Take away, for an instant, that modest diffidence of yourself (which, pardon my freedom, my dear General, is sometimes too great, and I wish you could know, as well as myself, what difference there is between you and any other man) you would see very plainly that if you were lost for America, there is nobody else who could keep the army and the revolution for six months." He warns him in an eager, boyish, almost passionate, manner against Conway, as "an ambitious and dangerous man," telling how Conway had tried to seduce him from his allegiance to Washington, how "he had engaged me by entertaining my head with ideas of glory and shining projects, and I must confess, to my shame, that it is a too certain way of deceiving me. . . . My desire of deserving your satisfaction is stronger than ever, and everywhere you will employ me you can be certain of my trying every exertion in my power to succeed. I am now fixed to your fate, and I shall follow it and sustain it as well by my sword as by all means in my power. You will pardon my importunity in favour of the sentiment which dictated it. Youth and friendship make me, perhaps, too warm, but I feel the greatest concern at all that has happened for some time since.

"With the most tender and profound respect, I have the honour to be, etc.

"LA FAYETTE."

Washington replied: "Your favor of yesterday conveyed to me fresh proof of that friendship and attachment, which I have happily experienced since the first of our acquaintance, and for which I entertain sentiments of the purest affection. It will ever constitute part of my happiness to know that I stand well in your opinion; because I am satisfied that you can have no views to answer by throwing out false colours, and that you possess a mind too exalted to condescend to low arts and intrigues to acquire a reputation." He then refers feelingly to the troubles that La Fayette wrote of, and closes with: "But we must not in so great a contest, expect to meet with nothing but sunshine. I have no doubt that everything happens for the best, that we shall triumph over all our misfortunes, and in the end be happy; when, my dear Marquis, if you will give me your company in Virginia, we will laugh at our past difficulties and the folly of others; and I will endeavor, by every civility in my power, to show you how much and how sincerely I am your affectionate and obedient servant.''

The clouds blew over; General Washington's fame is one of the brightest in the history of mankind, and Conway is but remembered by the phrase "Conway's Cabal.''

There was not much variety in the life at Valley Forge. December wore away, and January came in. Here is a letter from La Fayette to his wife:

"Camp near Valley Forge,
"January 6, 1778
"Dear Heart:

"What a date! and what a place to write from in the month of January! I am in camp, in the middle of woods, fifteen hundred leagues from you, imprisoned in the middle of winter. A short while ago we were only separated from the enemy by a little river; at present we are twenty miles away, and it is here that the American army will pass the winter in little huts that are about as gay as a prison cell. . . . The bearer of this letter will tell you of the agreeable spot that I choose instead of being with you and all my friends, in the midst of all possible pleasures. On my word, dear Heart, don't you believe that I must have good reasons to decide upon this sacrifice. Everything bids me go, but Honor says stay, and really when you shall know all the circumstances in detail concerning me and the army and my friend the Commander-in-Chief, and the whole American cause, you will forgive me, dear Heart, you will excuse me, and I almost dare say that you will approve of me. . . . Besides these reasons, there is another that I could not tell to everybody, as it would appear to make myself ridiculously important. My presence here is more necessary to the American cause than you can think. There are a great many foreigners who have not been given appointments, or have found their ambitions neglected, and have entered into powerful conspiracies; they have tried by all sorts of tricks to make me lose my liking for this revolution and for its leader, and they have done their best to spread abroad a report that I was about to leave the country. The English, also, proclaim aloud the same story. I can't in conscience justify those people. If I go, many Frenchmen, who are useful here, will follow my example. General Washington would be really unhappy if I spoke to him of going away. His confidence in me is greater than I dare avow, on account of my age. In the place he occupies, one is likely to be surrounded by flatterers or secret enemies; in me he finds a trusty friend, to whom he can unbosom himself and who will always tell him the truth. Not a day passes but he has long conversations with me or writes me long letters, and he consults me on very important points. At this very time there happens to be a particular matter in which my being here is useful; and so it is not the time to speak of going away. I am also engaged in an important correspondence with the President of Congress. The humiliation of England, the advantage to my country, the happiness of humanity whose interest it is that there should be in the world a people absolutely free, all compel me not to go at a time when my absence would cause harm. Besides after a little success that I had in New Jersey, the General, according to the unanimous wish of Congress, has asked me to take command of a division of the army, and drill it as I think best, so far as my limited capacities will permit. It would not be right to answer these marks of confidence by asking what I can do for them in Europe."

CHAPTER V

THE IRRUPTION INTO CANADA

The clouds I spoke of had blown over, but they reassembled in another shape. The attempt to get La Fayette away from Washington, with the added hope, perhaps, that if La Fayette were involved in failure it would discredit Washington, was not abandoned. An expedition, officially known as an "irruption into Canada," was proposed, and sanctioned by Congress. The instructions for it were sent out by General Gates, as president of the Board of War. An army of two thousand or three thousand men was to start from Albany, cross Lake Champlain in mid-winter on the ice, march northward across the border, burn British shipping at St. Johns, and then perform some further exploit, such as taking Montreal. La Fayette was to command the expedition, and Generals Conway and Stark, both men of twice his age, were to serve under him. The Congressional appointment was enclosed in a packet to Washington, who had not been consulted; he disapproved of the plan, and had reason to feel hurt by the slight. He merely handed the document to La Fayette with the words: "I had rather it was for you than for any other."

La Fayette was greatly flattered, and the prospect of winning back provinces that had but lately been wrenched from France fired his imagination. Nevertheless, he refused to accept a command wholly independent of Washington. He asked that he should be considered merely as one of General Washington's subordinate officers detached for special service, and that he should address his reports direct to him, sending mere duplicates to Congress. These conditions were agreed to; and full of bright anticipation he wrote the news to his wife.

"York, February 3, 1778

"Dear Heart:

". . . I shall not go into long details as to the mark of confidence that America honors me with. Let it suffice to know that Canada is oppressed by the English; all that immense country is in the enemy's possession. They have a fleet there, troops and forts. I am to go there with the title of General of the Army of the North, at the head of three thousand men, to see if I can do some harm to the English there. The idea of setting New France free, delivering it from a heavy yoke, is too dazzling not to follow it up. My army will grow enormously, many French will join it. I am undertaking a tremendous work, especially with little means. As to my own deserts, they are nothing for such a position; at twenty, one is scarce fit for the head of an army, burdened with all the details that are piled on a general, and with a vast extent of country under my direct orders. . . . I am leaving at once for Albany and from there go to another place near five hundred miles from here, and there I shall get to work. I shall go part way by a sledge. Once up there I shall have nothing but ice to travel on."

He left York in Pennsylvania, where Congress was

Madame de La Fayette with her son, La Fayette, about seven years old

From *France and New England*.   Photograph by Giraudon, Paris

Wounding of La Fayette at the Battle of Brandywine

After a painting by Alonzo Chappel, engraved by C. H. Jeens, reproduced from *Battles of America by Sea and Land*

then sitting, on February 3, 1778, and, crossing the Susquehanna, started off on horseback with a guide to Albany where he expected to find an army. He proceeded by way of Flemington, from where he wrote to Washington:

"February 9, 1778

"Dear General:

". . . I go on very slowly, sometimes drenched by rain, sometimes covered by snow, and not entertaining many handsome thoughts about the projected incursion into Canada; if successes were to be had, it would surprise me in a most agreeable manner by that very reason that I don't expect any shining ones. Lake Champlain is too cold for producing the least bit of laurel, and if I am not starved I shall be as proud as if I had gained three battles. . . .

"Mr. Duer had given me a rendezvous at the tavern, but nobody was there. I suppose that he and Mr. Conway have gone faster than he had said. Perhaps they will conquer Canada before I come, and I expect to find them in the Governor's mansion at Quebec. . . .

"Could I believe, for one single instant that this pompous command of *a northern army* will let your Excellency forget a little us absent friends, then I would send the project to the place it comes from. But I dare hope that you will remember me sometimes. I wish you, very heartily, the greatest public and private happiness and successes. It is a very melancholy idea for me that I can not follow your fortunes as near your person as I could wish; but my heart will take, very sincerely, its part of everything which can happen to you, and I am already thinking of the agreeable moment when I may come down to assure your Excellency of the most tender affection and highest respect.''

The whole expedition was little more than a hollow sham, but I will let La Fayette tell his own experiences.

''To General Washington
                    ''Albany, February 19, 1778
''Dear General:

''Why am I so far from you? And why did the Board of War hurry me through the ice and snow, without knowing what I should do, neither what they were doing themselves? You have thought, perhaps, that this project would be attended with some difficulty, that some means had been neglected, that I could not obtain all the success and the immensity of laurels which they had promised to me; but I defy your Excellency to conceive any idea of what I have seen since I left the place where I was quiet and near my friends, to run myself through all the blunders of madness, or treachery, (God knows which). Let me begin the journal of my fine and glorious campaign!

''. . . I went by Coryell's Ferry to Ringo's tavern, where Mr. Duer had given me a rendezvous; but there no Duer was to be found, and they did never hear from him. From there I proceeded by the State of New York, and had the pleasure of seeing the friends of America so warm in their love for the Commander-in-chief as his best friends could wish. . . . At length I met Albany. . . . General Conway had been here only three days before me, and I must confess I found him very active and looking as if he had good intentions, but we know a great deal upon that subject. His first word has been that the expedition is quite impossible. I was at first very diffident of this report, but have found that he was right. Such is, at least, the idea that I can form of this ill-concerted operation within these two days."

The situation did, indeed, render the expedition impossible. Letters from three generals, Schuyler, Lincoln and Benedict Arnold, said so most positively; the soldiers, too, were most averse to going. Everybody agreed that it would be a fool's errand. La Fayette was mortified and disappointed. He had hoped so much from this first command. Congress had pledged him at the lowest two thousand five hundred men, and there were but one thousand two hundred fit for service, and most of those without clothes suitable even for a summer's campaign. General Stark who was expected with a good sized corps, wrote to ask how many, where and when, should he begin recruiting. Colonel Biddle said that he would have done something if he had had any money. Eight hundred thousand dollars was owed to the troops; two hundred thousand were forthcoming. There was no help for it. La Fayette wrote his mortification and disappointment to General Washington:

"Albany, February 23rd, 1778
"Dear General:
"I sent you a little while ago an account of my painful and ridiculous situation. I was sent with loud shouts at the head of an army to do great things. This continent was all expectant, France will be too, Europe, and what's more, the English army. How they will be deceived, and how they will laugh at us! You can judge of this by the plain tale I have sent you.

In some matters, I venture to say, they have sought to impose upon me. . . . When I look about me, I am sure that they are spreading a mist before my eyes. . . . I admit that I can not suppress my feelings when my reputation and my hopes of renown are touched. It is hard indeed that this side of my happiness without which I can not live, should depend on plans which I did not learn of till it was too late to carry them out. I assure you, my dear and venerated Friend, that I am more unhappy than I have ever been."

TO HON. HENRY LAURENS

"Albany, the 23rd. February, 1778

"Dear Sir:

"I am so busy the whole day and so troubled for trifles that I am obliged to spend the nights in writing and it is at three a clock in the morning that I come to recall the Canadian Commander-in-Chief to your memory. You will have received, my dear sir, a long letter of mine where I let you know all the disappointments met with. You can not conceive at which point I am distressed and unhappy by that affair—it is the most disagreeable I have found, and I dare say, I'll find in my life—— More I consider the matter, more I see that it was impossible to go on—let it be a deception, a treachery, what you please, it was impossible for one single man to run through that dark cloud I was always surrounded with. I want rather to omit an occasion of distinguishing myself than if I was to loose an army trusted to my care and bring an eternal dishonor upon the American arms. . . . I hope you will be so good as to let me know everything which has been told me even by the public. I send this night to General Gates the copy of two letters from gnl conway and gnl fellow which I desire him to present to Congress—— I hope you will take care he don't forget them.

"I confess, Sir, that after such a noise made on account of my commanding an army, I expect and wish much to be put in a separate command to do something. I am told an attack upon new york is not looked on impossible, and the people is very willing to go on that expedition . . . in all, my dear sir, I speak here as a friend because this letter is a private one, I want much to be enabled to mind my reputation and the honor of the army under my command, on account of theyr not going to canada—but take care of Connway—if however things don't go in a decent way I'll have alwais the pleasure to see you and embrace you *at the french fashion* before leaving this country . . . if there are some niews, some niews papers etc etc be so kind as to forward them to me. I beg you above all to be very particular about everything which has been said publikly or privately of the canadian expedition and the commander in chief—don't be afraid to forward any disagreeable compliment. . . .

"Your most obedient servant
"the Mis. de La Fayette.

"the gentleman who was to carry this letter has forgotten it, I give to one of general connway's acquaintances, be so good sir as to answer me soon because I don't know how to do in the present circumstances."

The high flying young man was dejected by what Mr. Laurens called that "ill digested romantic affair"; but worse came on its heels, as the next letter, also to Mr. Laurens, shows:

"the 12th March, 1778

"Dear sir:

" . . . Gen'l Gates tells me that a niew arrangement will be made for the general officers in this part of the continent—that sentence I don't understand, but was interpreted to me in this way—*the marquis and general Kalb will leave to gn'l connway the chief command of the troops.* If it is so (unless such a disposition has been made out of a particular consideration for General Washington's recommendation) I'll beg leave to object that in my country we hold a particular military command as an honorable mark of confidence—that if I am recalled to leave this command in the hands of a gentleman who comes from Europe as well as myself, who is not above me neither by his birth neither by his relations or influence in the world, who has not had any more particular occasion of distinguishing himself than I have had, who has not had the advantages I can glory myself in, of being born a french man, I will look upon myself as not only ill used but very near being affronted—and such will be the sentiment of all those of my nation and europe whose opinion is dear to me.

"I am very far from making complaints—but as I hope Congress returns me some of the warm attachment I have showed for theyr country, they will permit and approve my going to france immediately—— I am sorry that this going away will take of from the army many french officers more useful than myself—but I should be very ungrateful for general de Kalb, gn'l portail, and the engineer le Ms. de Catoylne and almost all the french officers now in the continental army, was I to refuse theyr instances for following me in my going over to france—those who are at albany have renewed them to me when they heard of general conn-way commanding here and my being recalled.

"Don't believe, sir, that I speack here out of any particular ambition of supreme command—I was very well, I was very happy and quiete near the most respectable friend and the best general I can meet with—but I have been sent to command in chief in a particular place, the expedition is stopped, and immediately after a chief command is given to one of my officers when I am directed to repair to the main army—how do you think such a treatment will look? how can I agree to it?

"I am writing here upon an uncertainty for the intelligence of gn'l connway Commanding this army is not yet given to me *in form,* but, sir, if the niews is true I desire my intentions should be known soon, if not, I have no objections to the Congress knowing what I think my reputation would have obliged me to do in such a case. My heart schall alwais be opened, my frankness is as well known in courts as any where else, and I don't fear to tell freely my sentiments upon every happened or to happen occasion. Congress can read in my mind, and they will find the warmest attachment for theyr cause joined to the love of my own glory.

"I am sure I'll never meet with disagreements of this kind from the court of france *not even in favor of monsieur connway,* but even then the case would be different—love and duty bound me to the service of my country and there I'll serve as chearfully grenadier as general. In america, sir, I am only bounded by a friendship independent of any duty as soon as I am out of the service. * * * * *

"I beg you would oppen my public letters and then you will see that I need only to send you some fiew private lines on the subject—recalling me and leaving gn'l connway in a separate command is a thing which neither me neither any friend of mine will ever suffer. And I beg you would read my letters to Congress with those directed to general gates.

"I see nothing in the conduct of general connway and the board of war but deception and treachery—the conduct of the board schall be brought to the light and I'll take care of the insolent fellow who oppened my letter to you."

The report as to his being superseded by Conway was erroneous, and Washington wrote him the kindest and most considerate letter about the Canadian expedition:

"Headquarters, 10 March, 1778

"My dear Marquis:

"I have had the pleasure of receiving your two favors of the 19th and the 23rd of February, and hasten to dispel those fears, respecting your reputation, which are excited only by an uncommon degree of sensibility. You seem to apprehend that censure, proportioned to the disappointed expectations of the world, will fall on you, in consequence of the failure of the Canadian Expedition. But, in the first place, it will be no disadvantage to you to have it known in Europe, that you had received so manifest a proof of the good opinion and confidence of Congress, as an important detached command; and I am persuaded, that every one will applaud your prudence in renouncing a project, in pursuing which you would vainly have attempted physical impossibilities. . . .

However sensibly your ardor for glory may make you feel this disappointment, you may be assured, that your character stands as fair as ever it did, and that no new enterprise is necessary to wipe off this imaginary stain."

General Washington's letter evidently soothed his ruffled feelings for in a letter to Laurens written on March twentieth, he says: ". . . don't be angry against me, my good friend, and if I have made blunders you must impute them to my too quick feelings, and forgive the sinner on account of his repentence . . . But consider that by the first intelligence I got from you, it was likely they would fall upon a plan which every one will look upon as an affront for me. The only idea of it fired my head, and as even the suspicion of any uncivil treatment in such occasions will never be suffered by me from any one in the world, I sent immediately down Colonel armand to let know, *not what I was doing but what I should do in case such a thing would happen.* I have been too quick perhaps, but such is my temper and that temper of mine can't be altered." And Congress, in order to soothe La Fayette's feelings passed a resolution that they "entertain a high sense of his prudence, activity and zeal, and that they are fully persuaded nothing has or would have been wanting on his part, or on the part of the officers who accompanied him, to give the expedition the utmost possible effect."

In April La Fayette was back again at Valley Forge, and so ended the plan of the "Canadian irruption."

CHAPTER VI

BARREN HILL AND MONMOUTH

LA FAYETTE returned to Valley Forge with chagrin and disappointment. But chagrin and disappointment were soon forgotten, swept away by tumultuous joy over the news that France had recognized the independence of the United States and made an alliance with them. The Comte de Vergennes had long held the doubtful balance of policy, weighing bankruptcy at home against subservience to a triumphant and colossal British Empire, laying also in the scales his fear lest, if England should win or be reconciled by concessions to the revolted colonies, the two antagonists might reunite and both fall upon France. The defeat of Burgoyne turned the scales. The news of the alliance arrived on May 1, 1778, and there was great jubilation. La Fayette wrote to Mr. Henry Laurens:

"Valley Forge camp the 1st May, 1778
"houra, my good friend, now the affair is over, and a very good treaty will assure our noble independence. Very happy I find myself to see things so well brought to the common glory and satisfaction—*france* I am told has behaved with frankness and generosity— every circumstance affords me the Greatest pleasure. I hope we schall receive an authentic intelligence from Congress, and every one in the army evidently expects

68

to hear the signal from them, that they may abandon themselves to the solemn expression and acclamation of theyr happiness. I hope a grand, noisy *feu de joie* will be ordered, it will give high spirit to our soldiers, it will run through the whole continent."

Washington held a review of the army, with Lord Stirling commanding on the right and La Fayette on the left. La Fayette was entitled—though of course it would have been exaggerated and boastful to say *pars magna fui*—to feel that he had contributed to bring the alliance about; his romantic and adventurous departure had quickened interest and sympathy among people of great influence at Court, and ever since his arrival in America he had neglected no opportunity to preach and urge the American cause upon his friends in France. After the treaty had been signed on February sixth, the American envoys, Franklin, Deane and John Adams, were presented to the King and the royal family, and then they went to call upon Madame de La Fayette, still a girl of seventeen, in order to testify how much they believed themselves indebted to her husband for their happy success.

England recognized the need of prompt action before French aid could arrive. The easy-going Sir William Howe was superseded by Sir Henry Clinton, and signs were visible that the army in Philadelphia was going to do something. It was important to know what. Washington detached a body of twenty-two hundred men, the pick of the army, to reconnoiter, and put La Fayette in command. This choice was influenced, probably, by the wish to pay a compliment to France, partly perhaps by the wish to comfort La Fayette's vanity wounded by the fiasco of the

"Canadian irruption," but the determining cause
certainly was Washington's confidence in La Fayette's
ability and common sense. The instructions issued
state: "You will remember, that your detachment is
a very valuable one, and that any accident happening
to it would be a very severe blow to this army. You
will therefore use every possible precaution for its
security, and to guard against a surprise."

La Fayette left Valley Forge on May eighteenth,
crossed the Schuylkill at Swede's Ford to the north
side, and marched eastward, roughly parallel to the
river, a dozen miles to Barren Hill, which is about half-
way to Philadelphia. Here he took a good position on
high ground up above the river, with his right wing
protected by beds of rock, and his left by some stone
houses and a copse. Besides the road that he had come,
there were three roads running to the opposite quarter,
one toward Whitemarsh, one toward Germantown, and
the third to Philadelphia. It was possible for the
British to get to his rear by the Whitemarsh road, as
that passed Barren Hill somewhat to the east, and
therefore La Fayette ordered one of his subordinates,
General Potter, with six hundred men to guard it.

Scouts carried news of La Fayette's position to
Sir Henry Clinton, who jumped to the conclusion that
the Lord had delivered the young Frenchman into his
hands. He acted promptly. He sent eight thousand
men under General Grant by the Whitemarsh road to
make a long forced march and take their stand behind
La Fayette across the Swede's Ford road. This detachment should have been confronted by Potter and
his militia, but for some unexplained reason they were
not there, and the British marched by Barren Hill unmolested and took a position according to their in-

structions, and so cut off La Fayette's retreat in that direction. Clinton also sent a second detachment, consisting of two thousand men, under General Grey, who took (as I understand it) the road that led direct from Germantown to the village of Barren Hill, where La Fayette's left wing was stationed; and Clinton, himself, accompanied by General Howe, with the main body of the army took the direct road from Philadelphia, to attack La Fayette from the front. Clinton was so confident of success that, at least so the story went, he invited some ladies to meet Marquis de La Fayette at dinner that night, and Admiral Howe designated a frigate to carry the distinguished captive, the first fruits of the French alliance, in triumph to England.

Scouts reported to La Fayette that red coats were seen on the Whitemarsh road, but as he expected some dragoons in red jackets, he supposed that they were the men reported; nevertheless he sent for definite information. At this juncture Grey's division appeared on his left, approaching by the Germantown road; to meet them La Fayette shifted his front, making his men take shelter behind the stone houses, and in the cemetery, and also in the little wood. He had hardly completed this maneuver when orderlies rushed up, reporting all the enemy's movements, and cries rose, "We are surrounded! We are surrounded!" The young French general, with Washington's words ringing in his ears that the loss of these picked troops would be a severe blow to his army, had as the French say a *mauvais quart d'heure*. He smiled unconcernedly and dispatched some aides to make their way to Valley Forge and ask help of Washington. They returned and reported that they could not get through the encompassing lines. In Philadelphia, the Tory ladies were deciding what smocks they should wear to Sir Henry's dinner party.

There was one hope. Aides reported that Matson's Ford, a little more than two miles west of Barren Hill, was not yet occupied, though the British detachment of eight thousand men under General Grant was nearer to it than La Fayette. It was a stirring moment, but the young Frenchman was cool. By great luck the way to Matson's Ford ran over low land that was hidden from the upland occupied by General Grant. La Fayette hurried part of his force at once to the ford; he himself stayed and sent one thin line to the cemetery to halt Grey's attack, and another, so placed as if it was the front rank of a large body behind, to the border of the wood opposite Grant. Both Grey and Grant, seeing American soldiers facing them, paused to draw their men into fighting lines. Grey, in particular, proceeded cautiously, examining every rock and hollow in fear of some trap. La Fayette took advantage of these precious minutes to conduct his main body by the lower road unseen, and slip by Grant's troops which were still advancing prudently on the high land above; he was soon followed by his skirmishers, who must have run as hard as they could. It is said that Grey's men coming up by the cemetery, and Grant's men through the wood, nearly fired on one another. The Americans crossed the ford, and took so advantageous a position to defend it, that when Clinton came up, he did not venture to attack, and there was nothing for the British generals to do but lay the blame on one another, march back to Philadelphia and countermand the dinner party. As the troops under Grant had marched about forty miles, there may have

been grumbling. In the meantime Washington, hearing the cannon shots asking for help, had been very anxious. He gave La Fayette a warm welcome, and wrote to the President of Congress as follows:

"On the night of the 19th, the enemy moved out in force against the detachment under the Marquis de La Fayette, mentioned in my letter of the 18th, which made a timely and handsome retreat in great order over the Schuylkill at Matson's Ford. Our loss was nine men in the whole. The enemy's loss is supposed to be something more. Their march was circuitous and rapid, and I should imagine many of their men suffered from it. General Clinton, it is said, commanded in person."

And later in a letter to Franklin he speaks of, "The brilliant retreat by which La Fayette eluded a combined maneuver of the whole British force." Henry Laurens, president of Congress wrote to congratulate him; La Fayette wrote back:

"dear sir:

"I have received your late obliging favor and return you my very sincere thanks for it—if there is something to be praised in our late retreat it is much more owing to the intelligence and exertions of the officers, to the spirit and good order of the soldiers I had the honor to command than to any merit of my own. . . ."

La Fayette, ever since his drive to Bethlehem, had been on most friendly terms with Mr. Laurens, and at Valley Forge he made close acquaintance with Mr.

Laurens' son, who was somewhat older than himself. In one letter to the father he says:

"Valley Forge Camp 25th. May, 1778

"Dear Sir:

"I make you my warmest thanks to have projenited a son like yours whose company and friendship is so agreeable to me in camp, whose activity, zeal, intelligence and military knowledge have been so useful to me in the field during our detachment, and tho' you didn't think much of me when you did get him, I however acknowledge myself under great obligation to you for that so well performed work of yours. . . .

"Your most obedient servant

"the MARQUIS DE LA FAYETTE."

A month later General Clinton evacuated Philadelphia and marched northeastwardly across New Jersey toward New York. Washington with his army followed by a parallel road, some twenty to twenty-five miles farther west, biding his opportunity either to harass or to attack. He held a council of war as to which course to pursue. Some of the generals including Charles Lee, an Englishman by birth then second in command, were in favor of doing no more than harass, while La Fayette and a few others were in favor of the more spirited course. In spite of the disapproving majority, Washington decided to attack, and, perhaps partly in recognition of La Fayette's fighting spirit, put him in command of an advanced detachment of four or five thousand men, with orders to hang upon the British flank and rear, and attack if a favorable opportunity should show itself. Remember that La Fayette was not yet twenty-one years old. The command of this advanced division had been offered to Charles Lee, who had declined it. By this time the British army had taken the road from Allentown, which lies a little east of Trenton, and had marched eastwardly toward Monmouth Court House. It was now June twenty-fifth. La Fayette set out in pursuit and reached a place called Cranberry. From here he wrote that evening in high spirits to General Washington. Next morning, stirring with the lark, he dispatched a second letter:

> "At Cranberry, 5 O'clock
> "June (26) 1778

"Dear General:

"I have received your orders for marching as fast as I could, and I have marched without waiting for the provisions, though we want them extremely. . . . General Forman is firmly of opinion that we may overtake the enemy,—for my part I am not so quiet upon the subject as he is, but his sentiment is of great weight on account of his knowledge of the country. It is highly pleasant to me to be followed and countenanced by the army that if we stop the enemy and meet with some advantage they may push it with vigor. I have no doubt but if we overtake them we possess a very happy chance. However, I would not have the army quite so near as not to be quite master of its motions, but a very little distance may do it. . . . I beg when your Excellency will write to me, that you could let me know the place you have reached, that I might govern myself accordingly.

"With the highest respect I have the honor to be, etc.

> "LA FAYETTE."

But La Fayette was doomed to disappointment, as on the fantastic "irruption into Canada," in his hopes of reputation from a triumphant attack. General Lee, a little older than Washington, was second in command, he had fought in the French and Indian War, he had served both in the Polish and Russian armies, and had a large knowledge of military affairs; he was also a man of force and persuasiveness, and bore himself with such an assumption of superiority that virtually everybody had accepted him at his own valuation. Nobody even now knows what his real motives were; but his conduct at this juncture indicates that he wished to save the British army from defeat or loss, and did his best to give his wishes full effect. Perhaps he was jealous that a mere boy, and a Frenchman at that, should take his place in what was obviously a very important post. He had refused, as I have said, to accept this command, but that same day he thought the matter over, changed his mind, and wrote to Washington:

"Camp, at Kingston, 25 June, 1778

"Dear General:

"When I first assented to the Marquis de La Fayette's taking command of the present detachment, I confess I viewed it in a very different light from that in which I view it at present. I considered it as a more proper business of a young, volunteering general, than of the second in command in the army; but I find it is considered in a different manner. They say that a corps consisting of six thousand men, the greater part chosen, is undoubtedly the most honorable command next to the Commander-in-Chief, that my ceding it would of course have an odd appearance. I must entreat, therefore, after making a thousand apologies for the trouble my rash assent has occasioned you, that, if this detachment does march, I may have the command of it. . . . If this detachment . . . is to be considered as a separate, chosen, active corps, and put under the Marquis's command until the enemy leave the Jerseys, both myself and Lord Stirling will be disgraced.

> "I am, dear General, yours etc.
>   "CHARLES LEE."

He also wrote to La Fayette begging him to give up the command in his favor: "I place my fortune and my honor in your hands. You are too generous to destroy both the one and the other."

La Fayette was already fully absorbed in the exciting pursuit. Soon after leaving Cranberry very early in the morning of June twenty-sixth, he reached Hightstown, which he calls both Hidestown and Icetown, showing that his ear has not become as yet completely attuned to local pronunciation. Here he wrote again at quarter past seven to General Washington:

"I should be very happy if we could attack them before they halt, for I have no notion of taking one other moment [*i. e.* of taking any other time of attack] but this of the march. If I can not overtake them, we could lay at some distance, and attack to-morrow morning, provided they don't escape in the night, which I much fear, as our intelligences are not the best ones. I have sent some parties out, and I will get some more light by them."

In the meantime Washington had already written

a letter that conferred chief command upon Lee, limited merely by the condition that if La Fayette had already started upon some plan of attack, too far advanced to be advantageously abandoned, Lee should accept the plan and carry it out; but as yet La Fayette had not received the letter, for he goes on to say:

"Sir, I want to repeat to you in writing what I have told to you, which is, that if you believe it, or if it is believed necessary or useful to the good of the service and the honour of General Lee, to send him down with a couple of thousand men, or any greater force; I will cheerfully obey and serve him, not only out of duty, but out of what I owe to that gentleman's character. I hope to receive, soon, your orders as to what I am to do this day or to-morrow, to know where you are and what you intend, and would be happy to furnish you with completing some little advantage of ours.
"LA FAYETTE."

General Washington, as always, in answering was exceedingly careful of La Fayette's sensibilities, and his letter ends: "General Lee seems satisfied with the measure, and I wish it may prove agreeable to you, as I am, with the warmest wishes for your honour and glory, and with the sincerest esteem and affection——
"Your most obedient servant
"Geo. Washington."

In the meantime, while La Fayette's corps had been following the British, Washington with the main body of the army had reached Cranberry, and then fearing lest La Fayette should advance beyond easy reach, he sent orders for him to withdraw a little to English-

town. These orders arrived late on the evening of the twenty-sixth. La Fayette answered:

"Dear General:

"Your orders have reached me so late and found me in such a situation that it will be impossible to follow them as soon as I could wish. It is not on account of any other motive than the impossibility of moving the troops and making such a march immediately, for in receiving your letter I have given up the project of attacking the enemy, and I only wish to join General Lee. . . . I do not believe Gen. Lee is to make any attack to-morrow, for then I would have been directed to fall immediately upon them, without making eleven miles entirely out of my way. . . . I beg your pardon, Sir, if my letter is so badly written, but I want to send it soon and to rest one or two hours.

"I have the honor to be, etc.

"LA FAYETTE."

La Fayette proceeded to Englishtown early on the morning of the twenty-seventh, and handed over the command of the advance corps to General Lee. The next day the battle of Monmouth was fought. The story is confused. Washington, judging that the situation of the two armies was favorable for an attack, ordered Lee to hold his troops in readiness. At four o'clock in the morning La Fayette, who, now that he had been deprived of the command, regarded himself as a volunteer, asked Lee where he should go, and was told, if it should be agreeable to him, to go with the picked troops. But before those troops had proceeded a mile they received orders from General Lee to halt. After waiting and waiting La Fayette became impatient, and went to Lee to ask what was the matter. Lee replied that the intelligences he received did not hang together. After a time, however, the picked troops advanced but got into a hollow where both cannon and troops were useless. From that time on there were orders to retreat and great confusion. Nobody seemed to know what the matter was. Finally General Washington came up with the rest of the army; he was very angry at the situation, stopped the retreat and posted some troops in a position to hold the enemy, until he had time to form the main army in order of battle. The fight then lasted till evening. During the night the British army moved off, and had gone far enough by daylight to make pursuit impracticable. Washington won great credit by changing the fate of the day. La Fayette says: "General Washington seemed to turn back Fortune by a glance, his noble dignity, his grace, and presence of mind were never more manifest." Lee was tried by a court-martial at which all the principal officers, including La Fayette, testified. He was condemned for disobedience of orders, and for misbehavior in the presence of the enemy, "by making an unnecessary and in some few instances, a disorderly retreat," and for disrespect to the Commander-in-Chief, and suspended from any command for a year.

CHAPTER VII

THE EXPEDITION AGAINST NEWPORT

In spite of La Fayette's unhesitating and courteous acceptance of Lee's change of mind in asking for the command of the advanced corps at Monmouth, it is natural enough to assume that he felt great personal disappointment at the loss of an opportunity to gather laurels. Another disappointment, the third, was to follow on the heels of this. The Comte d'Estaing with a strong French fleet arrived in Delaware Bay, in the beginning of July, 1778, too late to block Lord Howe in Philadelphia; he then made an attempt to attack New York and the British fleet at anchor there, but was prevented because the French ships drew too much water to cross the bar beyond Sandy Hook. The next object of attack was the British garrison on Rhode Island, the island on which Newport lies, and a plan was concerted between the Comte d'Estaing and General Washington for a joint attack by land and sea. At this time Washington was in camp at White Plains, keeping an eye on General Clinton in New York, while General Sullivan was in charge of the American troops in the state of Rhode Island. It seemed prudent to strengthen Sullivan; so Washington sent a detachment of continental troops, and put La Fayette in command.

"White Plains, 22 July, 1778

"Sir:

"You are to have the immediate command of that detachment from this army which consists (etc.). . . . You are to march them, with all convenient expedition and by the best route, to Providence in the State of Rhode Island. When there, you are to subject yourself to the orders of Major-General Sullivan, who will have the command of the expedition against Newport.

"Having the most perfect reliance on your activity and zeal, and wishing you all the success, honor, and glory, that your heart can wish, I am with the most perfect regard,

"Yours, etc.

"GEORGE WASHINGTON."

La Fayette was very happy and proud to command two thousand American regulars in what there was good hope to expect would be a victory over England. He had already written the Comte d'Estaing:

"I rejoice to think that you are about to deal the first blow to an insolent nation, because I know that you will rightly value the pleasure of humiliating it and because you are sufficiently acquainted with it to hate it. I have the honor to be united with you in this sentiment as well as by the ties of kindred and by our common origin as *Auvergnats,* and there is no consideration in the world that is wanting to make me wish for your success with an ardor which it is impossible for me to express. . . . If I can be of service to you, Monsieur le Comte, command me; the more you give me to do for you the happier you will make me. The opportunity of being useful, even in the smallest matter, to my country, which is dearer to me every day that I realize its excellence above all others, will always give me the greatest happiness. . . . I hope you may defeat them, I hope you may send them to the bottom. . . . I hope you may now begin the great work of their destruction and put their nation under our French feet. I hope you will show them to their cost what a Frenchman can do—a Frenchman and an Auvergnat!

"Your very humble and obedient servant
"the MARQUIS DE LA FAYETTE."

But La Fayette, as I say, was destined to face more disappointments. In the first place, General Greene, whose home was in Rhode Island, wished to take part in the expedition. As there were no more troops to be spared, there was nothing to do but divide La Fayette's Continental detachment and give Greene half. General Washington, who had long been accustomed to deal tenderly with the susceptibilities of his officers, wrote one of his kind letters to explain the situation:

"Headquarters, White Plains
27 July, 1778

"Dear Marquis:

". . . I have concluded to give him [General Greene] a command in the troops to be employed in the descent. I have therefore directed General Sullivan to throw all the American troops, both Continental, state and militia, into two divisions, making an equal distribution of each, to be under the immediate command of General Greene and yourself. . . . Though this arrangement will diminish the number of Continental troops under you, yet this diminution will be more than compensated by the addition of militia, and I persuade myself your command will not be less agreeable, or less honorable, from this change in the disposition. I am with great esteem and affection, dear Marquis, your most obedient servant,

"GEORGE WASHINGTON."

There are a number of celebrated friendships in history, in which both friends have mutually shown constancy, tenderness, loyalty and sympathetic appreciation, but there is none that I have read of which sets off the characters of both friends in so vivid and high colored a manner: George Washington in his vigorous maturity, with his kindliness and soldierly breeding that cover and half conceal the massive steadfastness of his nature, and La Fayette, brimming with the new wine of youth, enthusiastic, impetuous, yearning for glory, yet ready to renounce his high hopes, ready to turn from the laurel bush, and draw back his extended hand though itching to pluck, at his friend's desire.

"Providence, August 6, 1778

"Dear General:

"I have received your Excellency's favour by General Greene, and have been much pleased with the arrival of a gentleman who, not only on account of his merit, and the justness of his views, but also by his knowledge of the country and his popularity in this State, may be very serviceable to the expedition. I willingly part with the half of my detachment, though I had a great dependence upon them, as you find it convenient to the good of the service. Anything, my dear General, you will order, or even wish, shall always be infinitely agreeable to me, and I will always feel happy in doing anything which may please you, or forward the public good.

". . . Though I have no account, neither observations to give your excellency, as I am here a *man of war of the third rate,* I will, after the expedition, scribble some lines to you, and join to the account of General Sullivan, the assurance that I have all my limbs, and that I am, with the most tender affection, and entire confidence, yours, with high respect,

"LA FAYETTE."

"White Plains, August 10, 1778
"My dear Marquis:

"Your favor of the 6th instant, which came to my hands yesterday, afforded a fresh proof of the noble principles on which you act, and has a just claim to my sincere and hearty thanks. . . . The courier to Count d'Estaing is waiting. I have only time therefore to assure you, that with the most perfect esteem and exalted regard I have the honor to be, my dear Marquis, your obedient and affectionate servant.

"GEORGE WASHINGTON."

To La Fayette's disappointment in sharing his command was added the far greater disappointment of the complete failure of the whole expedition. He arrived at Providence on August fourth; the French fleet was already off Newport, but General Sullivan had not been able to assemble the New England militia. The French admiral was put out by this delay for he had neither fresh food nor fresh water, and scurvy had broken out among his crews. Had a combined attack

by the fleet and the American army been made at once,
it seems that it must have succeeded. Sullivan asked
for a delay of nine days. During this time the English
general was able to concentrate his men and strengthen
his fortifications. La Fayette went to and fro between
Sullivan and d'Estaing, smoothing, encouraging, and
looking after all sorts of matters that were required
by the ships on the one hand and by the army on the
other. The Admiral, who was considerably more than
twice as old as La Fayette, recognized at once his
value. "No one is in a better position," he wrote to
the French Ministry, with more prophetic truth than
he could imagine, "than this young general officer to
become an additional bond of unity between France
and America. He enjoys here the highly merited
consideration which is due to his zeal, his gallantry,
and his wisdom."

Difficulties, however, arose over the plan of attack.
The Americans wanted to make a landing at a single
point, whereas the Comte d'Estaing preferred land-
ings at two points or more. The Americans also proposed that they should land on the island first and the
French after them, but the French commander was not
willing to accept for his troops a position of inferior
honor; the Americans wished to hold their troops together as the main army, but La Fayette's ambition
and patriotism led him to advocate the detachment of
a body of American regulars to unite with the French
troops, the whole being under his command. Allies
usually find it difficult to cooperate, each thinks that
the other is shirking its fair share of the common task
or seeking its own ends; besides, it is natural for different minds to approve different plans. La Fayette
was ambitious, and, not without reason, felt that his

relations with both armies would further harmonious action if he were in command of combined forces; on the other hand, American officers, far older than La Fayette, and others near his age but of far lower rank, were inevitably jealous of his sudden elevation to honor and power.

An accord was at last reached that a regiment of regulars and a thousand militia should get together with the French, under La Fayette's command. It was agreed that the attack should take place on August tenth; the Americans were to land on the island from the mainland to the east, and La Fayette's command from Canonicut Island to the west.

On August ninth, the day before the date agreed upon, General Sullivan thinking that he saw a good opportunity, crossed over and landed first. The French were extremely indignant at this breach of the agreement, and regarded it as a blow to their national pride. They thought that Sullivan was trying to win laurels without sharing them; the Americans on their part, thought that the French were over-sensitive. Finally when the Comte d'Estaing was about to transfer his troops from Canonicut to Newport Island, the look-out reported that the English fleet was approaching. The French troops were hastily reembarked, and the ships collected from their scattered positions.

The next day, taking advantage of a favorable wind, the Comte d'Estaing bore down upon Admiral Howe's fleet, which being inferior in strength, turned and sailed away. The French pursued. La Fayette was watching with happiest expectations. Just as the French fleet was drawing up to the English a terrific storm burst upon them, drove ships every which way, did great damage impartially, and effectually separated the fleets. A week later, Comte d'Estaing managed to bring his crippled ships back to Rhode Island, but merely to say to the Americans that he could not take part in an attack on Newport, but must go to Boston for repairs. His reasons were that his ships were greatly damaged and that he had learned that a fresh British fleet, under Admiral Byron was on its way to join Admiral Howe. "His express orders from the King were to go to Boston in case of an accident or a superior fleet."

The Americans were greatly taken aback. La Fayette went aboard the French flag-ship to see if a reconsideration were possible, or if at least some French troops could not be left. But the French officers had lost confidence in General Sullivan. No agreement could be reached, and the fleet sailed for Boston. The Americans were bitterly disappointed and angry, they believed themselves dishonestly abandoned, and they railed against the French. Sullivan and his officers signed an angry protest, alleging that such a departure injured the honor of the French nation. Comte d'Estaing answered with dignity that "the paper imposed upon the commander of the King's squadron the painful but necessary duty of profound silence." Washington and Congress, in alarm lest there might be a possible breach with France, did their best to calm General Sullivan and hush the matter up. La Fayette was deeply incensed. He wrote at once to the Comte d'Estaing:

"The state I am in, the feelings that animate me, and the outbursts of impatience, to which I have given way, make it impossible for me to talk or write to you with a quiet mind. Can you believe that I was summoned to attend a council where a protest was made against a measure taken by the French fleet? I told these gentlemen that my country was dearer to me than America, that whatever France does is right, that M. le Comte d'Estaing was my friend, and that I was ready to support these opinions by my sword, which had never been put to a better use. I added that if they had shown very little delicacy, upon their part, in summoning me, I also should show little in my choice of expressions. They all apologized, and said they were far from requiring me to give my vote. In the meantime, M. le Comte, imagine my situation; for from now on I shall be in fear lest I have to resent every word I hear spoken."

Even after that, on August twenty-fourth, General Sullivan in a general order to the army, stated that France had refused her assistance. La Fayette felt "obliged to pay a visit to General Sullivan" to demand retraction. Sullivan returned the visit, and hot words were exchanged. Sullivan, not afraid of a duel, understood the ills that might follow if La Fayette continued angry, and in an order two days later explained and modified his earlier language. La Fayette poured out his indignation to Washington:

"Camp before Newport, 25 August, 1778
"My dear General:
". . . My reason for not writing the same day the French fleet went to Boston was, that I did not choose to trouble your friendship with the sentiments of an afflicted and injured heart, and injured by that very people I came from so far to love and support. Don't be surprised, my dear General; the generosity

of your honest mind would be offended at the shocking sight I have under my eyes. . . . It is not to the commander-in-chief, it is to my most dearest friend, General Washington, that I am speaking. I want to lament with him the ungenerous sentiments I have been forced to see in many American breasts. . . . The people turned mad at their departure, and wishing them all the evils in the world, did treat them as a generous one would be ashamed to treat the most inveterate enemies. You can not have any idea of the horrors which were to be heard in that occasion. . . . I am sure it will infinitely displease and hurt your feelings, I am also sure you will approve the part I have taken in it, which was to stay much at home with all the French gentlemen who are here, and declare, at the same time, that anything thrown before me against my nation I would take as the most particular affront.''

To this affronted, troubled, sensitive young man, George Washington answered in his noble and sympathetic way. And after a few days passion subsided, and La Fayette again felt happy in his purpose to serve with perfect loyalty in the American army. General Greene wrote to Washington: ''The Marquis' great thirst for glory and national attachment often run him into errors. However, he did everything to prevail upon the Admiral to cooperate with us that man could do.'' The very day this was written La Fayette gave additional proof of his desire to heal the breach; in spite of his extreme reluctance to miss his part in the fighting which looked imminent, he rode nearly seventy miles to Boston, at Sullivan's request, to urge the local authorities to help repair the

French fleet, and to urge the Comte d'Estaing to send his soldiers to Rhode Island. Two days later on a Sunday, he rode back, covering the seventy miles in six hours and a half.

But in the meantime word had come that Lord Howe's fleet was on its way, and there was nothing for the Americans to do but withdraw from before Newport. There was some fighting at the north end of the island; the enemy was the stronger, and that same Sunday, late at night, Sullivan was busy transferring his men in all secrecy to the mainland. La Fayette arrived an hour before midnight and took command of the rear guard. "He returned in time enough," Sullivan reported, "to bring off the pickets and other parties which covered the retreat of the army, which he did in excellent order; not a man was left behind, nor the smallest article lost." So ended the ill-starred expedition. The French fleet sailed away.

Congress, now thoroughly alive to the young man's sensitiveness, passed the following resolution:

"That Mr. President be requested to inform the Marquis de La Fayette, that Congress have a due sense of the sacrifice he made of his personal feelings in undertaking a journey to Boston with a view of promoting the interest of these states, at a time when an occasion was daily expected of his acquiring glory in the field, and that his gallantry in going on Rhode Island when the greatest part of the army had retreated, and his good conduct in bringing off the pickets and out-sentries; deserves their particular approbation."

It was in acknowledgment of this resolution that La

Fayette wrote to Henry Laurens, the President of Congress, his well known words: "The moment I heard of America, I loved her; the moment I knew she was fighting for freedom, I burnt with a desire of bleeding for her; and the moment I shall be able to serve her at any time, or in any part of the world, will be the happiest one of my life."

CHAPTER VIII

AUTUMN 1778

THIS resolution passed by Congress might well have been addressed to a man of mature years and broad experience. And, in many ways, La Fayette was old beyond his years, but in others he manifested the temperament and the ardent affections of youth, as well as traits that we, whether rightly or wrongly, more commonly attribute to the French than to ourselves. These traits had quite as large a share as his courage in forming what the Comte d'Estaing designated as an additional bond of union between the two countries. They appear most clearly in his letters home:

"To the Duc d'Ayen
"Bristol, 11 September, 1778

". . . I have already tried to express to you a part of the joy that your last letter gave me, but I can't begin this without speaking of it again. . . . I bless the ship a thousand times that brought your letter, and the favoring wind that sped it to the American shore. It speaks with a kindness and friendliness that has sunk deep in my heart; and I appreciate its value. The indulgence you show me is much above what little I could ever lay claim to; and your approbation is so dear to me, and my pleasure at receiving it so keen, that I do not look at it too critically, and I am as much delighted as if I were convinced that I deserved it. I love you too much not to be enchanted, and overcome with joy, whenever I receive marks of your kindness. You will find men more worthy of it, but I make bold to challenge you to find any who are more sensible of it than I, or who desire it more. I am perfectly sure of that, and if I were so unfortunate as to be disapproved of, I venture to hope that you will never cease to love me. The greatest pleasure that I could enjoy would be to have you embrace me and hear you say that you do not disapprove my conduct, and that you still have that affection for me that makes me so happy. It is impossible to depict all the delight your letter caused me, and the sentiments of affection that prompted it.

". . . . You understand how impossible it is for me to foresee when I shall have the happiness of being with you again. I shall act according to circumstances. The great reason for going back would be the idea of an invasion of England. I should almost think myself dishonored if I were not there. I should be so angry and ashamed that I should wish to drown myself, or hang myself according to the English fashion. My greatest happiness would be to drive them out of here, and then go to England, and serve there in the command that you would have. [And he ends his long letter] . . . . My heart is full of the liveliest gratitude to you, of the most profound respect, and will always feel them, in every land and on every occasion until my last breath.

"LA FAYETTE."

"To Madame de La Fayette

"Bristol, September 13, 1778

"Dear Heart:

"If anything could trouble my pleasure in writing to you, it would be the bitter thought that I am still writing from a corner of America, and that all I love is six thousand miles away. . . . Your last letter arrived at the same time with the fleet; since that immeasurable time, since two months, I have been waiting for more, and nothing comes. . . . . Don't leave me in this cruel ignorance, dear Heart. . . . I conjure you to answer at once and at great length, just as if I were merely waiting for your letter to get up and go. Bid them fetch pen and paper, and tell me at once by every opportunity that you love me and will be very glad to see me again. O my Heart, it is not that I do not know it well. My affection bandies no compliments with you. . . . But it is always a fresh pleasure to hear you say that you love me. . . . And what can my love bid you say to our dear Anastasie [the baby]? You will find them in your heart and in mine, which you know equally well. Cover her with kisses. Teach her to love me in loving you. We are so united that to love one must be to love the other. Good-by, dear Heart. When shall I be allowed to see you and never leave you again, to make your happiness as you do mine; to beg for pardon on my knees? Farewell, farewell, we shall not be separated long."

He entertained a hope to go to France, if not to take part in an invasion of England, at least to see his wife and family while there was a lull in the fighting in America, and also to lay before the King's

Cabinet a new plan. His imagination, building castles of glory, had conceived the idea of another expedition to Canada. The French Government should send five or six thousand men by sea up the St. Lawrence, and the Americans should raise an army of twelve thousand men, to enter Canada at three vulnerable points. "He lays down," so young Laurens says, who in spite of La Fayette's candid praises of him, was a little jealous, "as self-evident that Canada can not be conquered by American forces alone; that a Frenchman of birth and distinction at the head of four thousand of his countrymen, and speaking in the name of the Grand Monarque is alone capable of producing a revolution in that country." And, indeed, La Fayette, with all his gentleness and prudence had a touch of Hotspur in him, and thought it was "an easy leap to pluck bright honor from the pale-faced moon." He expected the Comte d'Estaing to take part in this expedition. He wrote to him: "I can think of nothing but of the happiness of going with you, of Halifax surrendering, of St. Augustine taken, of the British islands on fire, and all confessing that nothing can withstand the French!"

He spoke of the plan to Washington who did not encourage him. Indeed, the plan, although but an enlargement of the earlier projected "irruption into Canada," had to face many grave objections. There was plenty for the American army to do in the United States, and it would neither be a wise nor a popular policy to give the French a footing in their old province. To be sure Comte de Vergennes understood the opposition in America to any reestablishment of the French power on the northern border, and had pronounced loudly against any such attempt; but nations are suspicious, and allies, as Vergennes had just found out, had enough difficulties to maintain harmony without adding another. Besides, the French Government had no mind to make the United States, powerful as it expected them to become, more powerful still by the addition of Canada. Nevertheless, La Fayette laid his plan before Congress, and, so well did he present it that Congress brought in a favorable report, and directed that it be submitted to the French Government. But Washington declared himself strongly opposed; apparently his old feelings, got in the French and Indian War, flared up so briskly that he, at least for a moment, suspected that La Fayette, though affecting to put forward the plan as his own, was really acting on the instigation of the French Government. There is not the slightest reason to suppose that this suspicion was justified, and Washington probably thought no more than that La Fayette might have been used as a cat's paw, to judge from an extremely kind letter he wrote him at the time, and ever afterward his letters are full of genuine respect and affection. Here are Washington's words: "It is far from impossible, that the plan had its birth in the Cabinet of France, and was put into this artful dress to give it the readier currency." If this suspicion constitutes the shadow of a shadow upon the mutual trust and affection of these two men, it is the only one.

Certainly there never was a shadow on La Fayette's part and even while the plan was being discussed, Washington gave fresh proof of his kindly interest in La Fayette. Henry Laurens, who perhaps knew of Washington's surmise, wrote to him to say that the scheme originated in La Fayette's own mind, and was the "offspring of the purest motives."

The British Government, feeling little hope of reducing America to obedience by force, attempted a conciliatory policy, and sent over a commission headed by the Earl of Carlisle, to discuss conciliation. La Fayette, who had seen or heard of these men in England, wrote a few humorous comments upon them to Mr. Laurens; of Carlisle he said: "He is a fine gentleman, very well powdered, and a man of *bon goust*—he began by ruining his own fortune, and wanted to get the reputation of a man belov'd by the ladies. While I was in england he was much in love with a fair dutchess and pretty ill treated by her—however he is a good poet." The commission was imprudent enough to speak ill of the French, accusing them of "a perfidy too universally acknowledged to require any new proof." The French officers in the American service were very angry and deputed La Fayette to act as their spokesman. La Fayette, aged twenty-one, felt there was but one course for a gentleman to follow. He consulted d'Estaing who disapproved, and also General Washington, who wrote back: "The generous spirit of chivalry, exploded by the rest of the world, finds a refuge, my dear friend, in the sensibility of your nation only. . . . Besides, supposing his Lordship accepted your terms, experience has proved that chance is often as much concerned in deciding these matters as bravery; and always more than the justice of the cause." But La Fayette, without waiting to hear what Washington's advice would be hastily sent a challenge to Lord Carlisle: "I do not deign to refute your language, my Lord, but I am anxious to punish you for it. M. de Gimat, a French officer, will make such arrangements for me as will suit your convenience. As for me, Milord, all are satisfactory, pro-

La Fayette about twenty years old

Photograph by Giraudon, Paris

Madame de La Fayette, wife of La Fayette

From *France and New England*. Photograph by Giraudon, Paris

vided that I may add to the glorious advantage of being a Frenchman, the pleasure of proving to a man of your nation that nobody attacks one of mine with impunity.'' Of course Lord Carlisle declined. He said that as the offensive language was contained in a public document, there was therefore no private responsibility, and that the English and French fleets would decide the public issue. La Fayette afterwards admitted that Carlisle was right, yet at the time he scored a point, for the general sympathy was with the challenger and not with him who refused the challenge.

Not long afterward, La Fayette, foreseeing an inactive period ahead and still harboring his Canadian plan, asked and received permission for leave of absence to enable him to go to France.

"To Henry Laurens
"President of Congress:

"Sir:

"Whatever care I schould take not to employ the precious instants of congress in private considerations, I beg leave to lay before them my present circumstances, with that confidence which naturally springs from affection and gratitude. The sentiments which bind me to my country can never be more properly spoken of than in the presence of men who have done so much for their own. As long as I thought I could dispose of myself I made it my pride and pleasure to fight under American colours, in defence of a cause which I dare more particularly call ours, because I had the good luck of bleeding for it. Now, Sir, that france is involved in war, I am urg'd by a sense of duty, as well as by patriotic love, to present myself before the King, and know in what manner he judges proper to employ my services. . . . I dare flatter myself that I schall be look'd on as a soldier on furlough, who most heartily wants to join again his colours, and his most esteemed and belov'd fellow soldiers. In case it was thought that I can be any way useful to the service of America, when I schall find myself among my countrymen, in case any exertion of mine is deem'd serviceable, I hope, Sir, I schall always be considered as the man who is the most interested in the welfare of these United States, and who has the most perfect affection, regard and confidence for theyr representatives.

"With highest regard I have the honour to be, Sir, Your Excellency's most obedient humble, servant.

"LA FAYETTE."

The President replied:

"Sir:

"I had the honour of presenting to congress your letter, soliciting leave of absence, and I am directed by the house to express their thanks for your zeal in promoting that just cause in which they are engaged, and for the disinterested services you have rendered to the United States of America. In testimony of the high esteem and affection in which you are held by the good people of these states, as well as in acknowledgment of your gallantry and military talents, displayed on many signal occasions, their representatives in congress assembled have ordered an elegant sword to be presented to you by the American minister at the court of Versailles . . .

"I have the honour to be, with the highest respect,

and with the most sincere affection, Sir, your most obedient and most humble servant.

"HENRY LAURENS, President."

These compliments were not all. He was known in the army as *The Marquis* or *The Soldiers' friend,* and the newly arrived French Minister, Marquis Gérard, wrote to Comte de Vergennes that La Fayette had created for himself during his service in the United States, by his good breeding, prudence and courage an extraordinary position, and had become "the idol of Congress, of the army and of the people of America." And to crown all, Congress wrote to the King of France:

"To our great, faithful and beloved friend and ally, Louis the Sixteenth, King of France and Navarre:

"The Marquis de La Fayette having obtained our leave to return to his native country, we could not suffer him to depart without testifying our deep sense of his zeal, courage, and attachment. We have advanced him to the rank of major-general in our armies, which, as well by his prudent as spirited conduct, he has manifestly merited. We recommend this young nobleman to your Majesty's notice, as one whom we know to be wise in council, gallant in the field, and patient under the hardships of war. . . .

"Done at Philadelphia, the 22nd. day of October, 1778 by the congress of the United States of North America, your good friends and allies.

"HENRY LAURENS
"President."

And Samuel Cooper wrote to Benjamin Franklin: "This young nobleman has done honor to his nation, as well as to himself, by the manner in which he has served these States. His intrepidity and alertness in the field are highly distinguished. His prudence and good temper are equally remarkable. He is highly esteemed and beloved in Congress, in the army, and through the States; and though we are not without parties, and his situation has been sometimes very delicate, I have never heard that he had made a single enemy'' (Jan. 4, 1779).

La Fayette, however, was delayed at Fishkill many weeks by a fever, taken as a consequence of exposure, fatigue and anxiety. He himself says: ''A very severe fit of illness did put me very near of making a greater voyage than this of Europe,'' and he assigns the cause as follows: ''Overdone by rides and fatigues, and still more by disappointment at Rhode Island, and on top of that, having sat up late, worked, and drunk a great deal in Philadelphia.'' He came close to death's door. Washington's physician, Doctor Cochran, took care of him, and Washington, whose quarters were eight miles away, came every day to ask after him, with tears in his eyes and bade the doctor care for him as if he were his own son. La Fayette repaid Washington's tenderness in full; he is never tired of eulogies of the man ''who [as he says] united in himself all that is good and all that is great, and is still more sublime by his virtues even than by his talents. . . . In creating him on purpose for the American revolution, Nature did herself honor.''

Good care from Doctor Cochran, and, as he believed, Madeira wine, set him in health again, so that he was ready to sail, but the ship lacked a crew. The Boston Council offered to send out press gangs, but La Fayette would not consent. At last English deserters and prisoners were enlisted and the ship was manned. As it turned out, La Fayette's consideration bore dangerous fruit. The frigate sailed on January 11, 1779. La Fayette was a bad sailor. Off the Banks they met a terrible storm. On board was also the captain of one of d'Estaing's ships who, having lost an arm in the battle off Rhode Island, was going home; he had never seen such a storm and thought the vessel would sink. "Confound it," La Fayette in his bed, seasick, replied to this, "nevertheless, I have done well. But at my time—barely twenty years of age—with my name, rank and fortune, after having married Madamoiselle de Noailles, to leave everything and serve as a breakfast for codfish!" Later a worse peril assailed them.

The British Government offered rewards, at least so it was said, to mutineers bringing in rebel ships. At any rate, when the frigate was still several hundred miles from France, the English seamen aboard plotted a mutiny. The mutineers were to divide into groups, one group was to go to the ship's magazine, kill gunner, carpenter and boatswain, while a second group was to capture cabin, wardroom and quarter-deck. The captain was to be put in a cutter and let go without provisions; the lieutenants, if they refused to navigate the ship, should walk the plank; La Fayette was to be put in irons and sent to England. Everything was prepared. The forecastle guns were loaded and ready for use. The cry, "A sail!" was to be raised, and as soon as the officers and passengers went up on deck, four cannon loaded with grape-shot would in case of resistance have blown them to bits. The hour for action was shifted from four in the morning to four in the afternoon. During this interval the mutineers, misled by the Irish accent of an American who had lived a long time in Ireland, revealed their plan to him and offered him command of the ship. This man pretended to agree and, only an hour before the time set, managed to tell La Fayette and the captain. They, with the other officers and passengers, sword in hand, went on deck, gathered together the loyal sailors, and then called the thirty mutineers one by one to come up and as they came, put them in irons.

CHAPTER IX

HOME AND RETURN, 1779-1780

THE vessel arrived safe at Brest on February 6, 1779, and La Fayette hurried to Versailles to report to the ministers, and then on to Paris to see his family. His wife says: "My mother prepared me for the happy moment and told me of it herself. I should not try to describe how she shared my delight, nor what she herself felt when she found that everybody judged La Fayette's character and conduct just as she had done long before, that he had behaved as she had expected him to behave, and how happy his wife was after so much apprehension." His daughter amplifies the record: "My mother's intoxicating joy was beyond all description."

At Versailles he had interviews with Marquis de Maurepas, and the Comte de Vergennes, and was presented to all the ministers. Being in technical disgrace he was bidden keep on bounds within the Hôtel de Noailles, but that was the extent of his punishment. Everybody went to see him; all the ladies kissed him. At the end of a week his "exile" was forgiven; he had an interview with the King, who after giving him a *"douce réprimande,"* asked him many questions, and complimented him on his success. At the Queen's solicitation (according to report), he received permission to buy the regiment of the King's Dragoons which cost him eighty thousand livres. In fact honors dropped like manna. Even the jealous spleen of the old Duc de Choiseul, who dubbed him *Gilles-le-grand,* is proof of the wave of enthusiasm that swept over Paris. At the Comédie Française, some verses in his honor were interpolated into the play, the first time, it is said, that a living man was ever so honored. And in due course the sword that Congress had ordered was presented to him by Franklin's grandson, together with a letter from Franklin about it:

"Passy (Paris)

"Sir:

". . . Some of the principal actions of the war, in which you distinguished yourself by your bravery and conduct, are therefore represented upon it. These with a few emblematic figures, all admirably well executed, make its principal value. By the help of the exquisite artists of France, I find it easy to express everything but the sense we have of your worth, and our obligations to you; for this, figures, and even words, are found insufficient. I, therefore, only add that, with the most perfect esteem, I have the honour to be,

"B. FRANKLIN."

The papers were full of this presentation, and everybody talked of him. Madame du Deffand wrote to Horace Walpole, "No doubt you know of M. de La Fayette's return from America. He arrived on Thursday the 11th, two hours after midnight, and got down at Versailles at the Prince de Poix's who was giving a ball; he went to bed and the next day, Friday, he had an interview of two hours with M. de Maurepas. He went to Paris after dinner; he hasn't seen the King, and his orders are to see nobody except his relations; but he has so many, that they are almost all the Court. He is nephew, *à la mode de Bretagne* [a courtesy title], of the *Idole* [Comtesse de Boufflers, a charming lady old enough to be his grandmother] consequently he took supper with her on Sunday with a pretence at secrecy. She was visibly hidden (to use an expression of Pontdeveyle's in the *Punished Ass)*." All the young nobles wished to become "petits La Fayettes." And yet in spite of this celebrity his modest demeanor did not forsake him. The Duc de Croy speaks of meeting him: "He is nice looking, very simple and very modest. This young hero (as I may call him) behaved exceedingly well in America, where he won immense distinction *(honneur infini)* and enhanced it by his modesty. We talked for half an hour. He listened with deference, a very rare thing now-a-days."

Where there is so much fire there must be some smoke. A backbiter in *Mémoires secrets* says: "Madame la Comtesse d'Hunolstein is a pretty young woman in the suite of Madame la Duchesse de Chartres. . . . It is known that his Royal Highness, the Duke, was in love with her. . . . The Marquis de La Fayette, who was smitten at the same time, failing in any success, out of chagrin, went and joined the American Insurgents, so that she was indirectly the cause of his fortune and glory. The first time that he came back from America, his passion was not extinguished. . . . Madame d'Hunolstein was less unkind. . . ." One may judge the truth of this scandal by the cause it assigns for his going to America. The origin is worthy of it. The version published in London, says *"tel était hier le bruit général de l'opéra et au palais royal,* (such was the talk going about the opera house and the palais royal).'' It was repeated later by the Comte d'Espinchal, who was a violent royalist, in a story full of unfriendliness to La Fayette. Very likely it was concocted in order to explain his going to America. Another story says that he went to America because he was refused advancement in the army. A third, that he went because Madame de Simiane urged him to go. You see that the scandal mongers do not agree.

As to the last tale, Monsieur Bardoux says in *La Jeunesse de La Fayette:* ''The 18th century asserted its rights, and this model husband none the less inspired *une passion fort tendre qui se changea en fidèle amitié* (a very tender passion that turned into faithful friendship). The lady in question was Madame de Simiane, the loveliest and most charming lady at Court. The Vicomtesse de Noailles said that she had never heard any one speak of the effect produced by the sight of Madame de Simiane's face otherwise than as a sort of rapt enthusiasm. She was gay, delightful, charming, amiable, with an adorable heart, noble feelings and great good sense.'' I suspect Monsieur Bardoux of a romantic disposition, picturing all high society of the eighteenth century as we see it in Lancret, Boucher and Fragonard; he forgot the Duchesse d'Ayen who talked on high and holy things in a fashion so clear, so noble, so simple, that it was like a page of Pascal, and that young La Fayette lived with her for two years and loved her tenderly.

Monsieur Bardoux does not say where he got his gossip, but I presume from a lively rattle-pate, the Comtesse de Boigne, who was not born till several years afterwards. She says that Madame de Simiane

was the prettiest woman in France, very elegant and
charming, etc., and that La Fayette paid court to her
before he went away. On his return all society wished
him every success. On one occasion the two were
sitting in an opera box, when a song was sung—"Love
under laurels finds no lady unkind—and the people
in the boxes found the words most appropriate."
Really there is not much here to justify Monsieur
Bardoux's expression *une passion fort tendre*. The
Marquis de Condorcet, also, has a reference to
Madame de Simiane in his memoirs: "She is," he
says, "that very pretty lady who showed the noblest
feelings in making use of her influence on M. de La
Fayette's heart and head to inspire him, at the age of
eighteen, with the love of glory, since it was she who
bade him leave her in order to go to America."

Out of all this foolish gossip a few facts appear:
Madame de Simiane was pretty, for Madame Vigée
Lebrun painted her, and agreeable, for Madame de
Staël invited her to dinner, and she was a fine person,
for she refused to save herself during the Terror and
leave her brother behind. Monsieur Bardoux is, also,
quite right about the *fidèle amitié,* only he omits to
include Madame de La Fayette, for when the La Fayettes were living in Holstein, after their release from
an Austrian prison, Madame de Simiane, who had
then escaped from France, made a visit to
their aunt, Madame de Tessé, in order to be near them;
and ten years later, Madame de La Fayette from her
death-bed sent to this same lady, her *tendres amitiés.*
Miss Edith Sichel, who wrote a book on *The Household of La Fayette,* closes her comment on what she
calls "an approach to flirtation" with the words: "But
we do not need this evidence to know that La Fayette's

wife had nothing ignoble to complain of." I agree
with her. And Philip Gibbs, who following the way-
ward guidance of Hilaire Belloc permits himself some
highly flavored rhetoric in denunciation of La Fayette,
admits that his private life was above reproach. But
in order to put before the reader all the scandal that I
have chanced upon, I will add what Madame de La
Tour du Pin, a very charming and high-bred lady, who
had been in waiting upon Marie Antoinette and came
of right by the most extreme aristocratic prejudices,
says in her memoirs: "Madame de La Fayette was
always treated by her husband with the cruelest indifference, and she certainly could not forget the
numerous infidelities with which she was overwhelmed,
etc."

Over this sweeping calumny I must stop for a
minute. The course of my story will prove how false
this statement is concerning the relations between La
Fayette and his wife, and, it is likely enough, *falsum
in uno, falsum in omnibus,* but I am not willing to leave
the reader in a moment's doubt concerning what La
Fayette calls, "the thirty-four years during which I
was bound by the tenderest ties that perhaps ever
existed." That La Fayette, in these youthful days of
intoxicating glory, "kissed by all the ladies," the
cynosure of every eye, may have had certain *égarements* is possible enough; and I think a statement by
his daughter that her mother never felt jealousy implies that she may have had some occasion, but the
feeling of the aristocratic ladies became so bitter
against La Fayette that no scandals they tell carry any
weight. If there were any such *égarements* they were
very transitory; the one certain thing is that his love
for his wife and hers for him were worthy of Brutus

and Portia. His wife speaks of her first meeting with the man, then but a boy, "toward whom my heart was drawn in a way that foreshadowed the deep feeling that has always united us in the closest and tenderest fashion." And her daughter says: "Her feeling for my father was above and beyond all her other affections, without detriment to any of them. One might say that it was the most passionate feeling, if that expression were in harmony with the enchanting delicacy that put away from her jealousy of any sort, or at least the ungenerous emotions *(les mauvais mouvements)* which usually follow after jealousy. My father never perceived in her any wish that might vex him, and never in the bottom of her heart did she have a sad impression to hide." And when she came to die, while speaking to him of the noble character of her daughters' husbands and of their happiness, she said: "But I have not been able to make them as happy as I have been. It would have required the power of God to do a thing like that; you are incomparable."

I have touched upon this matter, or rather I have gone out of my way to mention it, lest some reader, mindful of the times, of the manners of the French Court, of the freedom (if that be the word) of behavior practised in Paris by young noblemen of the old régime, might think there was something to conceal. Possibly a tedious search among the evil tongues of the period might bring other slanders to light; but to dispel all such accusations one need but read in full the letter that La Fayette wrote on his wife's death which I shall quote hereafter, for if there is deep and holy human love it is depicted there. But I leave my digression, and take up my story. At this time then, La Fayette at twenty-one was the most distinguished man of his years in all Europe. William Pitt, his nearest rival, did not make his maiden speech in Parliament till two years later.

This year in France was busy enough. At home his wife was ill for a long time; the coming of a new baby (George Washington de La Fayette), who was born on December 24, 1779, was attended with pain, and she was under constant anxiety as to what might happen to the men of the family. La Fayette's brother-in-law, Monsieur de Noailles, went with his regiment to the West Indies, the Duc d'Ayen was expected to take part in an invasion of England, and nobody knew what La Fayette might do. His plan of an invasion of Canada had to be given up; Congress, under the influence of Washington, abandoned the idea, and the French Government was also opposed to it. He at once had new suggestions, and dinned them in turn into Vergennes' ears. One of them was to obtain the aid of Paul Jones and raid the coast towns of England. Another was a descent upon Ireland, a plan in its details confined to Maurepas, Vergennes and La Fayette; but Ireland was found to be "not ripe" for revolution; and that plan was abandoned for a proposed invasion of England. La Fayette was itching to go. The Hotspur in him overflowed its confinements. He tried to endue Vergennes with his effervescing spirit (June 10, 1779):

"Monsieur le Comte, I should not be frank with you if I did not admit that my blood is boiling a little in my veins. My imagination starts off into the enemy's country at the head of an advanced guard, or of a separate corps of grenadiers, dragoons and chasseurs. You may think me too ardent, perhaps, but since you are kind enough to be my friend, remember that I love the profession of war passionately, that I believe myself born on purpose to play at that game, that I have been spoiled during two years by the habit of having large commands and of enjoying great confidence! Remember that I need to justify the benefits that my country has heaped upon me. . . . Remember that I adore my country; that the thought of seeing England crushed and humiliated makes me tremble with delight. . . . Judge if I ought not to be impatient to know whether I am destined to be the first man to step on that shore and plant the first French flag in the midst of that insolent nation."

Next he had a plan for hiring ships of the line from Sweden, and of obtaining a loan for America in Holland; indeed, he was well justified in referring to his "repeated urgent representations for getting ships, money and support of any kind." John Adams wrote: "He has been indefatigable in endeavors to promote the welfare and comfort of our army, as well as to support their honor and character, and had success in both. . . . He has had a share in convincing this Court of the policy and necessity of transferring their exertions into the American seas, and I hope he will in time assist in bringing Spain into the same system" (February 21, 1780). During the summer he was at Havre in expectation of the invasion of England, but also very busy in urging Vergennes to send several thousand French troops to America. This was the beginning of the plan that led to the famous expedition of Rochambeau. La Fayette wrote with the confidence of youth, and the zeal and importunity of ill-regulated impatience, but he was carefully heeded. He drew up a long paper discussing such an expedition with Newport as its first object, and then Halifax, but dependent upon circumstances. After the invasion of England had been definitely abandoned, this new plan stepped into the forefront of possibilities, as both practicable and expedient. La Fayette, full of self-reliance, and knowing the high value of his familiarity with the American army, the people and their ways, believed that he was the best man to command the expeditionary force, and said so with frankness and persistence, and yet he says to Vergennes (July, 1779): "I suppose that I shall be thought too young for this command, but I shall certainly be employed in it." But by February, 1780, he gives his word of honor that he believes it would be most advantageous to the public interests of France in relation to the Americans for him to have the command; nevertheless, while pressing this view, he states what should be done in case another general is named.

The whole matter of an expeditionary force was exceedingly delicate, as the Americans were very jealous of the presence of foreign troops, and particularly of French troops, so much so that La Fayette had been enjoined not to ask for any; but so convinced had he become of the necessity of French military aid that he took upon himself, on his own responsibility to urge it. The government decided not to appoint La Fayette; it chose instead a distinguished veteran of the Seven Years' War, Lieutenant-General the Comte de Rochambeau, and promised him an army of six thousand men. There is nothing to show that La Fayette expressed the least disappointment; on the contrary he accepted with alacrity the mission of going ahead to concert with General Washington what should be done to prepare for the arrival of the French troops. It was in accordance with his advice that the very sensible instructions were given to Rochambeau, that he was to be subject while in America to the orders of General Washington, and that the French, as auxiliaries, should always yield precedence to American troops. He sailed on March 14, 1780, and arrived at Boston on April twenty-eighth. When he landed the city turned out, and conducted him in triumph to Governor Hancock's house. It is said that there were tears in Washington's eyes at the news of his return, and when he reached the army there was great rejoicing.

CHAPTER X

THE VIRGINIA CAMPAIGN

IN THE meantime the disposition of the British forces had changed. Their troops had been withdrawn from Newport, and in pursuance of the new policy a campaign had been begun against the southern states. These were sparsely populated and easily overrun. Charleston had been captured. North and South Carolina (in spite of General Greene's efforts and the daring of Marion's men), as well as Georgia, were considered safely British, and Virginia became the next object of attack. General Washington was uncertain what was best to do. The American army was poverty-stricken, their numbers were reduced to six thousand with hardly half fit for duty. They needed clothes, they needed food, they had eaten as Washington said, "every kind of horse food but hay," and often had gone hungry; they had no proper supplies of any sort. Paper money had fallen to a ratio of forty to one and there was little of it at that. Congress had no power to tax; it could only beg the states to provide. The only hope lay in the French expeditionary force. But as usual joint action had its difficulties.

The first plan had been to attempt to recover New York; but Clinton's return from Charleston rendered that plan dangerous. Then, after Rochambeau and his five thousand men, for the promised number had shrunk by a thousand, had come to Newport another

116

English squadron arrived, which gave the English the superiority at sea and put the French on the defensive. For two weeks La Fayette was at Newport with the French army, acting as the intermediary between Rochambeau and Washington, doing all in his power to provide both French and Americans with what was necessary, urging speed and action, and showing a surprising self-restraint, and capacity, as well as tact. It was very hard to prevent friction and to bring different minds to a common view. At Newport La Fayette had quarreled with General Sullivan, this time he irritated Rochambeau. So he wrote a letter of explanation:

"If I have offended you, I beg your pardon, for two reasons; first because of my affection for you, second, because I mean to do everything that you would like. Wherever I am merely a private citizen, your orders will be my law, and for the meanest Frenchmen here I would submit to any sacrifice rather than fail to contribute to their glory, their satisfaction and their union with the Americans. . . . I was wrong to have written officially, and hotly, what you would have forgiven to my youth if I had written to you privately as a friend, but I acted in such good faith that your letter surprised me as much as it grieved me, and that is saying a good deal."

The old soldier wrote back:

"My dear Marquis:
"Be assured of my most affectionate friendship, and that when I drew your attention, very gently, to the things which displeased me in your last despatch,

I understood that the warmth of your heart and spirit
had somewhat heated the coolness and wisdom of your
judgment. Employ this latter quality in the council,
and conserve all of the former for the time of action.
Remember that *le vieux père* Rochambeau is talking to
his dear son La Fayette, whom he likes very much and
whom he will continue to like and esteem until his
latest breath.

"LE COMTE DE ROCHAMBEAU."

Of this La Fayette says in a letter to his wife:
"When I saw that I could not persuade him, as it is
necessary for the general weal that we should be good
friends, I swore roundly that I had made a mistake,
that I was in the wrong, and in good set phrases
begged for forgiveness, and this had so wonderful an
effect that we are on better terms than ever." La
Fayette's character never shows in a better light; absolutely unaffected by his disappointment in not getting the command, he acted with complete loyalty both
to France and to America.

An unsuspected danger nearly shipwrecked their
plans. During this autumn Benedict Arnold plotted
his treachery. Washington and La Fayette had just
arrived at West Point from a conference at Hartford
with Rochambeau. It was the twenty-fifth of September. They were on their way to join Arnold at his
house, but stopped to inspect the fortifications. At
that very hour Arnold received word that André had
been captured, he bade good-by to his wife, slipped
away and escaped on board an English ship. That
same day La Fayette wrote to tell of it to the French
Minister, the Chevalier de La Luzerne. There is a
touch of Don Quixote in this letter, I think.

"Robinson House opposite West Point
"September 26, 1780

"Monsieur le Chevalier:

"When I left you yesterday morning to come here to breakfast at General Arnold's, we were far from suspecting the event I am going to tell you about. . . . That Arnold—a man who, although not so highly esteemed as has been supposed in Europe, had nevertheless given proof of talent, of patriotism, and, especially of the most brilliant courage—should at once destroy his very existence and should sell his country to the tyrants whom he had fought against with glory, is an event, M. le Chevalier, which confounds and distresses me, and, if I must confess it, humiliates me to a degree that I can not express. I would give anything in the world if Arnold had not shared our labors with us, if this man, whom it still pains me to call a scoundrel, had not shed his blood for the American cause."

He sat on the court-martial that condemned Major André to be hanged. It was a hard duty. He wrote to Madame de La Fayette: "He behaved with such frankness, highmindedness and delicacy that I can not help being very, very sorry for him." But apart from this painful incident, although always fretting at the restraints imposed by circumstances, his time was spent pleasurably enough. He wrote to his aunt, Madame de Tessé: "My health is good; that's my custom. My situation is as agreeable as possible. And I think that I get on very well with the French army. In the American army they pile kindness on kindness. I am in command of a scouting corps, the pick of the army. . . . My friend, General Washington, always behaves toward me as I have described." And to his wife (February 2, 1781), "The Americans always overwhelm me with kindness; not a day passes without proofs of affection and confidence, both from the people and the army."

He did not exaggerate his situation. The Marquis de Chastellux, distinguished as a soldier and writer, who had come with Rochambeau, visited him at his quarters in a New Jersey camp: "Where," he says, "I warmed myself with great pleasure, partaking from time to time of a large bowl of grog, which stands always on his table, and is offered to every officer that comes in. . . . We found all his troops in order of battle . . . and himself at their head expressing by his air and countenance that he was happier in receiving me there than at his estate in Auvergne. The confidence and attachment of the troops are precious possessions, well acquired riches, of which nobody can deprive him; but what, in my opinion, is still more flattering for a young man of his age, is the influence and consideration he has acquired with the politicians, as well as with military men. I shan't be contradicted when I say, that his mere letters have frequently produced more effect upon some states than the strongest exhortations of the Congress."

In the meantime Washington had watched the progress of the British arms in the south with great disquiet. He concerted with the French Admiral Des Touches a plan to surround and capture Benedict Arnold who was at Hampton Roads in Virginia, to "burgoynizer Arnold" as they said in Paris; the French fleet should proceed to the mouth of Chesapeake Bay, and he would send an army by land. In accordance with this plan he entrusted La Fayette

with the command of twelve hundred men, composed
of New England troops, and directed him to proceed
to the Head of Elk at the northern extremity of
Chesapeake Bay. Baron Steuben was to come up with
Virginia militia and cooperate. La Fayette arrived
at the Head of Elk on the third of March. The French
admiral, however, for one reason and another, was
delayed in starting, and when he put out from Newport met a British fleet and was driven back. The
chance of cooping up Benedict Arnold and capturing
him was lost; in due course General Phillips with more
troops joined Arnold, and La Fayette, who had advanced his army to Annapolis, was obliged to return
to Head of Elk (April eighth).

Here he received orders from Washington to join
General Greene; for if Cornwallis should march
against Greene from the south, and Benedict Arnold
from the north, Greene's little army might be in the
gravest danger. In obedience to these orders, La Fayette crossed the Susquehanna (April thirteenth). His
troops were in need of shoes, shirts, ammunition and
what-not; but the sorest trial in the eyes of these New
Englanders was a summer in the hot south, with its
malaria and general God-forsakenness, and the men
began to desert. Some of the best soldiers were reported missing. The prospect was dark. It looked as
if La Fayette would not have six hundred men left
when he reached his destination; but he was not wanting to himself. In order to stop desertions, he announced that he was starting upon a difficult and
dangerous campaign, to fight an enemy of superior
numbers, that the General was going, even if he went
alone, and hoped that the soldiers would go, also, but
that any man that wished was free to leave at once

by applying for permission to join the main army in
the north. This order read like Harry the Fifth's
speech before Agincourt:

Rather proclaim it, Westmoreland, through my host,
That he which hath no stomach to this fight,
Let him depart; his passport shall be made,
And crowns for convoy put into his purse.

And the effect was the same. From then on, not a
man wished to leave, and an under officer, unable to
march on account of a bad leg, hired a cart. This
same measure had no retroactive effect, and was not
to be misconstrued as an act of weakness: two deserters were caught, one of whom was hanged and the
other dismissed from the division. The difficulty of
destitution he met by other shifts. In Baltimore he
borrowed two hundred guineas on his own notes of
hand, and bought linen which the ladies of the city
made up into shirts.

It became evident by this time that the immediate
purpose of the British army under Phillips, who
ranked Arnold, was to capture Richmond, where large
stores of supplies had been collected. La Fayette
hurried off in order to get there first, leaving tents and
artillery to follow, making forced marches and sub-
jecting to requisition along the way all the horses and
carts he could lay hold of. He left Baltimore on April
nineteenth, arrived at Fredericksburg on the twenty-
fifth, and entered Richmond on the twenty-ninth. He
arrived but just in time. The next morning General
Phillips, who had been delayed by the duty of destroying as he went, appeared on the other side of the river,
twenty-four hours too late. La Fayette held too
strong a position to be attacked, so Phillips withdrew,

to continue the work of destruction on the south side of the James.

La Fayette's army contained less than a thousand Continental troops, and, with "more militia going off than coming in," and those undisciplined and ill armed, he had no choice but to keep out of danger and hinder the enemy as much as possible. So he marched forward and back, sending urgent messages to General Wayne to come and join him with his Pennsylvania troops as fast as possible. During these weeks La Fayette was kept on the alert with a vengeance. It might be that Phillips's army would go south, join Cornwallis, and then proceed to hem in General Greene, or it might wait for Cornwallis to come up and then force the evacuation of Richmond, perhaps attack Fredericksburg and even Baltimore. Greene's danger was his greatest fear; but when Cornwallis came marching northward and picked up the other British army (now under Arnold for Phillips had died), it was apparent that Richmond, not Greene's army, was the object threatened. It was impossible to risk a battle, and yet it was imperative to defend all the territory he could, for not only his army but Greene's, was dependent upon Virginia for their supplies. Washington wrote him to prolong the defense as much as might be. Cornwallis at this time had under him about four thousand men, eight hundred of whom were mounted. He advanced; La Fayette retreated. Both armies, in order not to impede their motions, carried with them only bare necessaries; there was hurried marching, La Fayette falling back as the British van approached his pickets. He wrote to Wayne: "I detest this runaway kind of war," and he says several times in his *Memoirs* that he was more afraid of his own hot temperament than of the enemy. Cornwallis on his part was confident. He wrote (in an intercepted letter) "the boy can not escape me"; and with La Fayette's army out of the way it would have been easy to take Baltimore and then march on Philadelphia. Sir Henry Clinton advised the British Government of Cornwallis's hopes.

To do justice to La Fayette's conduct during the Virginia campaign would require space disproportionate to the scale of my book. I can only give an outline. La Fayette, largely outnumbered, retired until he met General Wayne with troops of the Pennsylvania line. Then he came back to hamper Cornwallis. It happened that in the meantime Sir Henry Clinton in New York, fearful lest Washington and Rochambeau should attack him, ordered Cornwallis to retire to the sea, fortify himself and send on all the spare soldiers. Cornwallis, therefore, marched back to the coast, followed by La Fayette, who had been further strengthened by Virginia militia. There was one "smart action" on the way, and another at the crossing of the James River. In the second General Wayne's impetuosity nearly got the army into serious trouble, but again there was neither victory nor defeat. Nevertheless, La Fayette's military reputation was increased; he had certainly shown prudence and good judgment. He asked Washington what he thought of his generalship. Washington answered: "You ask my opinion of the Virginia campaign. Be assured, my dear Marquis, your conduct meets my warmest approbation, as it must that of everybody. Should it ever be said, that my attachment to you betrayed me into partiality, you have only to appeal to facts to refute any such charge." And after the campaign was over the Comte de Vergennes wrote to him: "Monsieur le Marquis, I have been following you step by step throughout your Virginian campaign; and I should often have been anxious for your safety if I had not had confidence in your prudence. It required a great deal of skill to maintain yourself, as you did for so long a time, in spite of the disparity of your forces, before Lord Cornwallis, whose military talents are well known." And Madison wrote to a friend: "Will not the Assembly pay some handsome compliment to the Marquis for his prudence and zealous services, while the protection of the country was entrusted to him? His having baffled and finally reduced to the defensive, so powerful an army as we now know he had to contend with, and with so disproportionate a force, would have done honor to the most veteran officers, and, added to his other merits and services, constitutes a claim on our gratitude which, I hope, will not be unattended to." The General Assembly of Virginia "as a lasting monument of his merit and their gratitude," ordered Houdon, the great sculptor, to make a marble bust of the meritorious general.

CHAPTER XI

CORNWALLIS withdrew to Portsmouth and the troops asked for by Sir Henry Clinton sailed for New York. Then La Fayette began to fear that the main action would take place at New York, and asked Washington to let him go there, too. But Washington gave him a hint of what was to happen. He, the Comte de Rochambeau and the French admiral at Newport, had come to an understanding for joint action. Washington had been inclined to attack New York, but Rochambeau proposed an expedition by sea and land to the Chesapeake, and when it became known that the Comte de Grasse, admiral of the French West Indies fleet, would cooperate, there was no further question as to which was the wiser plan. It had happened, however, that the letters sent by Washington to Congress to appraise them of the proposed attack on New York had fallen into English hands and it was for that reason that Sir Henry Clinton had ordered Cornwallis to send him all the soldiers he could spare.

La Fayette had been in suspense for weeks, guessing as to what Cornwallis's troops would do—sail for New York, make an attack on Baltimore, or march south to act against General Greene—so Washington's advices, bidding him expect Admiral de Grasse any day and not to let Cornwallis escape to the south, were

126

most welcome. A letter to his wife, written August 24, 1781, shows how good his spirits were:

"The *amour propre* which you are kind enough to impute to me, was perhaps, flattered by the rôle that has been thrust upon me; you would hardly expect me to be equally awkward on every stage! But I accuse you of a terrible attack of vanity (for, since we have everything in common, it is vanity in *you* to think too highly of *me*) if you have not trembled at the dangers I have run; I am not speaking of cannon balls, but of much more dangerous strokes that Lord Cornwallis frightened me with. It was not sensible to entrust me with so much of a command; if I had had bad luck, the people would have regarded my appointment as blind partiality. . . . I ought to speak of my health; that matter becomes a little monotonous, for every time I can only repeat a eulogy of my constitution; the Virginia sun has a very bad reputation . . . but the climate is as good to me as any other, and the only effect hardship has had upon me is to double my appetite."

On August thirtieth Comte de Grasse arrived in Chesapeake Bay with twenty-eight ships of the line. Washington was already on his way with his Continental army, reduced to a beggarly two thousand men, and the French contingent of four thousand under Rochambeau. But before his arrival, General Saint-Simon and three thousand soldiers had disembarked from the fleet at Jamestown, had put themselves under La Fayette's orders, and the combined army, now about seven thousand five hundred strong, advanced to Williamsburg, ten miles west of Yorktown (September 7). Cornwallis was now blockaded by land and by sea. La Fayette may tell of what might well have been a dangerous temptation to a young man of just twenty-four, thirsting for glory: "The French admiral was impatient to return to the West Indies, and he wanted to take Yorktown by assault. The Marquis de Saint-Simon was of the same opinion. Both represented to La Fayette that it was but right, after a long, successful campaign that had been full of hardships, that the glory of making Cornwallis lay down his arms should belong to the man who had forced him into that position. The admiral offered to send to the assault not only his marines, but all the sailors that might be asked for. La Fayette was deaf to the temptation." He wrote to Washington: "I am not so hasty as the Comte de Grasse, and think that having so sure a game to play, it would be madness, by the risk of an attack to give anything to chance." As La Fayette was major-general commanding, the Marquis de Saint-Simon, although a much older man, had put himself under his orders, but La Fayette, as usual, showed the prudence that was as marked a trait in his character as his impetuous zeal for glory. He wrote to Washington: "With whatever politeness the Marquis de Saint-Simon has been pleased to say that he was ready to serve under me, I shall do nothing without showing him the deference due to age, talents and experience; but I rather incline to the cautious line of conduct that I have of late adopted." That he acted wisely may be best judged from Washington's commendations: "Nothing could have afforded me more satisfaction than the information . . . of the measures you had taken. . . . I have . . . an additional pleasure in finding, that your ideas on every occasion have been so consonant to my own, and that by your military disposition and prudent measures, you have anticipated all my wishes." Washington was very circumspect and very polite but he said what he thought, and he would not have put La Fayette over the heads of Wayne, Muhlenberg, Gregory and other generals much older than he, and kept him there, if La Fayette had not proved his mettle and his merits. Of his prudence there can be no question. The French officers also, General du Portail for one, reported their admiration of the "maturity of his judgment"; Rochambeau wrote to Vergennes: "La Fayette behaved very well. . . . He behaved admirably in every respect."

The British fleet under Admiral Graves came up to attempt Lord Cornwallis's deliverance, but was driven off, and, finding itself distinctly inferior in ships and guns, sailed back to New York. There was to be no succor for Cornwallis by sea. On September fourteenth, General Washington and the Comte de Rochambeau and their suites arrived amid great rejoicing. "An elegant supper" was served that night to the leading officers, and "to add to the happiness of the event and evening, an elegant band of music played an introductive part of a French Opera, signifying the happiness of the family, when blessed with the presence of their father, and their great dependence upon him." The sky looked fair; but one black cloud rose high. Word came that the British fleet at New York had been strongly reinforced, and Admiral de Grasse concluded that, as the two fleets would be nearly equal in strength, it was his duty to put out to sea and fight on the ocean where he would have full elbow room. Washington was troubled; he wrote his profound discontent and La Fayette bore the letter. The scales of Fortune hung uncertain. The Admiral held a council of war, and La Fayette had the pleasure of announcing to Washington that the fleet would stay.

La Fayette had now returned to his more modest position of major-general commanding a division of light infantry in the Continental army. On the twenty-eighth Washington advanced to a new position two miles from Yorktown. From that time on the allies advanced upon the doomed fort closer and closer. On October sixth, they were within six hundred yards of the British lines; on the eleventh, within three hundred yards. On the evening of the fourteenth two projecting redoubts were to be carried; the Baron de Vioménil was to assault one with a detachment of French troops, La Fayette the other with his American light infantry. The French General expressed to La Fayette some doubt as to whether the latter's light infantry could attain their objective. La Fayette's men—Alexander Hamilton was with him—charged with bayonets, carried their redoubt with ease, and made the defenders prisoners; and La Fayette sent his compliments to Baron de Vioménil, to ask if he needed any American help. To be sure the French were opposed to the stronger redoubt. Washington begged the two generals to accept his warmest acknowledgments for the excellence of their dispositions, as well as for their own gallant conduct, and to thank their troops for their spirit and firmness. On October seventeenth Cornwallis asked for terms of surrender, and on the nineteenth the surrender was made. Here is La Fayette's letter to Monsieur de Maurepas:

"Camp near York, October 20, 1781

"The play is played, Monsieur le Comte, the fifth act is just ended. I was a little worried during the first acts, my heart leaps up at the last, and I have no less pleasure in congratulating you on the happy issue of our campaign.

"Please be kind enough, Monsieur le Comte, to present my compliments to Madame la Comtesse de Maurepas, and accept the assurance of my affection, my gratitude and my respect.

"LA FAYETTE."

Cornwallis affected illness and did not march out with his troops. Washington, Rochambeau and La Fayette sent their respective *aides-de-camp* to him with their compliments. He detained La Fayette's aide, Major George Washington, a nephew of the general, and said that, as he had made a long campaign against General La Fayette, he wished, because of the value that he set on his good opinion, to render him the full particulars of the reasons that compelled him to surrender. Lafayette went next day to see him. "I know," Lord Cornwallis said to him, "your humanity toward prisoners, I commend my unfortunate army to you." As this recommendation implied lack of confidence in the Americans, La Fayette answered, alluding to the capture of General Burgoyne, "You know, Milord, that the Americans have always been humane towards captured armies." When they met years later, Cornwallis wrote of the meeting: "La Fayette and I were the best of friends possible."

Washington and La Fayette wished Admiral de Grasse to attack Charleston, but the Admiral answered that his time was up. He sailed back to the West

Indies. There was to be no more fighting that year, and La Fayette, believing that he would be of more service in France for the furtherance of Washington's plans for a campaign the following year than if he stayed in America, asked for leave of absence. His request was answered by the following resolutions:

"Resolved, That major-general the Marquis de La Fayette have permission to go to France; and that he return at such time as shall be most convenient to him.

"That he be informed, that on a review of his conduct throughout the past campaign, and particularly during the period in which he had the chief command in Virginia, the many new proofs which present themselves of his zealous attachment to the cause he has espoused, and of his judgment, vigilance, gallantry and address in its defence, have greatly added to the high opinion entertained by Congress of his merits and military talents. . . .

"That the Secretary of Foreign Affairs acquaint the Minister Plenipotentiary of the United States, that it is the desire of Congress that they confer with the Marquis de La Fayette, and avail themselves of his information relative to the situation of public affairs in the United States;

"That the Secretary of Foreign Affairs further acquaint the Minister Plenipotentiary at the court of Versailles, that he will conform to the intention of Congress by consulting with, and employing the assistance of the Marquis de La Fayette, in accelerating the supplies which may be afforded by his Most Christian Majesty for the use of the United States;

"That the Superintendance of Finance, the secre-

The Surrender of Lord Cornwallis' Army

After the work of Barbier, Peintre du Roi

Reunion of the generals of the American and French Armies after the Capitulation of York Town.
Washington, Rochambeau, La Fayette and Lincoln

tary of Foreign Affairs, and the Board of War, make such communication to the Marquis de La Fayette, touching the affairs of their respective departments, as will best enable him to fulfill the purpose of the two resolutions immediately preceding."

Congress also wrote to the King commending La Fayette to his favor, saying that "in the last campaign he had added greatly to the reputation he had already won."

He sailed on December twenty-third. His last letter was to Washington:

"My last good-bye must be addressed to my well beloved General. . . . I assure you that my love, my respect, my gratitude for you, are above expression. . . .

"Farewell, dear General, your respectful and affectionate friend,

"LA FAYETTE."

He arrived in the port of Lorient late at night on January 17, 1782, and at Paris unexpectedly on Monday the twenty-first. Somehow word of his arrival had got abroad and the women from the fish market crowded in front of the Hôtel de Noailles, holding up branches of laurel. Madame de La Fayette was at the Hôtel de Ville, where there was a great fête in honor of the birth of the Dauphin; on the news coming, the Queen bade her get into one of the royal carriages, for had she in strict etiquette waited for her carriage in its ceremonial place, she would have been delayed for hours. The royal procession stopped in front of the Hôtel de Noailles to let her get down. La Fayette was up-stairs, heard her voice, dashed to the front door, caught her in his arms as she all but swooned from excess of joy, and carried her into the house, amid the cheers of the crowd.

The next day he went to Versailles and was most cordially received by the King. And at the ball given at Versailles, the Queen, dressed after the picture of *La Belle Gabrielle,* most politely, graciously and charmingly danced a quadrille with him. He received the rank of maréchal de camp, skipping that of brigadier, and ceded his regiment of dragoons to the Vicomte de Noailles for sixty thousand livres. He was invited to dinner with all the marshals of France by the old Maréchal de Richelieu. And at the opera, where they gave Gluck's *Iphigénie en Aulide,* when the chorus sang ''Achilles is crowned by the hands of victory,'' the prima donna walked toward his box and held up the laurel crown. The parterre redoubled its applause; while the *talons rouges* in other boxes were green and silent with envy. Benjamin Franklin wrote, ''The Marquis of La Fayette was at his return hither received by all ranks with all possible distinction. He daily gains in the general esteem and affection, and promises to be a great man here.''

He had left in disgrace, he returned in glory.

CHAPTER XII

PHILANTHROPY

CORNWALLIS's surrender had decided the issue of the war, nevertheless negotiations for peace moved on slowly. To force England's compliance, France and Spain made ready a great fleet at Cadiz, with the Comte d'Estaing as admiral and La Fayette chief of staff, to attack Jamaica and then sail for the coasts of North America. La Fayette was at Cadiz ready to start, when news arrived that the preliminaries of peace had been signed on January 20, 1783. "Humanity," he wrote, "has won its case, and liberty will never more be without a place of refuge."

In the meantime La Fayette had been working with Franklin, Adams and Jay, to borrow money from France, and to further in many other ways America's interests. Adams noted in his diary that La Fayette's too great success and popularity had stimulated his vanity, "he would be thought the *unum necessarium* in everything." But Adams had a sharp tongue at times. Yet it is likely that La Fayette's immense success had rendered him a little uppish, as the phrase is. For example, the Queen consulted him about a present for Washington with an accompanying message. La Fayette deemed it lacking in the superlatives that he thought becoming. But, she said, the phrases suggested had been lately used to crowned

135

heads: "They, Madam," he replied, "were only kings; Washington is the general of a free people." At the military reviews he wore his American uniform which bore an emblem on the belt. The King asked what that was, and on examination saw a liberty tree planted on a broken crown and scepter. And, when in 1783 he had taken a house for himself, he hung on the wall the American Declaration of Independence, with an empty space beside it awaiting, he said, "the Declaration of Rights for France." His ostentatious republicanism was to him a sort of insignia of honor, which he wore as Nelson did his medals: "In honor I won them." However, when he made parade of these incorporeal medals to Frederick the Great in 1785, the King recounted to him how a certain young man, having helped establish a republic in another country, came back to establish one in his own, and asked him if he knew what happened to him. "No, Sire." "He was hanged."

That Adams's countrymen did not agree with any adverse criticism was plain enough, when La Fayette next year made a six months' visit to America. He was received everywhere—at New York, Philadelphia, Mount Vernon, Albany, Portsmouth, Boston, Richmond, Trenton—with affection and cheers. Here and there, perhaps a little petulant jealousy showed itself; Colonel William North speaks of that "Don Quixote La Fayette." But that is all that I have met with. At Marblehead the widows of those soldiers who died in the war (more than half the male population able to bear arms) went to do him honor in place of their husbands. While in New York State, he went with James Madison to an Indian council at Fort Schuyler. Madison saw him intimately. He says: "The time I have passed with the marquis, has given me a pretty thorough insight into his character. With great natural frankness of temper, he unites much address and very considerable talents. In his politics, he says his three hobby horses are the alliance between France and the United States, the union of the latter, and the manumission of slaves.'' And again: ''Though his foibles did not disappear, all the favorable traits presented themselves in a stronger light on closer inspection. He certainly possesses talents which might figure in any line. If he is ambitious, it is rather of the praise which virtue dedicates to merit, than of the homage which fear renders to power. His disposition is naturally warm and affectionate, and his attachment to the United States, unquestionable.'' And as I am on the matter of his character, I will quote other testimony. Baron de Kalb said: ''He has extended to me numerous proofs of regard since the beginning of our friendship. I shall thank him as long as I live, and value and esteem him most highly.'' And Washington's letter of good-by said: ''It is unnecessary, I persuade myself to repeat to you, my dear Marquis, the sincerity of my regards and friendship; nor have I words which could express my affection for you, were I to attempt it. My fervent prayers are offered for your safe and pleasant passage, happy meeting with Madame de La Fayette and family, and the completion of every wish of your heart.'' La Fayette wrote back: ''Everything that admiration, respect, gratitude, friendship and filial love can inspire is combined in my affectionate heart to devote me most tenderly to you. In your friendship I find a delight which words can not express.'' I suppose that in the whole range of American history, of all men from whom one would most wish praise, George Washington stands preeminent. His approval may well express the voice of history.

Madison quotes La Fayette as saying that one of his hobbies was the manumission of slaves. In the first letter La Fayette wrote to Washington from Cadiz on hearing of the signature of the preliminaries of peace, in the midst of congratulations and a description of the projected expedition and so forth, he says:

"Now, my dear General, that you are to taste some repose, permit me to propose a plan to you which might become extremely advantageous to the black portion of the human race. Let us unite to buy a small estate where we can make the experiment of enfranchising the negroes and employ them only as farm hands. Such an example given by you, might well be generally followed, and if we succeed in America, I shall joyfully devote a part of my time to make this idea fashionable in the Antilles. If this is a crazy plan, I had rather be crazy in this fashion than be deemed wise for contrary conduct."

La Fayette's boyish enthusiasm for liberty that carried him to America might have been thought to have sprung from a spirit of adventure and a thirst for glory, but in this proposal to Washington, by the very letter that carried the first news of peace, asking him to begin an enterprise that should lead to the enfranchisement of the negroes, he shows himself, what he was, if not an innovator, at least an exponent of the liberal ideas that dominated the better part of the upper classes in those years that precede the Revolution. And, again on behalf of liberty, he steps forward as champion of the Protestants in France. Here too, he turns to Washington for sympathy as the noblest and wisest man of the time:

"My dear General:

". . . The Protestants in France are subjected to an intolerable despotism. Although at present there is no overt persecution, they depend on the caprice of the King, Queen, *parlement* or of one of the ministers. Their marriages are not legal; their testaments have no validity in the eyes of the law; their children are considered bastards; their persons exposed to the gallows. I want to effect a change in their situation. With this object, I am going, veiling my motives, with the permission of M. de Castries [secretary of the navy] and of another minister, to visit their chief places of residence. I shall then try to get M. de Vergennes's support, also, *parlement's,* and also that of the keeper of the seal who performs the functions of chancellor. It is a task that requires time, and is not without inconvenience to me, because nobody will give me a scrap of writing, nor support any plan whatever. I take my chances. . . . But when you learn, during the course of the autumn or winter that something has been done in this matter, I like to have you know that I have contributed to it."

These two humanitarian courses, and his interest in reforming the cruel criminal code, mark the trend of his general ideas for a more liberal society. These ideas were no private property of his. The last generation had said a great deal concerning the natural rights of man; they asserted that man was of himself good; that it was ignorance, superstition and wrong institutions that had made him bad, wherever he was bad; and that enlightened men should bend their efforts to freeing humanity from the prejudices of creed and dogma, as well as from the fetters of an absolute despotism. Rousseau had touched the hearts of his generation by his eloquent preaching of man's innocence and virtue; Voltaire had mocked and satirized all forms of tyranny. These two men of genius had died in 1778; but others followed in their wake. Condorcet reiterated their teachings; l'Abbé Raynal cried out against the exploitation of colored races; Marmontel wrote novels to plead the cause of tolerance and a return to nature. Less known men had taken up the same cry. The Marquis de Chastellux, who visited Washington and La Fayette at their camp in New Jersey, expressed ardent hopes for liberty and tolerance. Such ideas of liberty were in the air, and La Fayette, having fought for political liberty in America, now turned to work for other liberties in France. Perhaps, he had heard slavery condemned by the Moravians, among whom he lived during convalescence after the battle of Brandywine, or perhaps, by the Quakers of Pennsylvania; and he may have met Anthony Bénezet, the son of a French Huguenot, who devoted himself to propaganda in favor of abolition. In England, also, among the Quakers in 1783, a society had been formed for the relief and liberation of negro slaves in the West Indies. But the movement in America and in England was primarily religious and Christian, whereas in France the feeling that prompted La Fayette and others was a general enthusiasm for liberty and humanity.

La Fayette's friends shared many of his sentiments. Madame de Tessé, his aunt by marriage, with whom he was on the friendliest terms, received in her salon the enemies of "absolutism" and "arbitrary power." And La Fayette found sympathy in a lodge of Freemasons; the lodges had just become the fashion among gentlemen imbued with philanthropy, the Duc de Chartres was Grand Master, and other members of the high aristocracy and of the intellectual world were also members. Nevertheless, the feeling in favor of Protestants was not general. There had been a temporary sympathy for them among the intellectual classes when Voltaire, twenty years before, had caused the rehabilitation of the memory of the two Protestants, Calas and Sirven, both executed on the accusation of having respectively murdered their children because they had turned Catholic; and in consequence of this sympathy the last Protestants condemned as such to be galley slaves had been set free. And though (as La Fayette says) the laws remained unchanged, Protestants were suffered to celebrate their religious services in houses and barns. The General Assembly of the clergy, however, continued to demand the rigor of the old laws, and Louis XVI, in spite of Turgot's encouragement, did not dare omit from his coronation oath a promise to suppress heretics on French soil.

Such was the situation when La Fayette was free enough from American affairs to give his attention to these other humanitarian causes. In February, 1786, he writes again to Washington:

"Between ourselves, I hope that during the course of next winter the affairs of the Protestants will take a better turn. I confide another secret to you also, I have bought in the colony of Cayenne [French Guiana, South America] a plantation for 125,000 livres, and I am going to work to set my negroes free, an experiment you remember that is my hobby."

Washington wrote back: "Your last acquisition of a plantation at Cayenne, with a view to emancipate the slaves, is a generous and noble proof of your humanity. Would to God that a similar spirit might animate all the people of this country. But I despair of witnessing it. Some petitions were presented to the Assembly during the last session, but they could scarcely obtain a reading."

La Fayette also wrote to John Adams:

"Paris, Feb. 22, 1786

"My dear Sir:

". . . In the cause of my black brethren I feel myself warmly interested, and most assuredly side with them against the white part of mankind. Whatever be the complexion of the enslaver, it does not, in my opinion, alter the complexion of the crime which the enslaver commits, a crime much blacker than any African face. It is a matter of great anxiety and concern to me to find that the trade is sometimes perpetrated under the flag of liberty, our dear and noble stripes, to which virtue and glory have been constant standard bearers."

In August 1786, La Fayette wrote again to Washington: "My plan for Cayenne looks better; the last letters I have received are very good." And in October; "You will be glad to learn that I have great hopes to see the situation of Protestants in this kingdom much improved, assuredly not as much as they should be; but the absurd and cruel laws of Louis XIV will be greatly amended."

In 1785, under pretext of speaking about commercial affairs concerning the United States, he journeyed from Chavaniac to Nîmes, where he saw an old apostle of Protestantism, Paul Rabaut, who had suffered much persecution. Monsieur Rabaut, after having talked with La Fayette, repeated *Nunc dimittis,* and it was agreed between them that when La Fayette should have prepared the way at Paris and at Versailles, Rabaut's eldest son, also a Protestant minister, should go to the capital. La Fayette, on his return, spoke to his friend the Duc de La Rochefoucauld, and they two spoke to Malesherbes, a very distinguished old man, formerly magistrate and at one time minister, now living in retirement, and much attached to both of them. They also had an interview with Breteuil, Minister of the Interior, who adopted their ideas. Afterward young Rabaut came up, and La Fayette took him to see Malesherbes.

Of all this La Fayette's daughter writes: "In 1787 my father busied himself with the civic rights of Protestants. In the Assembly of Notables he prepared a resolution to this end which was supported by M. de la Luzerne, bishop of Langres. My father had been to Nîmes to inform himself in detail of all the vexations that he was working to put an end to. My mother shared his feelings, and welcomed with great interest the Protestant minister who in consequence came to the house. Her enlightened zeal for religion made her wish that no further injustice should be committed in its name. . . . There was in her a union of the most liberal principles of tolerance with a most ardent religious zeal."

These efforts were finally crowned with success. In the Assembly of Notables La Fayette proposed a motion to confer civil rights upon Protestants, which was carried; and, afterward, Malesherbes, once more in office, drew up an edict granting civil rights to those who did not profess the Catholic religion, with respect to marriage, legitimacy of children and so on, and the right to practise professions and trades. This edict was duly registered, according to the practise under the old régime, by the *parlement.*

On the other hand, the experiment in Cayenne terminated badly. The *Société des amis des noirs* to emancipate negroes was founded in 1788 by Brissot (who subsequently became leader of the Girondins in the Assembly) and other men of philosophic mind. La Fayette soon joined. But the movement was swept aside in the Revolution. At Cayenne he put an abolitionist as superintendent in actual charge of his plantation which he called *La Belle Gabrielle,* and then turned over the general care to Madame de La Fayette, who gave it her particular attention. Her daughter says: "In my mother's heart an ardent desire to add to what is good, and a horror of all injustice, were very vigorous. She was delighted when my father went to work to abolish the slave trade. He bought a plantation at Cayenne, in order to set an example of gradual emancipation. Her energetic zeal for doing good made her eagerly look about for means to put the plan into practice, and my father placed most of the details of this enterprise in her hands, for besides sharing in my father's desire to bring the negroes of the plantation up towards liberty, she wished to instruct them in the elementary principles of religion and morality. She chose, in concert with him, a superintendent, M. de Richeprey, who was worthy of the undertaking and devoted himself to it; and she got into relations with the priests of the seminary of the Holy

Ghost who had a house at Cayenne. . . . Her charity caught fire at the hope of teaching the negroes to know and love God, and also of teaching the philosophers, *Amis des Noirs,* that the success of their enterprise would be in great measure due to religion. The events of the Revolution did not allow us to realize her hopes; but at least we had the consolation of learning that the negroes on our plantation *La Belle Gabrielle,* did not commit the horrors that took place on other plantations."

Here, then, we have the guide to La Fayette's general ideas on liberty: the right of men to govern themselves, as in America; the right to practise such religious worship as their consciences dictated; and the right of dark-skinned men to be their own masters. He seems to have entertained a happy belief that these reforms could be accomplished by the efforts of men of good will without any social convulsion. Most people of liberal ideas were of his way of thinking. Michelet suggests that Mesmer's remarkable psychical experiments in hypnosis, that he attributed to *animal magnetism,* inspired people with the notion that miracles could easily be wrought. La Fayette was among those that were greatly interested; when he left for America in 1784 the King asked him: "What will Washington think when he learns that you have become *le premier garçon apothicaire de Mesmer* [head apothecary clerk to Mesmer]?" Wherever that notion came from, it was misleading; and the events now to be related bear witness to its falsity.

La Fayette, then, on the eve of the Revolution stands out in the first place as the hero of American independence; for instance, a young man, the Marquis de Valady, asking Brissot for an introduction to La

Fayette, says: "Marquis de La Fayette, by his chivalric enthusiasm for the liberty of the New (and real) Atlantis, has called forth all the outpourings of my soul; I have envied his good luck and his fame a thousand times; I have burned a thousand times with the wish to know him and see him close to, but I have felt too shy to introduce myself, etc." La Fayette, also, even then, represented the bond between France and America; when in 1787 the *Société Gallo-Américaine* was formed, he is appealed to: "Sir, you are in our country the protector of the United States; it is to you principally that the increasing and solid commercial relations which are growing up between them and France are due, etc." And he is also one of the standard bearers of liberal ideas. Brissot, who thereafter was destined to be one of La Fayette's most virulent enemies, says: "For a long time I found him a noble enthusiast for all that was high, all that was for the good of mankind." But under the passionate pressure of differing notions concerning the good of France, of humanity, and of individual selves, old values and appreciations were swept away, and men judged other men by personal prejudice, until the standard of good became "What I think," and of evil "What you think," to a degree unparalleled except in religious wars. But till then, on the eve of the Revolution, radicals like Brissot and his friends looked to La Fayette as a leader, and even aristocrats, like Madame de La Tour du Pin, who, oddly enough, deemed themselves liberal-minded, agreed that he "desired as much as any of us the establishment of a reasonable liberty and the abolition of abuses." In short, La Fayette was in the front rank of the vanguard of the reformers.

CHAPTER XIII

THE ASSEMBLY OF NOTABLES

THE first great episode in La Fayette's life is over, the episode of his adventurous youth in America, and now we come to the second, more adventurous still, in which he attempted to establish in France the principles and the practise of liberty and equality controlled by law and order, that he had learned from Washington and the leaders in the cause of American independence to regard as most likely to promise, in the political order, human happiness.

The French monarchy was a venerable, a majestic institution. Its strength and absolute power were the consequence of services rendered to the cause of domestic peace and public order. Those services, in great measure, constitute the political history of France for a thousand years. Under Louis XI, to go back no farther, the centralizing needs of the kingdom had striven with feudatories and barons who endeavored to maintain local and independent despotisms. To the evils of feudalism succeeded similar evils of civil wars between great nobles and religious leaders that wrought untold destruction throughout France. The imperative need of order, of which Henri IV made use, set the monarchy on a firm foundation. The genius of Richelieu buttressed it. The alarm caused by the silly civil wars of la Fronde, supplemented by the dexterity of Mazarin and the sagacity of Louis XIV, raised the monarchy to its proud position, dominating Europe. Then came the downward course. The King's ill-regulated ambitions begot war after war. These wars, the building of Versailles at the cost of grinding taxation, the conversion of warrior nobles into courtiers dancing attendance in the royal antechambers, the King's bigotry in revoking the Edict of Nantes—these and other destructive factors, pulled out great props from underneath the throne. Then followed the regency, and the long reign of Louis XV, with Madame de Pompadour and Madame du Barry, pulled out others. When La Fayette came to manhood the whole political edifice was loosened, sagging, cracking, like a house built upon sand.

The condition of the nation at that time was after this fashion. Louis XV had been a handsome, clever, cynical profligate; his last mistress, Madame du Barry, had begun her career as a prostitute. The young King, Louis XVI, was utterly different, he was a kindly soul, with excellent intentions, he was no fool but he was ignorant, boorish, infirm of purpose, caring for little but hunting and things mechanical. Madame de La Tour du Pin describes him as a stout man, with high shoulders, of medium height, with the worst possible bearing and carriage, and the air of a peasant walking with a sort of lubberly roll as he follows the plow. The young Queen—with (I quote Madame Vigée Lebrun) "so much grace united to so much distinction, her little hands were of perfect shape, and her feet charming"—was elegant, aristocratic, uneducated, haughty and—how could it be otherwise with such a husband, in such a Court?—intensely eager for amusement. The King's brother, Monsieur, the Comte de

Provence, was an amiable egotist, with few ideas, no passions and a profound sense of his own divinely conferred dignity; his younger brother, the Comte d'Artois, was a gay, narrow-minded, light-hearted, pleasure-lover; he ruined himself for the sake of one actress, and after the King had paid his debts ruined himself again for another. At twenty-four he owed twenty-four million francs. So much for the royal family. Below them came the three orders, the Clergy, the Noblesse, the Third Estate, and the unconsidered rag-tag and bobtail of proletariat and peasantry.

The Clergy was divided in two. The great prelates were members of the high aristocracy and lived like *grands seigneurs,* enjoying life and paying little or no heed to their sees, except to pocket the revenues. Some were accused of disbelief. When it was proposed, so it is said, that Loménie de Brienne should be appointed archbishop of Paris, the King replied: "The archbishop of Paris ought at least to believe in God." The lower clergy, parish priests, vicars and such, were humble folk, for the most part very poor, and separated from the prelates by a social abyss. The Clergy constituted a privileged order and were not taxed.

The Noblesse were likewise divided into two unequal parts. The greater part of the high nobility waited upon the King and Queen at Versailles, they quarreled with one another and intrigued for places and pensions. Montesquieu described a *grand seigneur* as a man with ancestors, debts and pensions. They were personally brave, but usually ignorant of military or any other matters, except those who served regularly in the army. The humbler nobles were poor, sometimes very poor, too poor to buy a commission in the army, and promotion was confined to Court favorites; they lived in the country in a mean fashion. The *noblesse de la robe,* if not of equal consideration with the *noblesse de l'épée,* held themselves as proudly; they were judges, members of *parlement,* and so forth. Their offices were hereditary, bought and sold. For many judicial positions, indeed, a university degree was necessary, but these, it seems, could be procured at small cost. It was the custom for judges to accept bribes. The *parlements,* judicial bodies, possessing or claiming certain political duties and rights, were very conservative, especially with regard to the privileges of the *noblesse de la robe.* They made an excellent target for liberal attacks. Voltaire detested "the parliamentary rabble"; Diderot said that the *parlement* was "intolerant, bigoted and stupid, hugging its Gothic and Vandal customs." The Noblesse, like the Clergy, constituted a privileged order and were not taxed.

The Third Estate consisted of the rich and well-to-do burghers of the cities,—bankers, merchants, manufacturers, professional men and country proprietors. Below the comfortable bourgeoisie, came the inarticulate many, the work people of the towns, the peasants. The peasants ranged from serfs up to petty farmers, owners and cultivators of land. The Third Estate paid all (I believe not literally but virtually) the taxes, and most of these fell on the peasants, for the land in their hands, and also their labor, was subject to all sorts of exactions. There were the *taille,* the *gabelle* and *aides;* there were tithes to the church; there were dues to the seigneur; they must buy his wine, leave forests untouched for his game, not scare his pigeons from their own seeded fields; they must grind their grain at his mill, work a certain number of days at his tasks, and so on; and, though in many cases particular dues had been commuted into payments of money, the burdens were grievous. In Auvergne, according to La Fayette, peasant proprietors were abandoning their plows, the artisans their workshops, and the most industrious citizens, despoiled of what they earned at home, or got from abroad, would soon (he says) have to face the alternatives of beggary or emigration. And down below the peasants, at the lowest levels of society, a multitude of vagabonds led their valueless lives, mendicants, poachers, smugglers, robbers, galley slaves, who, afterwards came up from underground, as it were, to do the cruelest deeds.

But as to this it is better to call an eye-witness, so I quote from Thomas Jefferson, who was then our Minister to France. He is speaking of the popular pressure, in 1787, for a fixed constitution: "Nor should we wonder at this pressure when we consider the monstrous abuses of power under which this people were ground to powder; when we pass in review the weight of their taxes, and the inequality of their distribution; the oppressions of the tithes, the tailles, the corvees, the gabelles, the farms and the barriers; the shackles on commerce by monopolies; on industry by guilds and corporations; on the freedom of conscience, of thought, and of speech; on the freedom of the press by the Censure; and of the person by *Lettres de cachet;* the cruelty of the Criminal code generally; the atrocities of the Rack; the venality of the Judges, and their partialities to the rich; the monopoly of military honors by the Noblesse; the enormous expenses of the Queen, the Princes and the Court; the prodigalities of pensions; and the riches, luxury, indolence and immorality of the Clergy."

By the constitution the King was in theory absolute, he was the sole source of authority and law; but in fact there were various institutions, customs and immunities that hedged in and limited his power in one way and another. He has been called "the chief slave of a system." The Clergy could not be taxed, the Noblesse could not be taxed. There were the *parlements*, as I have said, more particularly that of Paris, whose jurisdiction extended over a third of the kingdom. The *parlements* were originally high courts of justice, but as they were charged with the duty of registering the royal edicts, they had drawn the inference that they had a right to decide whether they would register an edict or not. From their assumption of political jurisdiction many conflicts arose with the Crown. It is obviously difficult to govern when all the rich are exempt from taxation, where part of the clergy look to a foreign potentate for orders, where *parlement* refuses to register edicts of taxation that affect its own class, where serfdom is not wholly abolished, where there are all sorts of immunities, legacies from a long past, attached to provinces, to individual cities, to baronial estates, to this nobleman, to that bishopric, to religious orders, to monasteries, to guilds and so on. When Calonne, Minister of Finance, addressed the Notables he said: "One can't take a step in this vast kingdom without finding different laws, contrary usages, privileges, exemptions, freedom from taxes, rights and exemptions of all sorts; this general incongruity complicates administration, interrupts its procedure, embarrasses its jurisdiction and everywhere multiplies expense and disorder."

The King had the right to call on certain bodies for counsel and help. He might summon an Assembly of

Notables, inviting whom he wished; or he might summon the States-General. *Les États-généraux* was a national assembly, of the three orders, Clergy, Noblesse and Third Estate, that is of the bourgeoisie, for the peasants had no representatives; but as this assembly had sometimes claimed, though with little effect, that its consent was necessary to taxation, and had often been less a help than a hindrance to the royal will, it had not been summoned since 1614, and was regarded as obsolete.

In times of ease no government would have thought of convoking Notables or *États-généraux,* but now after the close of the American war, financial difficulties were piled high, Pelion on Ossa. Bankruptcy stared the nation in the eyes. One finance minister had followed another. The point had been reached where it was impossible to increase the existing taxes or to borrow. The new Minister of Finance, Calonne, proposed a radical revision of taxation that should subject the privileged classes to bear their equal share of the common burden. He admitted that *parlement* would not register any such decree and suggested an assembly of Notables. It was Hobson's choice. The King accepted the plan. A body of one hundred and forty-four distinguished persons—nobles, bishops, presidents of the *parlements,* mayors of cities—was selected, and summoned to meet at Versailles.

La Fayette's name was on the list, then stricken off, and then, again, on the instigation of two ministers, Breteuil and Castries, replaced. The same ill-natured critic who told the story concerning Madame d'Hunolstein, says that La Fayette went and begged Calonne to include him, that Calonne replied that he was too young, had shown no qualifications by administrative experience, but that he would propose his name on the understanding that he should support all the King's views. The story refutes itself. The true reascn of the government's hesitation to appoint him was his revolutionary and republican principles. These were well known and were obnoxious to the government. As far back as February 8, 1786, Jefferson had suggested to Madison a gift of land in Virginia to La Fayette, saying: "Nor am I sure that the day will not come when it might be a useful asylum to him." The assertion that the government did not think him of sufficient account is contradicted by the fact that when the Notables went to Versailles, out of one hundred and forty-four, La Fayette was one of twenty to be lodged in the château. Thomas Jefferson undoubtedly has the truth. He wrote on January 16, 1787: "Our de La Fayette was placed on the list originally. Afterwards his name disappeared, but finally was reinstated. This shows that his character here is not considered an indifferent one, and that it excites agitation. His education in our school has drawn on him a very jealous eye from a court whose principles are the most absolute despotism. The King, who is a good man, is favorably disposed towards him, and he is supported by powerful family connections and by the public good will. He is the youngest man of the Notables except one whose office placed him on the list." A little later, speaking of him in a letter to Madison (January 30, 1787), he says: "The Marquis de La Fayette is a most valuable auxiliary to me. His zeal is unbounded, and his weight with those in power great. . . . He has a great deal of sound genius, is well remarked by the King, and rising in popularity. He has nothing against him but the suspicion of Republican principles. I think he will one day be of the ministry. His foible is a canine appetite for popularity and fame; but he will get above them.''

La Fayette to Washington:

"Paris, January 13, 1787

"My dear General:

". . . Your own acquaintances in this assembly are the Comte d'Estaing, the Duc de Laval and your servant, named among the thirty-six members of the Noblesse. The King's letter announces the plan of submitting to the examination of the Notables the state of the finances that need to be settled, the means of lightening the people's burdens, and many abuses to be reformed. You will readily understand that at the bottom of all this lies the desire to get money, in one way or another, to reestablish the balance between receipts and expenses that profusion has rendered enormous. But to arrive at this end, there was no other way so patriotic, frank and noble. The King and his Minister, M. de Calonne, deserve a handsome acknowledgement; I hope that a tribute of gratitude and good will will recompense this popular measure. My ardent wish and dearest hope is to see this reunion lead to popular assemblies in the provinces, the destruction of many commercial fetters, and a change in the lot of Protestants, all matters for which I with my friends, are going to work with all my heart and devote my feeble efforts.''

To the same:

"Paris, February 7th, 1787

"I have already spoken to you of the Assembly of Notables, the evil-minded say 'not-ables,' who would have met, if those Ministers, le Comte de Vergennes,

M. de Calonne and the Keeper of the Seal, had not fallen ill very opportunely. I have a lively hope that this assembly will have good results. I flatter myself that we shall obtain a sort of chamber of representatives in each province, not (it is true) to fix, but at least to apportion taxes, and that many legal restrictions that interfere with the internal commerce of the kingdom shall be abolished. It is not probable that the affair of the Protestants will be submitted to the Notables; it might fail by the protestations of the clergy and of the bigots."

The King in person opened the session on February 22, 1787. Calonne made a frank—partly frank—speech in which he admitted a deficit, that up to then he had denied, of eighty millions of francs. Later he admitted one hundred and thirteen millions. Of course, the purpose in summoning the Notables had been to get their assent to taxes upon the privileged classes in order to fill in this deficit; and Calonne, garnishing his proposition with various liberal measures in order to conciliate the good will of liberal opinion, proposed a general land tax on all land. The reader expects to find La Fayette heartily supporting this measure; not at all, he joins with the others in disclaiming any power in the Notables to tax. Whatever the motives of the others may have been, his course in so doing was in accordance with a definite plan of action. He wished to force the King to accept certain constitutional principles, and did not propose, until he should have done so, to enable him to escape from the pressure of national bankruptcy. For that reason La Fayette did not support the land tax; he urged retrenchment and various collateral reforms.

But I shall confine myself to the particular issues to which La Fayette addressed himself. For convenience of deliberation the Assembly had been divided into sections; the Comte d'Artois presided over that in which La Fayette sat. First came a criticism upon sales of royal domains to royal favorites, with the implication that the Crown had not received the honest value of the properties. A distinguished magistrate raised this question. La Fayette supported him and bore the brunt of the discussion. The Comte d'Artois reported this to the King, who said that such serious accusations should be signed. La Fayette thereupon asked the Comte d'Artois please to thank the King for this permission, and handed in the following paper with his signature:

"Monseigneur,

"The King invites us not to point out grievances without signing our names. What I asserted last Saturday has secured for us this permission; I take advantage of it, Monseigneur.

"I proposed and I propose that this section petition his Majesty to make a serious investigation (into sales etc of royal domains, and purchases of land). . . .

"It is possible that I am mistaken, but great disorder implies great depredation. I ask why the ministers of finance propose to the King purchases and exchanges, which as they do not benefit him can only serve to benefit private persons. . . .

"And since this recommendation signed by me is to be submitted to his Majesty, I reiterate with redoubled confidence the observation that the millions which are squandered are raised by taxation; that taxation can not be justified but by the real needs of the State; that all the millions surrendered to depredation and greed are harvests of the sweat and tears of the people, perhaps of their blood; and that a reckoning of the amount of unhappiness that has been caused in order to raise the sums so lightly squandered is a fearful thing for the goodness and sense of justice that we know are his Majesty's natural sentiments."

Such a paper refuted the charge that La Fayette in return for his appointment to the Notables had promised Calonne to support the King's wishes. His statements were so strong that the Comte d'Artois interrupted him, but other members upheld a member's right to lay his views before the throne. When Calonne received the petition he went to the King and asked to have La Fayette committed to the Bastille. This was denied, but an oratorical battle between him and La Fayette was expected at the next session of the Notables. Before that time, however, a cabal had overthrown Calonne, and another minister of finance had taken his place. A new estimate of the deficit put it at one hundred and forty millions. This gave La Fayette another opportunity. His speech was in substance as follows:

There is great diversity among the statements as to the amount of the deficit. It is necessary to know the deficit exactly in order to determine what moneys must be raised by taxation in addition to those procured from loans and by retrenchments.

There has been a great increase of the public debt during the present reign: *Tout était donc perdu et même l'honneur* (all was lost, even honor, too), if the

King were not determined upon all possible economies in order to lighten the new burdens to be put upon people already crushed down. Under these circumstances the Notables should propose certain precautionary measures in order to prevent a future deficit:

1. Economy in the military establishment and in the royal household, and the appropriation of fixed sums for them; the suppression of hunting preserves not necessary for the King's pleasure, and of unoccupied royal palaces, and also of states-prisons "which the King, as well as the law, would disavow if he knew how useless and dangerous they are."

To fix the salary for each office; to suppress reversion of office; to forbid officials to derive private advantage from matters in their charge.

2. Expenses of all departments to be subject to rules, and, except for the department of foreign affairs, to be printed and published.

3. That a committee of Notables, chosen from the three estates should be present when accounts are submitted to the King, when the expenses for the following years are decided on, and when new regulations are considered.

4. Pensions and gifts to be conferred only for services rendered, or to encourage talent; for then "to publish such benefactions is to double them, and at the same time, the publication will stop improper gifts. Such homage rendered to the sovereign's munificence ought to be very dear to the grateful hearts of those whom he enriches."

5. When a tax is imposed as security for a loan, it should be diminished *pari passu* with the diminution of the loan and extinguished with the extinction of the loan.

6. No revenue shall be anticipated.

7. Finally, after the King shall have put the promised retrenchments into practise, "we will try to provide for the rest of the deficit by the painful miracle of increased taxation."

Provisions against a future deficit should precede those for wiping out a present deficit. And we are confident that the Notables will receive from the King a detailed statement of the disposition he means to take to prevent the danger of an arbitrary administration. For sad experience proves to his Majesty that his good intentions are not enough to set matters in good order; and this experience, which has cost the nation dear, does not permit it to rest at ease except upon a new order of things.

"May this disastrous period provoke unceasing opposition to the devouring luxury and habitual extravagance of the Court. May it make an impression as lasting on the hearts of those that can prevent the evil, as of those who are its innocent victims! Happily, this assembly is not the body to sanction new taxes. The imprescriptible right to determine public charges belongs only to the representatives of the nation; and taxes, only become legal after registration by *parlement*." Then he ends by saying: "It seems to me that this is an appropriate time for us to supplicate His Majesty to bring all these matters to a happy issue by the convocation of a National Assembly."

At these words the Comte d'Artois cried out: "What, Sir! Are you asking for the convocation of the States-General?" "Yes, Monseigneur, and even more than that." "Do you wish me to write down and carry to the King the words: M. de La Fayette proposes a motion to convoke the **States-General?"** "Yes, Monseigneur."

This dramatic demand **for** the convocation of the States-General reveals the purpose, to which I alluded, that lay behind La Fayette's prior actions and speeches. He strove to take advantage of the Assembly of Notables (an anomalous body with no legal authority), to make a breach in the absolute power of the Crown and extort certain constitutional rights for the nation. That he helped to set the movements afoot that led to the Revolution can not be doubted. The meeting of the Notables served mainly to show how impotent a body they were. It could merely make suggestions. A decree submitted by Calonne to establish provincial assemblies for the apportionment of taxes was approved, so, too, was the suppression of the gabelle, and on La Fayette's motion his section recommended the removal of disabilities from Protestants, and also a reform of the cruel and antiquated criminal code. The Assembly was dismissed on May twenty-fifth. La Fayette wrote to Washington:

"Paris, August 3, 1787

"My dear General:

". . . The spirit of liberty is making great gains in this country; liberal ideas are propagating from one end of the kingdom to the other. Our Assembly of Notables was a fine thing, except for those who fathered it. You know the personal quarrels that I have got into with respect to gifts to favorites at the public's expense. That has drawn down on me a great number of powerful enemies, but it was well received by the nation. Since then I have expressed some of my ideas in very clear terms. I can't say that

I am in favor at court, if by the court you mean the King, the Queen, and the King's brothers; but I am on friendly terms with the administration. . . . Nevertheless the *parlement*, stirred up by the example of the Notables, is opposing a stout resistance to the establishment of new taxes. It will be compelled to register the edicts; but it is good that it [also] has asked for a meeting of the States-General. I foresee that the States-General will come when the local assemblies that are establishing in every province shall have acquired the necessary importance and a sense of their own power."

"October 9, 1787

". . . French affairs are still in an undecided condition. It is necessary to make up an enormous deficit by new taxes, and the nation is tired of paying what it has not voted. Ideas of liberty have spread rapidly since the American Revolution. The Assembly of Notables set fire to combustible materials. When they had got rid of us, they had to fight the *parlements,* who though mere courts of justice charged with the registration of edicts, do not wish to sanction any tax not agreed to by the nation. . . . The Comte d'Artois was hooted at by the populace when he was carrying the King's orders. Some ministers have been burned in effigy. . . . You see that the King is often obliged to give way, without, however, satisfying the mass of the people. Discontent is so great that the Queen doesn't dare come to Paris any more for fear of a rude reception. After what has happened in these six months, we shall at least have succeeded in putting into everybody's head that the King has no right to tax the nation, and that nothing of that sort can be done without the consent of a national assembly. The King is all powerful in France; he has every means to constrain, punish and corrupt. The ministers incline to preserve the despotism and conceive it their duty. The court swarms with cheap and effeminate courtiers; their temper is enervated by the influence of women and the love of pleasure; the lower classes are stupid and ignorant. On the other hand, the French character is lively, enterprising and inclined to look with contempt on those that govern them. People's minds are clearing up under the influence of philosophical works, and of the example of other nations. . . . There is a strange contrast between the oriental power of the King, the efforts of the ministry to keep it intact, the intrigues and servility of the courtiers on the one hand, and on the other a general freedom of thought, of speech and of writing, in spite of spies, of the Bastille and the restraints on publication. The spirit of opposition and of patriotism, spread abroad in the highest class of the nation, including those in the King's personal service; the mocking insolence of the populace in the cities (always ready, it is true, to scatter before a detachment of the guards); and the much more serious discontent of the people in the country,—all these ingredients mixed together will bring us little by little, without a great convulsion, to a representative system, and as a consequence to a diminution of the royal authority. But this will be a matter of time, and will proceed the more slowly according as the interests of powerful men put a spoke in the wheels.''

CHAPTER XIV

THE STATES-GENERAL

La Fayette's letters, that I have just quoted, show the trend of events. His words *a great convulsion,* though employed only to be denied, are ominous. After the dispersal of the Notables the social fabric creaked worse than before with strange and portentous, rasping, irate noises. The King was soon at loggerheads with the *Parlement de Paris.* He sent in the proposed land tax and a proposed stamp tax; the *parlement* refused to register both edicts, and declared that only the representatives of the nation in States-General assembled had the legal authority to levy permanent taxes. The King, using his prerogative, attended the *parlement* and ordered the registration of the edicts. The next day *parlement,* amid the cheers of a waiting crowd, declared the registration null and void. The King, thereupon, exiled the *parlement* to Troyes. The other *parlements* supported their Parisian brethren and demanded radical reforms. There was rioting in Paris; troops were called out. In the provinces there was unrest and agitation. Béarn claimed its ancient privileges. Brittany was up in arms for its rights; La Fayette, who had estates there and was a Breton through his mother, joined in the protest; for which some signatories were sent to the Bastille, and La Fayette was deprived of a com-

164

mand in the army that had recently been given him. In Dauphiny there was nearly civil war; the local assembly demanded that the States-General be convoked, that the Third Estate, being two hundred times as numerous as the two privileged orders should have as many deputies as the two together, and that the vote should be, not by orders, but *per capita*. These demands passed from mouth to mouth and swept over the country. Everything was going wrong; the army was discontented, crops were bad, laborers were out of employment, taxes harder and harder to collect, the deficit in the treasury grew and grew. Everybody put their hopes in a States-General. A new party, *les nationaux*, was formed by people of all sorts, *grands seigneurs* such as La Fayette and the Duc de La Rochefoucauld; lesser nobles like Mirabeau; philosophers like Condorcet; lawyers of all sorts, Danton and others, and so on. Again Hobson's choice. Necker had been recalled, and at last upon his insistence, the King consented to convoke the States-General.

Then came the question of how the States-General should be constituted. The Notables were recalled to give their opinion (November 6, 1788). The important issue was the position of the Third Estate. The Notables were not disposed to part with their privileges, and voted overwhelmingly against the people's claim to a double representation; in La Fayette's committee his advocacy of the affirmative was only supported by eight out of twenty-four. The *parlements* held with the Notables, except the *Parlement de Paris* which evaded responsibility. At this, popular antagonism shifted from the King to the privileged orders. The issue was now between classes, the upper middle class against the aristocracy.

In the meantime La Fayette had taken his seat in the provincial assembly for Auvergne, and according to a fellow member, the Comte d'Espinchal, at once "manifested revolutionary principles. . . . Continually occupied in flattering the Third Estate, he tried to embitter their minds against the Government." I call attention to this, for it shows Espinchal's bias against La Fayette; he being one of those who circulated the gossip concerning Madame d'Hunolstein, and of La Fayette's bargaining with the government for a place among the Notables. I will now show what, in the Comte d'Espinchal's eyes, constituted La Fayette's main offense. The government had asked for an increase of taxes; the Auvergnat assembly protested against an increase. The King manifested his disapproval of their protest; thereupon, on La Fayette's motion, the Auvergnat assembly adopted a resolution to say that it had heard with deep consternation the unexpected announcement of the King's disapproval, and that "they would have had no consolation in their great grief, if it had not been that every member in adopting the resolution, had obeyed absolutely the voice of his conscience," and the assembly reasserted its refusal to increase the taxes. It seems very clear that the Comte d'Espinchal in attributing to La Fayette a willingness to truckle to the Court was quite at fault. Jefferson wrote to Washington (December 4, 1788): "The Marquis de La Fayette is out of favor with the Court, but high in favor with the nation. I once feared for his personal liberty, but I hope he is on safe ground at present."

Throughout the province La Fayette had been received with the most flattering marks of affection and confidence from all classes. At the town of Aurillac he was repeatedly cheered; a chronicler says: "He was the first hero they had seen, and they could not tire of staring at him." At Saint-Flour, he was given a fête that ended with a banquet at which verses were declaimed to the illustrious La Fayette, who,

Par ses nobles exploits dans les deux hémisphères
A su se donner sans choix tous les humains pour frères;
(By his noble exploits in two hemispheres
Has taken indiscriminately all men for brothers.)

But he was back in Paris early in October to do his part in bringing on political changes. He, together with Condorcet, Mirabeau, Sieyès, Talleyrand, the Duc de La Rochefoucauld-Liancourt and others, constituted the directing committee of the National party, and addressed themselves to the elections for the States-General. It was then that the Abbé Sieyès published his brochure with the famous question: *"Qu'est ce que le Tiers état?—Tout—Qu'a-t-il été jusqu'à présent, dans l'ordre politique?—Rien—Que demande-t-il? A y devenir quelque chose."* ("What is the Third Estate?—Everything—What has it been up to now in the political order?—Nothing—What does it ask for? To become something.") Not only in Paris but through the country there was clamor for a double representation in the Third Estate of so violent a character that the King and Queen yielded to Necker's arguments, and at the very end of the year it was announced that its representation should be equal to that of the other two orders.

La Fayette went to Chavaniac, in Auvergne, to stand for election to the order of the Noblesse. He writes March 8, 1789: "There is division and jealousy here between the orders, and between townships and between individuals. I have the disadvantage of an audience which is forewarned and prepared against my opinions, and whose interests are against them. Some of my friends among the nobles have let me know that with certain complaisances I shall be unanimously elected; without such complaisances, no. I answered that I wanted to convince not to flatter. The Third Estate was willing to go pretty far, and I had a chance for celebrity; but I preached moderation at the risk of displeasing. It would be quite possible that instead of nomination I shall take away from here only a lot of quarrels and esteem of various sorts; but I shall do my duty and be moderate, although, between ourselves, these nobles revolt me by their overbearing, and their egoism makes me indignant."

However, after some hesitation as to whether he should stand for the Noblesse or for the *Tiers état,* he was elected by a large majority of votes as a deputy of the Noblesse; but his constituents, disregarding his opposition, instructed their delegates to support the separation of the orders and separate voting. It is hardly necessary to add that the Comte d'Espinchal says that La Fayette intrigued with both Noblesse and *Tiers état* to secure his election as deputy. The Comte and his friends are probably referred to, when La Fayette speaks of "the cabals with which I was surrounded." In spite of his election, he was vexed by his instructions and by the position that the Auvergnat noblesse had taken, and wrote to Washington: "For my part, I ardently hope to obtain a Bill of Rights and a Constitution, and I should like to have the thing accomplished quietly, as far as possible, and in a manner satisfactory to all." Gouverneur Morris wrote to Washington that the Marquis, in spite of opposition from the Queen and the Royal Princes, had been suc-

Distant view of Château Chavaniac with the fountain in the foreground

Photograph by Maison Ad. Braun & Cie, Paris

Danton

From the painting in the Musée Carnavalet

cessful and had acquitted himself admirably as a speaker, and that the people adored him.

On May 5, 1789, the three orders assembled at Versailles in the *Palais des menus plaisirs*. This building stood on the left as you walk up the broad avenue that leads to the great château. The King opened the session, and Necker laid before the deputies the state of the finances, falsely, for he did not admit half the deficit. Then began the tug between privilege and democracy. The Third Estate, six hundred strong, was composed almost wholly of the upper middle class, among them were many men destined to fame, Mirabeau, Robespierre, Bailly, Barnave and others; supported by the great mass of the nation, they insisted on the union of the three orders in one chamber, and a vote by heads. Otherwise how idle it was to have given the Third Estate a double representation; and if clerical privilege and aristocratic privilege were each to sit in a chamber by itself with power of veto, there was an end to the hopes of reform. The King, under the influence of the Queen and the ultra-conservatives, said that the orders should sit separately. The inferior clergy, however, sympathized with their class and a number of them drifted into the Third Estate. The liberals among the Noblesse wished also to join, but the large majority stood firm for the privileges of their order. La Fayette, caught between his inclination and his instructions, was embarrassed as to what he ought to do. Thomas Jefferson advised him (May 7, 1787) to disregard his instructions, as the lesser wrongdoing, but he felt bound. As the Noblesse in consequence did nothing, he chafed at inaction, and thought of resigning and seeking a new election as a member of the *Tiers état*.

That Estate finally acted with vigor; after making, patiently and vainly, repeated overtures to the other orders to join them, they adopted the title of National Assembly (June seventeenth) and, proceeding to assume sovereign authority, declared that no taxes were valid without the consent of the nation. The Court, the *parlement,* and almost all the privileged people, both outside the States-General and within, took fright and besought the King to stop this rebellious insolence. The poor *bonhomme* King yielded to the reactionaries. On June nineteenth he announced a royal session for the twenty-second, and in the meantime closed the hall of *menus plaisirs* for the ceremonial preparations. The next morning the deputies, arriving at the hall in the rain, found workmen at work, and were not allowed to enter. They went round the corner, at the suggestion of Doctor Guillotin, and held their meeting in the *Jeu de Paume,* the tennis court, which you still see very much as it was with its plain walls, high windows, and no furniture, save for racquets, tennis balls, one table and a few benches. There, damp and indignant, they all—all except one—following the example of the president, Bailly, took an oath not to separate until they had set a constitution for the nation on a solid base.

At the royal session, a day or two later, the King annulled the action that the Third Estate had taken on the seventeenth, and directed the three orders to separate, and sit each by itself, independently of the others. The two privileged orders obeyed and withdrew to their rooms; the Third Estate stayed. A detachment of guards was sent to clear the hall, but La Fayette, La Rochefoucauld and a few liberal nobles opposed their entrance. The King was told; and the poor inconstant bewildered man said; "Well, damn it, let them stay." Thereupon the Third Estate reasserted the validity of their enactments on the seventeenth. This was flat disobedience, but they felt their growing power; public opinion ran strong in their favor. The majority of the Clergy came in to take part in common deliberation, then forty-seven members of the Noblesse. La Fayette still believed himself bound by his instructions, and the rest of the nobles held back. However, it was useless to kick against the pricks; the weather-cock King gave way and bade both orders join the commons (June twenty-seventh). The monarchy was losing ground.

Signs of the coming storm were visible in Paris. For the purpose of electing deputies to the States-General—an electoral college had been appointed, the *Assemblée des Elections du Tiers état;* this body, though it had fulfilled all its lawful functions, decided to remain and assume political power, disregarding the fact that at the Hôtel de Ville there was already a municipal body in the exercise of duly authorized powers. There was excuse enough! the old authorities were losing their hold upon obedience. The populace was restless. A number of the King's guards, won over by the people, refused to obey orders. Thunder was audible. The Court, apprehensive of the great city, ordered certain foreign regiments composed of Swiss and Germans, stationed in various places, to concentrate about Versailles and the capital. This caused the liveliest excitement in Paris, and great agitation in the National Assembly. Mirabeau suggested that a citizens' guard should be formed, and moved (July eighth) that the King be asked to countermand the soldiers. A proposal was made to send the motion to a committee. La Fayette got up and spoke for the first time:

"There are only two reasons for sending a motion to a committee; where there are doubts of fact to be cleared up or where there are doubts of what course to pursue. Now, gentlemen, the presence of soldiers, ordered to surround the Assembly, is a fact evident to all of us. As to the course to pursue, I shall not do the Assembly the wrong to believe that any one will hesitate. . . . I ask that, instead of sending the motion to committee, the chamber proceed at once to a vote."

The King sent a reassuring message about the troops, but the Assembly remained distrustful and disturbed, and more convinced day by day that there must be great political changes. On July eleventh, La Fayette presented a Declaration of Rights, the first proposed in Europe, as he liked to remember:

Nature created men free and equal; distinctions necessary to social order rest only upon grounds of general utility.

Every man is born with certain inalienable and imprescriptible rights: freedom of thought; protection of his honor and his life; the right of property; the complete disposal of his person, of his industry, of all his faculties; the right to communicate his thoughts by every known means; the pursuit of happiness; resistance to oppression.

No man may be subjected to laws, except by his consent, (or by that of his representatives) legally enacted and duly published.

The origin of all authority lies in the nation.

Every government has one purpose only, the common weal.

"For the people to love liberty all they need is to know it; for them to obtain freedom all they need is to deserve it!"

This declaration was printed that night and distributed in Paris. There was no need of fuel for the fires of excitement there. Necker, Minister of Finance, had been abruptly dismissed. Some one said it was as if the King of Naples had flung the sacred oil of Saint Januarius into the sea. Bondholders—and all the prosperous bourgeoisie held government bonds—went about, their hair on end, in fear of immediate bankruptcy. People cried that feudalism had triumphed, reform was at an end. In the garden of the Palais Royal Camille Desmoulins climbed upon a table and harangued the crowd, uttering wild words. He plucked a green leaf for a cockade and put it in his hat. The crowd cheered, put green leaves in their hats, and, collecting more men and women from every street, marched through the city. They met soldiers and began throwing stones. Barricades were erected; shops pillaged of firearms. Communication with Versailles was interrupted. In the Assembly, on La Fayette's motion, the King's ministers, "whatever place or rank they might have," were declared responsible for whatever might happen. The session was made permanent, with a shift for the night. La Fayette was elected vice-president, and for the nonce to preside (July thirteenth). He slept on a bench in the hall. At six o'clock in the morning he wrote: "Today will be interesting."

Reports came from Paris of clashes between the populace and the foreign soldiers. The National Assembly again sent a deputation to the King asking for the removal of the troops. In Paris, that same day, more radical action was taken. Members of the *Electoral College* assembled to the ringing of bells at the Hôtel de Ville and appointed a Permanent Committee, consisting of their own members and of the municipal officers, and called for a citizens' militia in defense of the city to be constituted by eight hundred men from each of the sixty districts into which the city was divided, and to be under the control of the Permanent Committee. The color of the cockade for the militia was to be changed from green, chosen by Camille Desmoulins, to red and blue, the colors of the city.

That day and the next, the fourteenth of July, crowds searched Paris for arms and ammunition—the Hôtel de Ville, the Invalides, the Carthusian Convent, the Arsenal—and laid hands on what they could find. Report said that great quantities of powder had hastily been transferred from the Arsenal to the Bastille. The crowd rushed to the Bastille, which girdled by its eight towers stood at the east end of the city, massive and grim, confronting the Faubourg Saint-Antoine. The Governor de Launay had a garrison of thirty Switzers, and eighty Invalides, with rations for two days. There were parleys between him and the Permanent Committee. The crowd swelled and swelled, growing impatient and suspicious. The Governor promised not to fire, unless attacked. Two fellows, apparently of their own accord, climbed into the court of the fortress, and broke the chains of the raised drawbridge. The drawbridge fell across the moat. The mob surged in. The Governor, believing himself attacked, commanded his men to fire; the mob thought that he had lured them in on purpose and fired back. More parleys, more misunderstanding. Soldiers of the French Guards, in sympathy with the mob, dragged up cannon, while other assailants maintained a lively fusillade from their muskets. During the fight ninety-eight of the besiegers were killed and seventy-three wounded. The Governor sent a message that he would blow up the powder magazine and with it the Bastille, unless the assailants would accept a capitulation. The officers of the Guards accepted the capitulation, and the gates were opened, but the crowd shouting "No! No!" swarmed in, disarmed the helpless garrison, sacked the building, and liberated seven prisoners (two feeble-minded, four confined for forgery, and one, a wastrel, at his father's request).

The mob dragged de Launay through the streets, beating and kicking him, to the Hôtel de Ville, where one of them, a cook, cut off his head with a penknife. Others murdered the Prevôt des Marchands, chief official of the old municipal government, whom they suspected of treachery, and putting the two heads on pikes, marched them round the town. Nevertheless the people, though drunk with victory, were full of apprehensions lest the King's troops should close in upon them; they rang bells, threw up barricades, fired cannon, paraded the streets and illumined the windows. All were mad with victory, fear and anger.

CHAPTER XV

LA FAYETTE IN POWER

At Versailles, the Assembly waited, not knowing what was happening; the Vicomte de Noailles, La Fayette's brother-in-law, brought news that the mob was attacking the Bastille. The Duc de Liancourt went to the King: "Sire," he said, "this is not rioting, it is revolution." And yet that very night, the Comte d'Artois and the Duchesse de Polignac fêted two German regiments that were at Versailles. The time was ill chosen. The next day Mirabeau declaimed in the Assembly: "Tell the King that the foreign hordes by whom we are encircled, received yesterday the visits of princes and princesses, of favorites, men and women, who bestowed upon them caresses, exhortations, gifts; tell him that all night long these foreign satellites, gorged with gold and wine, predicted in their blasphemous songs the enslavement of France, etc."

The Assembly attributed the uprising in Paris to the excitement over the presence of these foreign regiments, and La Fayette was about to lead a deputation to the palace with further remonstrances, when the King himself, thoroughly disturbed, for he seems to have been too phlegmatic ever to know the sensation of fear, came to the Assembly and announced that he had withdrawn the foreign troops. There was immense enthusiasm at this announcement, and the deputies escorted his Majesty back to the Château in transports of gratitude. But the fall of the Bastille had frightened the Court; the Comte d'Artois hurried out of the country and the emigration of the noblesse began. The King and Queen thought of flight to Metz, where the Marquis de Bouillé was in command, but there was no answer to the question put by the Maréchal de Broglie: "What shall we do when we get to Metz?" so they stayed.

The National Assembly, realizing that their petition had been granted by the King in consequence of what the Parisian populace had done, dispatched a deputation of eighty members with Bailly and La Fayette at their head to congratulate the city. It was a momentous occasion when the National Assembly accepted with gratitude the succor of the mob. The deputation was hailed with enthusiasm. The streets were thronged, the windows decorated, welcomes and blessings were shouted out: *Vive la Nation! Vive le Roi! Vivent les Députés!* At the Hôtel de Ville La Fayette addressed the newly installed Electoral College; he congratulated them, and all the citizens of Paris, on the liberty they had conquered by their courage, on the peace and happiness for which they would be indebted to the justice of a kind but misled King. He said that the National Assembly recognized with pleasure that France would owe the constitution which was going to assure her felicity to the great efforts that the Parisians had made for popular liberty. He also read what the King had just said to the Assembly. Almost every sentence of the speech and of the reading was interrupted by applause and cries: *Vive le Roi! Vive la Nation!*

In the meantime, earlier in the day, the self-established Electoral College, having decided that the city must have a militia, consulted as to who should be its commander. There, in the hall of the Hôtel de Ville, where they were assembled, stood Houdon's bust of La Fayette, presented to the city by the state of Virginia three years before. The presiding officer pointed to the bust, and started to speak but acclamations drowned his words, and La Fayette was elected unanimously; Bailly, who, having spent a life in scientific pursuits, mainly in astronomy, had been by a strange chance exalted to the position of president of the National Assembly, was acclaimed mayor of the city. Both gentlemen were notified amid immense enthusiasm. La Fayette drew his sword and swore to defend this beloved liberty entrusted to him with his life. Outside, a crowd, packing the square, shouted and yelled in a delirium of joy. Both men were obliged to remain in Paris and enter upon their new duties at once.

The next day, La Fayette says in a letter: "It was necessary for me to accept and to stay; the people in the delirium of their enthusiasm can only be quieted by me. I wanted to go to Versailles; the leaders of the city told me that the safety of Paris required me not to leave the city for a minute. Forty thousand people collect together, their excitement is at fever heat, I show myself and one word disperses them. I have already saved the lives of six persons whom they were about to hang in different quarters of the city; but this mad, drunken people will not hearken to me always. At this very moment that I am writing eighty thousand people are crowding round the Hôtel de Ville and say that they are being deceived, that the troops have not been withdrawn, that the King must come to Paris. They will not accept anything unless I sign it. When I am not there, their heads grow giddy. In any case my situation is not like anybody's else. I reign in Paris over a maddened people, stirred up by abominable cabals; on the other hand their complaints are justified by a thousand infamous tricks that have been played upon them. At this moment, they are making a terrible outcry. If I show myself, they will calm down; but other periods of fury will come."

Perhaps this is one of the occasions to which Mr. Bernard Miall, translator of Aulard's *The French Revolution,* refers when he says: "A certain chivalrous scrupulosity kept La Fayette from seizing opportunities that would have led a less honorable man to triumph and dictatorship." At this time, I do not believe that La Fayette wished for a dictatorship; he wished for the triumph of liberty through law. As Carlyle says, ironically but truly, "he sticks by the Washington formula." His attitude toward law, if not that of a lover, is at least that of a loyal husband. In this case, partly from his native prudence no doubt, but much more from his respect for the Washington formula, he did not rest content with the *viva voce* election of the Permanent Committee, but asked for a formal election by the sixty districts of Paris. He sent out a circular saying: "However dear the testimony of your confidence, I must observe that the General of the Paris Militia has been appointed by acclamation, which is no doubt very flattering, but lacks the legal character of the expression of the people's will, from which all power must emanate. To-day, Gentlemen, I ask my fellow citizens to elect regularly a Commander-in-Chief, reserving to myself in any event the honor of serving them like the most faithful of their soldiers. Therefore, I can exercise only provisionally the functions with which I am charged.'' His election was unanimous, and was afterward confirmed both by the National Assembly and by the King.

The Permanent Committee had asked for a city militia in order to defend Paris from the King's foreign troops, but a disciplined force was still more necessary for police duty. The city was heaving with passion. The populace had armed themselves with all sorts of weapons, guns, axes, knives, bludgeons, whatever they could lay hands on; and among them were many hundreds of soldiers who had deserted the King's service. All the old fabric of authority had fallen, tribunals, magistrates, laws. Ordinary occupations were largely stopped, and there was scarce food for twenty-four hours ahead. Suborned hirelings were at work to make disorder more hideous, some in the interest of the old régime, some in that of the Duc d'Orléans, a prince of the blood who posed as a liberal in the hope, so it was thought, that he might supplant the elder branch of the Bourbon family. There were, also, thousands of strangers roaming the streets. The only authority lay with the Permanent Committee and the local groups of electors in the several districts and that was self-conferred.

On July sixteenth, by order of the Permanent Committee, in the name of Monsieur de La Fayette, the demolition of the Bastille was decreed; subsequently Monsieur de La Fayette presented the key to Washington. The next day, the King, with but a scanty guard, for he never lacked passive courage, came from Versailles to Paris. The whirligig of time had been busy during the twelve years since young La Fayette was pursued by a *lettre de cachet* and the Bastille had loomed in the background. To-day, La Fayette, on his white horse, wearing a red and blue cockade, sword in hand, at the head of a vast multitude of armed men, met his Majesty on the road, and escorted him into the city. At the Hôtel de Ville, Mayor Bailly made a little speech and gave the King a red and blue cockade. When La Fayette came to escort him back, the King said: "Monsieur de La Fayette, I was looking for you to let you know that I confirm your nomination to the post of Commander-in-Chief of the Paris guard." There is a touch of pathos in this unasked-for confirmation of a rebellious officer in an illegal office.

La Fayette at once devoted himself to his new duties. He suggested as a name for the militia, the National Guard of Paris, advised a committee consisting of one man from each electoral district to assist him in the organization of the new force, and for its cockade added to the city's colors, red and blue, the ancient color of the French monarchy, white, making the tricolor its emblem. When La Fayette presented his plan of organization at the Hôtel de Ville he said: "I bring you a cockade that shall go round the world, and an institution at once civic and military, that shall triumph over the old tactics of Europe and reduce arbitrary governments to the alternative of being beaten if they do not copy it, or of being overthrown, if they do." Enlistments came in rapidly, but the guard was not a democratic organization, for the members paid for their own arms and uniforms, and as a consequence for the most part men of the upper classes formed it, men of business, bankers, merchants, men of property. Madame de La Tour du Pin says that every man "in society" under fifty had enrolled.

At this time La Fayette was the most influential man in France. "He!" said an orderly, "he makes revolutions as others sing songs." Gouverneur Morris dined with him on July twentieth, making it a condition that he might bring his own wine. "La Fayette tells me," he says, "that he has the utmost power his heart could wish, and is grown tired of it; that he has commanded absolutely a hundred thousand men, has marched his sovereign about the streets as he pleased, prescribed the degree of applause which he should receive, and could have detained him prisoner had he thought proper. He wishes, therefore, as soon as possible to return to private life."

But the ruler of a mob is never at ease and never absolute, as La Fayette was soon to learn. There was a certain rich man, Foulon, who for a few brief days had been assistant secretary of war; he was regarded as one of the evil counselors of the old régime, instrumental in bringing the nation to bankruptcy, and was charged in particular with having said that "the people should be only too happy if they were given hay to eat." The mob discovered him, hauled him to the Hôtel de Ville and demanded that he be tried on the spot and hanged. Bailly endeavored to interfere and La Fayette harangued again and again, and nearly succeeded. He said: "If he is guilty, I am far from trying to save him; I only wish him to be taken to prison and judged by a tribunal that the nation shall indicate. I wish the law respected, for were it not for law I should not work for the Revolution." At that moment some ruffians from the Faubourg Saint-Antoine, a quarter of the city "inhabited entirely by the class of day laborers and journeymen in every line," burst into the Hôtel de Ville, and laid hold on Foulon. La Fayette again harangued, shouting, "Take him to prison," and the crowd, momentarily won over, burst into applause, but the fool Foulon applauded too. Some one shouted: "They are in cahoots," and the ruffians pulled him away, and hanged him on a lamp-post. They had not long hanged him, when they came upon his son-in-law, one Berthier, and massacred him, too; they tore his heart out and placed it on the desk of the Electoral College. Both heads were cut off, fastened on pikes, and paraded through the streets, passing among others young Chateaubriand and his sister, also Gouverneur Morris, who ejaculated, "Gracious God, what a people!" La Fayette was outraged, and handed in his resignation as commander, but the universal consternation forced him to continue in his office. He writes: "You can't picture to yourself the consternation that my resignation caused. All the districts have sent to conjure me to stay: they fell on their knees, weeping and swearing to obey me in everything. What is to be done? I am in despair. . . . I can't abandon the citizens who put all their trust in me, and if I stay, I am in the terrible predicament of seeing evil without remedying it" (July twenty-fourth). This is the first clash between La Fayette and the forces of the slums. As he had truly said "this mad, drunken people will not hearken to me always." And not in Paris alone were atrocities committed but also almost everywhere throughout France, charters of privileges and title deeds were destroyed, nobles murdered, châteaux burned; in one district, Beaujolais, for instance, one hundred and fifty châteaux were burned.

La Fayette, as I have said, had immense influence, but he also had immense difficulties. He says in one of the letters I quoted, "The populace is led by an invisible hand . . . the cabal that encompasses me appears to be pushed by outsiders." He was right, though he probably does not give the populace sufficient credit for spontaneous rioting. There were plotters at work and underhand agents who had objects in view other than the welfare of France. The Duc d'Orléans, a plotter himself or an instrument in the hands of plotters, was a person of whom La Fayette entertained strong suspicions. He took great pains to win popularity. During the harsh winter 1788-89, in which poor people suffered horribly, he sold his famous collection of pictures and gave, it was said, eight million livres to charities. His democratic professions won for him the nickname, Égalité. He was a gross debauchee and not pleasant to look at. "A hereditary taint of blood and dissolute personal habits had disfigured his face and features." The Court party regarded him as a pure demagogue, and attributed all riots to his fomenting. And La Fayette inclined to agree with them: "Among the people who make themselves most conspicuous in the revolution, there are some whose views extend beyond the establishment of a constitution. I feel sure that M. le Duc d'Orléans, or at least the people that push him on, mean to sow disorder. Advances have been made to me. Yesterday I was told that the head of M. le Duc d'Orléans and mine were proscribed; that there were sinister plots against me as the only man able to lead an army; that M. le Duc d'Orléans and I must act in unison. I answered coldly. . . . But in the meantime I am watching him and perhaps I shall be in a position to denounce M. le Comte d'Artois as a factious aristocrat, and M. le Duc d'Orléans. . . ."

An incident corroborated his suspicions. One day he rode by the old convent of the Cordeliers, the seat of an electoral district, near the present *École de Medicine* off the Boulevard Saint-Germain, where the patriots of that neighborhood were assembled. He was invited to go in. There was a crowd, among them a large number of French Guards. After the usual applause at his coming, Danton, the president and orator of the day, informed him that in order to recompense the patriotism of the brave *Gardes-françaises,* the district had voted to petition that their regiments should be reestablished in their old form, and that the command should be given to the first prince of the blood, the Duc d'Orléans. "We can not doubt," he added, "of the consent of the *Commandant Général* to so patriotic a plan." Danton's speech was larded with compliments for La Fayette, and greeted with acclamations.

What La Fayette knew of Danton at this time, I can not say; afterward he distrusted him completely, perhaps because he believed him venal, perhaps also because the *grand seigneur* in him instinctively disliked a demagogue, or perhaps because a partisan of orderly revolution disapproves of partisans of revolution by riot and violence. He saw at once that the plan of Danton and the chiefs of the Cordelier Club was to separate the trained soldiers from the militia in the interest of the Duc d'Orléans. He began his speech in reply with great caution, and raising objections gradually succeeded in making his audience, both the civilians and the soldiers themselves, disapprove of the plan.

One now realizes the difficulties of La Fayette's position. There was he, whom a German scholar calls "the very noble European representative of the political ideas of the United States," champion of the "Washington formula"—law, order, equality of opportunity, with preponderant political power in the hands of education and property—opposing despotism and feudal privilege on the one hand, and on the other, opposing violence, riot and the domination of the proletariat. And confronting him on the right was the Court, headed by the Queen who hated him, and on the left, the down-trodden, hungry, miserable populace, with Danton hounding them on; Danton, a bold, passionate demagogue, filled with a fine frenzy of zeal for the proletariat, whom in his exalted moments he saw noble, just and heroic, so long as his ambition and theirs were at one, but ready in his desire for comfort and luxury to take money from the Court— so, at least, his biographer Monsieur Louis Madelin believes, and La Fayette, Mirabeau and Brissot, men not in accord, believed, as well as Saint-Just. "Where did you get all this luxury?" And Monsieur Hamel, in his life of Robespierre, says that it would require *"une bonne volonté infinie"* to believe him innocent; Danton, a volcanic kind of man, ready to approve murder for the sake of a France, where he and the proletariat should sit in luxurious power, and disdainful of the elegant scruples of the American-bred marquis.

This was the first time, and not the last, that the two men clashed.

CHAPTER XVI

OCTOBER 5-6, 1789

THE fall of the Bastille was caused by a mob animated by no further purpose than to obtain fire-arms; but its fall resounded throughout France like the last trump, and at the sound resentments, humiliations, dormant hopes, concealed hatreds, suppressed wishes, leaped to their feet, not yet wide awake, still bewildered, befogged, uncertain of the differences between realities and fears. A nightmare came over the country, they call it *la Grande Peur,* spreading the wildest rumors of invasions from England, Saxony, Germany, rumors of the Comte d'Artois returning with an army, of hordes of brigands coming to burn and pillage. The peasants ran amuck, they rioted in fury, they committed what are called, except when done by a whole people, the crimes of arson and murder; they robbed and pillaged; they insulted, outraged and murdered seigneurs, churchmen, Jews, creditors. It was a *jacquerie,* a class revolt. After a time it died away. But feudal privileges had been kicked and beaten down.

What the peasants and other unprivileged persons had done with fire and crowbar, the National Assembly completed by legislation. They laid the ax to feudal rights, customs and privileges. On August fourth the Vicomte de Noailles, La Fayette's brother-in-law, proposed the abolition of the corvée and personal servitude; other members, in generous rivalry, proposed abolishing this and that, giving up, surrendering and suppressing the mass of ancient burdens that had weighed so heavily on the lower social classes. The deputies from provinces renounced the privileges of the provinces, those from cities the privileges of their cities,—one dissentient said: "Everybody hurried to give away what did not belong to him," another called it the "Saint-Bartholomew of property"—and all was done amid wild enthusiasm, and with cheers for the King: *Vive Louis XVI, restaurateur de la liberté française!* The deputies then addressed themselves to a Declaration of Rights, a sort of Magna Charta, as prologue to a constitution. The preamble begins: "The representatives of the French people, now become the National Assembly, considering that ignorance, forgetfulness, or contempt of the rights of man, are the only causes of public misfortunes and of the corruption of governments, have decided to set forth in a solemn declaration of natural rights, etc." La Fayette, kept by his duties in Paris, no longer sat in the Assembly, but his draft of a declaration of rights had been largely followed. The committee on the project of a constitution invited Thomas Jefferson to assist them; but he did not think it becoming to accept. They soon came upon a great difficulty: What authority should the King have? Should he have any veto, should he be given the power of veto upon ordinary legislation, should he have a right to veto the great acts of reform, destructive and constructive, that the Assembly had just passed? Over these questions the reformers disagreed; and the disagreement raised the hopes of the Court and the reactionary aristocracy. The moderates thought that they had gone quite far enough, and wished the King to have substantial authority, while the radicals would not hear of any veto.

La Fayette was much concerned. He favored a suspensive veto, that is that the Assembly, after a delay that ensured deliberation, should have the power to override the veto. "You see," he writes to a friend, "that the power I enjoy has made me respectful and moderate." He was also inclined toward a second chamber, elective, on the principle of the American Senate, and for a long term. But he admitted that the whole matter was a task far out of the ordinary. He writes to a friend, "Don't be reckoning up my present power (I shall make no use of it) nor what I have done. I want no reward. Reckon up the public good and the liberty of my country, and believe that I shall not refuse any burden, any danger, provided that when the time of quiet arrives I may become a private citizen again. . . . If the King rejects the constitution, I shall fight him. If he accepts it, I shall defend him. And the day that he surrenders as my prisoner will render me more devoted to him than if he had promised me half of his kingdom." As to the veto, the main question before the Assembly, he keeps reiterating that he and the National Guard have no mind to influence their decisions, that the army must be subject to the civil powers.

That meant, of course, that he was not to use his influence as a military officer, for his private efforts to keep together the two parties, the moderates and the radicals, were unceasing. Thomas Jefferson writes: "In this uneasy state of things, I received one day a note from the Marquis de La Fayette, informing me that he should bring a party of six or eight friends to ask a dinner of me the next day. I assured him of their welcome.'' La Fayette brought seven, Duport, Barnave, Alexandre Lameth, Mounier, Maubourg and two others. ''These were leading patriots, [I am quoting Jefferson] of honest but differing opinions, sensible of the necessity of effecting a coalition by mutual sacrifices, knowing each other, and not afraid, therefore, to unbosom themselves naturally. . . . The cloth being removed, and wine set on the table, after the American manner, the Marquis introduced the objects of the conference, by summarily reminding them of the state of things in the Assembly, the course which the principles of the Constitution were taking, and the inevitable result, unless checked by more concord among the Patriots themselves. He observed, that although he also had his opinion, he was ready to sacrifice it to that of his brethren of the same cause; but that a common opinion must now be formed, or the Aristocracy would carry everything, and that, whatever they should now agree on, he, at the head of the National force would maintain. The discussions began at the hour of four, and were continued till ten o'clock in the evening; during which time, I was a silent witness to a coolness and candour of argument, unusual in the conflicts of political opinion; to a logical reasoning, and chaste eloquence, disfigured by no gaudy tinsel of rhetoric or declamation, and truly worthy of being placed in parallel with the finest dialogues of antiquity, as handed to us by Xenophon, by Plato and Cicero. The result was, that the king should have a suspensive veto on the laws, that the legislature should be composed of a single body only, and that to be chosen by the people. This concordate decided the fate of the Constitution. The Patriots all rallied to the principles thus settled, carried every question agreeably to them, and reduced the Aristocracy to insignificance and impotence." I have thought it worth while to give Jefferson's report of this discussion, for French writers are apt to dwell upon Mirabeau's eloquence, upon Danton's volcanic periods, upon Sieyès's logic, upon Talleyrand's ingenuity, upon the impetuous southern rhetoric of the Gironde, and take little notice of the quiet reasoning of these moderate men that commended itself to this no mean observer.

But this halcyon prospect was not of long duration. The King refused to accept this overthrow of royal authority, and ordered the regiment of Flanders, stationed at Douai, to come to Versailles (September fourteenth). He had his excuse, for Paris was in an angry mood. The sixty electoral clubs in the sixty districts were meeting daily in churches, convents or halls, and orators were haranguing them. Each district wished its advice to be followed by the municipal government at the Hôtel de Ville. The city was near anarchy. Thousands were out of work; bread was bad, dear and very scarce, for each province, apprehensive of famine, kept its grain for itself. At every bakery a long queue stood in line. The populace accused not only the aristocrats but also the moderate party in the Assembly of being the cause of their misery. The newspapers denounced monstrous plots against the nation; Camille Desmoulins published his paper, *Discours de la lanterne aux Parisiens,* with malice and art, Marat, *l'Ami du People,* with malice and ferocity, attacking La Fayette among other enemies of the people. All united to preach that salvation could only be attained if the people, that is the proletariat, dominated both Court and National Assembly. Plots of Jacobins, plots of aristocrats, plots of Orléanists, or rumors of such, increased and multiplied; dangers lurked at every corner. Then came the news that the regiment from Flanders had come to Versailles.

The Court felt easier, although the royal soldiers were few in number compared to the new National Guard of Paris, and it hoped to strengthen its position by winning over the all powerful Commander-in-Chief. They offered to create La Fayette constable of France, and make him lieutenant-general of the kingdom. They did not know how idle it was to try to bribe a man for whom George Washington was the great exemplar of noble manhood. Somewhere La Fayette says: "My ambition was always to be above ambition." He refused their offers, as he refused the command of other National Guards except those of Paris, as he refused a salary of one hundred and twenty thousand livres. Then the Court, in its folly, made a demonstration of its attachment to its soldiers. The *Salle de l'Opera,* at the end of the north wing of the Château, was put at the disposal of the officers of the *Gardes du Corps* who invited the officers of the Flanders regiment to a banquet. Wine flowed too freely, healths were drunk to the King! to the Queen! to the Dauphin! to the Royal Family! the nation was not mentioned; and some one shouted, "Down with the tricolor cockade!" It was a royalist, anti-national, drinking bout. And the ladies of the palace filled up the cup of rashness, by distributing white cockades. These were really the Queen's doings; the King when left to himself went a-hunting.

When Paris heard of all this, there was an outburst

of fury. Marat (Desmoulins said) made as much noise as the trumpets of the day of doom; Danton fulminated at the club of Cordeliers; miscellaneous patriots shook their fists in the Café de Foy (off the Palais Royal) and the women of the markets, in their Billingsgate, expressed indignation and wrath. There was a general cry that the Queen was to blame, and that the people must go out to Versailles. The flood of anger was well-nigh universal, and swept the National Guard with it. Cries went up for a constitution, for bread, for bringing the King to Paris, also others were heard, more sinister, "Death to the Aristocrats!" "Death to the Queen!" The next day, October fifth, a vast crowd assembled. According to an unsympathetic commentator, who was living at the time: "All the filth that the mud of the Faubourgs Saint-Antoine and Saint Marceau can uncover, all the vilest, lowest, most disgusting stuff that the cellars and sewers from the neighborhood of the *Place de grève* can spew forth, rushed upon the Hôtel de Ville, calling for bread and the heads of the aristocrats." The French have a turn for expressing discontent with dregs, filth, foulness, that loses its fastidious elegance when rendered into English. Evidently the memory of an elderly man still vividly retained the impressions of his youth.

This multitude, men and women,—the people, or a mob, according to your sympathies,—shouting for bread, under the lead of Maillard, one of the heroes of the Bastille, started for Versailles. Great numbers of the National Guard crowded about the Hôtel de Ville, where La Fayette had his headquarters; they were in full sympathy with the mob. One said to La Fayette: "General, the King is deceiving everybody, you as well as the rest; he must be deposed; his son

shall be king and you regent, and all will go well."
La Fayette, full of alarm at what might happen, did
all that a man could to prevent the perilous exodus,
he probably wished to save the National Assembly as
well as the King from being bullied, perhaps maltreated, by the mob. He forbade the National Guard
to go and refused to go himself. He held firm from
nine o'clock in the morning till four in the afternoon, in
spite of cries *à la lanterne,* in spite of a noose hung up
to a lamp-post, and though twenty times a gun was
pointed at him. Then, fearing what the mob might do,
he gave way. Clinging to the shadow of legality he
finally asked and received permission to go from the
municipality, and then at the head of fifteen thousand
National Guards, attended by as many more volunteers, he hurried off on the road to Versailles.

The mob, largely women, armed with pikes and
bludgeons had already arrived, wet with rain, tired
from trudging eleven or twelve miles, and raging:
"We'll make the slut pay dear." They found the Assembly deliberating on the constitution; Maillard, who
led the women, entered the hall and addressed them,
accusing the aristocrats of starving the people. The
Assembly, remembering the advantages gained by the
doings on July fourteenth, thought that the mob would
again enable them to bring pressure on the King and
force him to accept their Declaration of Rights and
such articles of a constitution as they had enacted;
they, therefore, sent a deputation to accompany the
women, who had already swarmed up to the Château
palings, clamoring for bread. The King received the
joint deputation from Assembly and mob graciously,
promised the women bread and accepted the Declaration of Rights and the articles of the Constitution.

Outside the Château the crowd howled angrily, and there was quarreling and some fighting between the Versailles militia, who sympathized with them, and the Royal Guards. Inside there was fear, hesitation and doubt. The King did not know what to do. Some counseled flight, and the King inclined to their advice. Preparations were begun. Then Necker appeared and protested that flight meant ruin. The hesitating King paced up and down, saying, *"Un roi fugitif! Un roi fugitif!"* and decided to stay.

Near midnight La Fayette arrived at Versailles with the National Guard, all sopping wet and tired. No one had opposed them; on the contrary the Flanders regiment sent to La Fayette for orders. He halted on the avenue de Paris, that leads to the Château, in front of the hall of the National Assembly and made provision for lodging his soldiers. He sent word of his arrival to the King, who answered that he was glad to know that he had come and that he "had accepted his Declaration of Rights." La Fayette then went, accompanied by two envoys from the municipality of Paris, to the gates of the Château. The Swiss Guards refused to open. La Fayette explained that he wished to enter alone with the two civilians. The Captain of the Guard was amazed at his daring. La Fayette replied: "I shall never lack confidence in the midst of these brave Swiss Guards." He crossed the court, so exhausted that he nearly needed support, mounted the stairs, passed through the gorgeously decorated rooms crowded with ladies and gentlemen in waiting. As he walked through the Oeil-de-Bœuf, under its gaudy frieze of cupids in gilt stucco, some one exclaimed: "There goes Cromwell!" To which he answered: "Monsieur, Cromwell would not have come alone,'' and hurried on to the King's apartments. Many persons were gathered there. ''Sire,'' he cried, ''you see before you one of the unhappiest of men, obliged to come under these circumstances and in this fashion. If I had believed that I should have served your Majesty more usefully to-day by laying my head on the block, you would not see me here.'' The King said that he was glad to see him and *''nos bons Parisiens,''* and bade the National Guard do duty outside the Château, leaving the enclosure within the gates to the *Gardes du Corps* and to the Switzers. From the Château La Fayette drove in a carriage to the barracks of the *Gardes du Corps,* which were surrounded by the mob. Men with pikes stopped the carriage. La Fayette put his head out and said: *''Mes enfants,* what do you want?'' ''We want the heads of the *Gardes du Corps.''* ''But, why?'' ''They have insulted, and trampled on, the National cockade; they must be punished.'' ''Be quiet; trust me; everything will be all right.'' His words and a few coins quieted the rowdies, and they let the carriage drive on.

At three o'clock in the morning the National Assembly adjourned. The mob continued singing and drinking. La Fayette finding all quiet retired to his headquarters hard by. He made some necessary dispositions for Paris, took something to eat, threw himself down in his clothes, and went to sleep. It was already daybreak. The aristocrats never tired of charging him with going to sleep that night to the neglect of his duty, they dubbed him, General Morphée; forty years later they still taunted him with it. But Madame de La Tour du Pin, one of the Queen's ladies in waiting, who was there in the Château with her husband, says that on arriving when he had dismounted, he was so tired that he could hardly hold himself up. "His fault, if there was one, did not consist in that hour of sleep that he took, all dressed, on the sofa in Madame de Poix's drawing-room, for which he has been blamed so much, but in his complete ignorance of the Duc d'Orléans' conspiracy." As to this ignorance we shall see later. In recounting the night he says: "I should have supposed that the exhaustion of my body, rudely tired for more than twenty hours, needed a little rest, if it had not been that a few minutes later a sudden alarm gave me back my strength." He was called in haste. The rabble was attacking the palace. It was about six o'clock. He ordered a band of grenadiers, in which Hoche, afterward very distinguished, was a sergeant-major, to run to the palace. He ran, too, and jumped on the first horse he met.

The mob had got within the fences, by a gate left unfastened, by neglect or more likely by collusion. The Royal Guards resisted; two fell. The rabble cut off their heads and fixed them on pikes. They swarmed on and up the marble staircase that leads to the Queen's apartments, on the left of the *Cour Royale* as you face the palace, and burst into the hall of the Queen's *Garde du Corps,* driving the guards there into the next room, the Queen's antechamber. They broke this door down and murdered a guardsman. Another guardsman, all bloody, ran shouting to the Queen's tirewomen, "Save the Queen!" One of these ladies locked an intervening door, and the Queen, scarcely dressed, ran through the *Oeil-de-Bœuf,* on into the King's apartments to the right of the *Cour de Marbre.* At this juncture the National Guards charged in and expelled the mob.

La Fayette, galloping up, saved on the way a band of the King's Guards. The mob was about to kill them. He cried out to the people: "I have pledged my sacred word to the King that no harm shall come to them." An angry crowd surrounded him, and one shouted, "Kill him!" But La Fayette thundered out, "Arrest that man!" and the crowd seized the fellow and dragged him along the ground. He then commanded the National Guard to see that his promise to the King was kept. In the King's apartment he found National Guardsmen already there, and they promised him with tears in their eyes to perish to the last man for the King. The King never forgot this. The sun was now up. The court before the palace was packed with people but the National Guard had arrived there in force. The King's Guards, still trembling, showed themselves at the windows wearing the tricolor cockade. They were greeted by shouts of approval: *"Vive le Roi! Vive la Nation! Vivent les Gardes du Corps."*

Overlooking the *Cour de Marbre* a gilded balcony projects. Here the royal family showed themselves for a moment, and from it La Fayette addressed the crowd. The people shouted for the Queen. She stepped out with the Dauphin. There were cries of "No children!" Some ruffians in the crowd made terrible gestures, and one man aimed his gun at her. She drew back. La Fayette said: "Madam, what will you do?" "I know," she answered, "what fate is before me, but my duty is to die at the King's feet, in the arms of my children." "Come out with me, Madam." "What! alone on the balcony? Didn't you see the gestures they made?" "Yes, Madam. Let us step out." The crowd howled so that La Fayette could not make himself heard. He bent over the Queen's hand and kissed it. The crowd responded to this act of chivalrous homage and shouted: *"Vive le Général! Vive la Reine!"* Next the King stepped out. The crowd howled: "Come to Paris." The King promised to go, and to bring the Queen and the Dauphin: "I trust my most precious possessions to the love of my dear and faithful subjects." After this some of the King's Guards stepped out on the balcony, and La Fayette embraced them. They cried: *"Vive le Roi! Vive la Nation!"* and the mob yelled back: *"Vivent les Gardes du Roi."*

So La Fayette and the National Guard saved the lives of the King and Queen, and of many of the *Gardes du Corps.* That same day, October sixth, the royal family returned from Versailles, after an absence of one hundred and twenty years, to Paris. La Fayette signed the passports of safe conduct for them and their suites. The procession started at one o'clock, with thousands and thousands of people in line, women brave in tricolor cockades and carrying be-ribboned branches, red, white and blue, men with guns and pikes, the National Guard, the King's Guards, wearing tricolor cockades, the Flanders regiment, the royal family in a carriage, and La Fayette riding beside. The royal family drove direct to the Hôtel de Ville. When they got there La Fayette felt his hand squeezed in gratitude; it was the King's sister, the Princess Elisabeth. At the Hôtel de Ville, Bailly made a pretty speech. The people were wild with joy; whenever they saw a member of the royal family they burst into frantic applause. They were gay for the victory was theirs; the National Assembly had triumphed over the King, but the commune of

Paris had triumphed over both, and the King was a prisoner in the city. La Fayette escorted the royal family back to the Tuileries. Madame Adelaide, the King's aunt said to him: "I owe you more than my life, I owe you the life of my poor nephew, the King."

CHAPTER XVII

DUC D'ORLÉANS, MOUNIER, BOUILLÉ

THE fourteenth of July had caused the overthrow of the feudal system, for it made manifest to the nation on how weak a base privilege stood, and on that revelation the nation had acted; in like fashion, the fifth and sixth of October overthrew the absolute monarchy, leaving the way free for a new political edifice. There was a king left, a remnant of nobles, a bourgeosie, a proletariat and peasants; what should be done?

This question concerned everybody. La Fayette was absorbed in it, but he could not attend the National Assembly, for he had supreme charge of public order. A nobleman, somewhat critical of him, described him at the time in this way: "He seemed to me devoured by a desire to put his name at the head of the revolution in this country as Washington had put his at the head of that in America, but only willing to employ honorable means; he had great presence of mind, a very good head, energy, though directing it with very mediocre judgment, much skill in taking advantage of opportunity, although without the genius that creates opportunity—on the whole an honorable man with capacity, though not a great man." This critic perhaps did not know, or perhaps would not have agreed, that the combination of traits that constituted La Fayette's character, a readiness to sacrifice even a passionate ambition to duty and honor, is rarer than the energy that wisely chooses its object, rarer even than the genius that creates opportunity, as rare, perhaps, as greatness in man.

And, having quoted the Marquis du Châtelet, I will also quote La Fayette's cousin, the Marquis de Bouillé, a confirmed aristocrat, whom we shall soon meet again: *"C'était un heros de roman* who, though at the head of the wickedest insurrection, thought that he could maintain honesty, honor and disinterestedness, and give free rein to the spirit of chivalry. . . . La Fayette was an enthusiast for liberty as Don Quixote was for knight-errantry; his stay in America had completely turned his head, just as reading romances had turned that of the Spanish knight. His only ambition was to make a noise in the world, maintaining and defending the liberty of peoples against kings and princes, whom he pretended were their oppressors. His fate was like that of the Gracchi. . . ." This seems to me a far more just estimate than that of Gouverneur Morris, who proffered a great deal of advice to La Fayette, and was vexed when he did not take it; "But in fact he is the lover of freedom from ambition of which there are two kinds: one born of pride, the other of vanity, and his partakes more of the latter."

La Fayette had at the outset two especial problems: the Duc d'Orléans and Mirabeau. The Duc d'Orléans, immensely rich, *immoral et crapuleux,* was regarded as a man of the first potential political importance; he was a member of the National Assembly, an advocate of liberal measures, and intrigued or let others intrigue on his behalf, with Jacobins, aristocrats, and even at one time, it is said, with the Court. La Fayette

thought him bad and dangerous, and believed that he
had set on the ruffians, revolutionists, patriots, that
assaulted Versailles. At this time the Duke was in
accord with Mirabeau, who entertained the idea that,
if Orléans were regent or lieutenant-general of the
kingdom, he would be prime minister. It was in fear
of such a plot that the Ministry offered to create La
Fayette constable and lieutenant-general himself. La
Fayette answered proudly that the position offered
would add nothing to his credit in France, nor to his
determination to defend the King against the attacks
of Monsieur d'Orléans.

La Fayette did not show the indecision, of which
Mirabeau frequently accuses him, in this instance.
The very day after the great doings of October fifth
and sixth, he asked *Monseigneur le Duc* to give him
orders as to when, how, and where he might see him.
The Duke accepted a rendezvous at the house of the
Marquise de Coigny, whom both knew very well, and
there they had a frank conversation that Mirabeau
called "very imperious on the one part and very sub-
missive on the other." La Fayette indeed spoke
plainly: "I have contributed," he said, "more than
any one else to tipping over the steps that rise toward
the throne. The nation has set the King on the last
step. I shall defend him there against you, and before
you take his place, you must pass over my body, and
that will not be easy." It was agreed that the Duke
should go to London under the color of some mission.

The Duke, however, after consulting with his
friends, changed his mind, and said that he would not
go. La Fayette demanded a second meeting for the
next day, and exacted a promise that the Duke would
leave within twenty-four hours; he took him to the

King, who was amazed, especially when the Duke
assured him that "in London he should try to discover
the authors of the late troubles"; La Fayette added
dryly, "It is more to your interest than to that of anybody's else, for you are the most compromised." But
a second time the Duke drew back; he concerted with
Mirabeau against La Fayette. Mirabeau was to make
a speech in the Assembly, (as he afterward told La
Fayette) denouncing him: "How he had caused the
Comte d'Artois and the Princes of Condé and Conti
to emigrate, how he had taken the King, the royal
family, and Monsieur [the King's next brother] into
custody, how he had now banished the Duc d'Orléans,
and with what ambitious views in mind the Assembly
might guess." In consequence of this tergiversation
there was a third interview. The Duke said: "My
enemies pretend that you have proofs against me;" to
which La Fayette replied: "It is rather my enemies,
that say so; if I were in a position to produce proofs
against you, I should have had you arrested," and
added, "I am looking everywhere for them." The
Duke, first writing a letter to the president of the
National Assembly that should prevent Mirabeau's
project of denunciation, left for London. The French
Ambassador wrote to La Fayette on the Duke's
arrival: "Although I may say that you are not very
popular among our refugees, there is not a Frenchman or French woman who does not think a thousand
times better of you since you have sent me an
ambassadorial confrère. I will admit, however, that
though I could have got on very well without him, you
have rendered a very great service to our country by
politely insisting that he should leave it. . . . His
person, or rather his name, would have given a good

deal of embarrassment to people like you, who desire the reestablishment of order and the establishment of a good government." La Fayette was so in accord with this opinion that he sent to inform the Duke, in case he should propose to return to France, that he must regard him on landing as a personal enemy, and that if he came to Paris, he would fight a duel with him the following morning, and then go and justify his conduct at the bar of the National Assembly.

This incident shows the immense prestige that La Fayette enjoyed at this time. The ministers complained of "his despotism." A letter of his sets forth his own state of mind: "Naturally, at this time, all those that have kindly feelings for me, or who hope for places near the place where I shall be, busy themselves with my future. Some want me to be constable, others generalissimo. The Ministers have proposed the bâton of a marshal of France. Alexandre Lameth, acting, I suppose, for M. de La Tour du Pin [Minister of War], spoke of the army of Flanders; this, *au fond*, when everything becomes quiet would suit me very well, for it is the principal army and would be the one to march in case of war. But to all this I answer that I can't concern myself with it till I become useless, and, I fancy, between ourselves, that ingratitude will then save me from the embarrassment of rewards." And he sets forth his views further in a letter that he wrote to Mounier, who had first raised the cry of double representation for the Third Estate and the voting of the three orders together, and had been president of the National Assembly on October fifth and sixth. Mounier, liberal though he was, shocked and alienated by the events of those days, had gone back to Dauphiné to work against the Assembly.

"Paris, Oct. 23, 1789.

"My dear Mounier,

". . . As for me I am astonished by my immense responsibility, but it doesn't discourage me. I am devoted to the cause of the people both by affection and duty, and I shall fight aristocracy, despotism and faction with equal ardor. I know the faults of the National Assembly; but to discredit it seems to me much more dangerous, really culpable. I hate too great influence in one's man's hands; but I feel more deeply than you think the necessity of strengthening the executive power. I believe that the only way to avoid civil war and do some good, is to start with things as they are and act with and through the National Assembly and the King, reunited in the capital. I believe this great work possible, I believe it certain, if leading citizens and men of capacity do not desert the commonwealth. . . . Don't sink into discouragement and vexation of spirit, and, if I persist in my efforts to save our country, at least don't let me be able lay the blame upon those whose help would save us and whose opposition may ruin all. Adieu, my dear Mounier."

I will also quote a letter he wrote a few weeks later to his cousin, the commander at Metz, Marquis de Bouillé, who, as I have said, was a stout royalist, and disapproved of La Fayette's revolutionary doctrines and actions.

"Paris, November 14, 1789

"My dear Cousin

". . . Both of us like liberty; I felt the need of a stronger dose than you, and you ought to be the less displeased, because you would take no part in it. But to-day we fear the same evils—anarchy, civil dissensions, the dissolution of all public authority; we want the same things—the reestablishment of credit, the strengthening of constitutional liberty, the return of order and a large measure of executive authority. A counter-revolution is happily not possible, besides it would be criminal, for it would bring on civil war. . . . Decent people, good citizens, can only hope to wind up the machine to go in the direction set by the revolution. The King feels this truth deeply. I think all able men should feel it deeply. The National Assembly after having pulled down at Versailles, is now going to build up in Paris, and it will be more reasonable now that all excuse for distrust is gone. The more you rally to the new constitution, my dear Cousin, the greater will be your power of serving the public. . . . As for me, put by circumstances and the people's trust in responsibility far above my talents, I believe that I have shown that I hate faction as much as I love liberty, and I am impatient for the time to come when I can prove as well that no thought of personal interest has ever touched my heart. I have opened myself to you, dear Cousin, with confidence and I eagerly seize upon every sentence in your letter that brings me close to you.''

Such were La Fayette's general views; I shall have occasion to harp on them again and again, and on his stubborn fidelity to them. The work of demolition had gone far enough, it was now time to build up rational doctrine upon rational doctrine, and fashion a constitution that men of all minds could rally to. Mirabeau also held the same general opinions, he wished to uphold the monarchy and royal authority as the most likely security for order in the rising tide of anarchy. They were the two most influential men in France, Mirabeau by his great talents, La Fayette by his vast popularity; and each made efforts to come to an understanding with the other.

CHAPTER XVIII

LA FAYETTE AND MIRABEAU

To THE cooperation between Mirabeau and La Fayette there were obstacles on both sides. Mirabeau was undoubtedly jealous and envious of La Fayette. Conscious of his own intellectual gifts, he was burning with ambition to use them, and having attempted in vain to rise to power by means of the Duc d'Orléans, he now tried to make use of La Fayette. Nobody will dispute that Mirabeau possessed greater talents than La Fayette; but stung by envy, and annoyed both to be dependent upon La Fayette and not to be readily accepted as an ally, he became unjust to him. He nicknamed him Cromwell-Grandison, and complained that he was undecided and irresolute: "You see," he wrote, "the sort of man he is, equally incapable of scanting his promise and of keeping it at the time agreed." Later on, when Mirabeau wished to make up to the King, he believed, or affected to believe, that La Fayette's loyalty masked republican ambition. If he really believed this, it is proof that he was not so perspicacious as his admirers assert. This is what he says in a memorandum on politics that has been preserved: There are three political parties in Paris: ". . . The third is that of M. de La Fayette; it is marked by a series of maneuvers which prove a steadily followed plan, the maneuver of February 28th

[1790] is of a *grande profondeur;* he affects attachment to the King and to royalty, but these sentiments mask republicanism. In short this party joins deceit and intrigue to the great means that circumstances give him." Perhaps this adverse opinion did not arise until the two had parted company: at any rate, whatever his opinion at this time, it did not prevent Mirabeau, on the nineteenth of October, 1789, at the first session of the National Assembly held in Paris, from pronouncing a pompous eulogy on La Fayette's services, and from writing to him the same day: "Whatever happens, I am yours to the end, for your great qualities have strongly drawn me, and it is impossible for me not to take a lively interest in a destiny, so noble, and so closely bound up with the revolution that is leading the nation to liberty."

La Fayette, on the other hand, knew that the conclusion of an alliance between them lay with him to determine. His popularity gave him nearly absolute power. To show what that popularity was at this time, I will quote Brissot, a Jacobin, who had worked with La Fayette for the enfranchisement of negroes and was to become the leading member of the political party known as the Gironde. It was written a couple of years later:

"Remember to what a height he was exalted, what enthusiasm his presence, even his name, aroused. He was a hero in the eyes of all women, who were made to write (by the hand of Kornmann) that they were all in love with him, and that they could not live without his picture. He was a god for all the multitude who had not words enough to tell his praises, or crowns enough to throw at his feet. At that time the newspapers talked of nothing but his glory and of his patriotism. Pamphlets, books as well, rained down to sing his praises; he was lauded in the tribune, he was lauded in the pulpit, lauded in prose and in verse. It seemed that one could not praise him too much, and woe to him that dared open his mouth and utter a reflection that did not express admiration for him!

"At that time the enthusiasm for the Commander-in-Chief had become with some people a real madness. Charton published a letter about the rewards that should be bestowed upon this defender of liberty! He proposed that the principal part of the building of the *École Militaire* be emptied for him, and that there should be an inscription over it, *A La Fayette, la patrie reconnaissante*. He wanted to send eighty-three bronze tablets, containing a brief record of his services, to the eighty-three departments [of France]; and he must needs have besides a standing statue cast in bronze, representing him holding a sheet of the decrees that had been enacted on his motion.

"Who does not remember all the addresses, all the congratulations that he received from one end of France to the other? The National Guards in every department disputed him and proclaimed him as the man who *la patrie régénérée* should put at the head of its defenders." This is the testimony of a man who had become his mortal enemy.

This giddy popularity had been caused in part by his American fame, but more still by his words and actions from 1787 to 1789. A fellow member of the *Assemblée constituante*, Adrian Duquesnoy, says: "In every detail France will owe La Fayette more than it is possible to say; friends of liberty can not utter his name without respect and admiration (December 30,

1789). . . . Of all the men who have played a part in these trying times, the only one whose name will last is La Fayette, because he has virtue, great virtue, a real love of the public weal, and love of true glory, of that pure glory that remorse does not disturb and public hatred does not know (February 19, 1790). . . . Always great and steadfast, he never yields to petty passions, to the intrigues of the hour. One doesn't yet know what France owes to M. de La Fayette. He is the man of the Revolution, perhaps the saviour of the state (March 21, 1790)." I cite these contemporaneous comments because, as time went on and La Fayette became a convinced partisan of constitutional monarchy, the partisans of democracy, Camille Desmoulins, Marat, Danton, Robespierre (followed by socialists to-day), were equally loud in their condemnation of his conduct, as soon as he, having hallooed the Revolution to a certain point, that of the Washington formula, tried to hold it back.

The Marquis de Condorcet (not the philosopher) was also a great admirer, but with reservations: he speaks of "La Fayette's most noble disinterestedness, his brilliant courage, remarkable serenity in danger, his power of discourse, popular manners, and a rare elevation of soul that counselled him better than the most consummate talent, *except in public affairs,* all of which would have made him most apt for a party leader, had it not been for indecision of character." But even Condorcet when he heard La Fayette criticized as weak and uncertain in action, replied: "Is he not between two enemies and is he not obliged to turn round and round all the time to confront them?"

As I shall say again, La Fayette's indecision was due to the extreme difficulty of steering a narrow

The Marquis de La Fayette, Commanding General of the National Guard of Paris

Mirabeau

course. Because he would not turn a few points nearer to the conservative interest, the Marquis de Condorcet judged him undecided, as Mirabeau judged him undecided because he would not veer in his direction. The real difficulty lay in La Fayette's inflexibility to his ideal of his *via media*. He was no Cromwell, but it may be doubted if Cromwell without his disciplined Ironsides could have controlled the course of the Revolution. He was no Napoleon; but when Napoleon came in, he had a victorious army at his back, and found a France weary of the wild revolutionists. The great Roman dictators all had legions behind them. I doubt if history can show an instance of a man, with nothing but the reed of popularity to lean upon, dominating a maddened people. Everybody, who wished him to do differently, found fault. He was overwhelmed with slanders. The best summing up of his character at this time, in my judgment, is that by Monsieur Suard (August 26, 1790): "M. de La Fayette has not enough capacity *(une tete assez forte)* for the part he plays in the Revolution. He has all the gifts of popularity; he is an excellent commander of the National Guard; he has right ideas on liberty, great courage, and an activity equal to a great enterprise. But he wishes to be moderator *(conciliateur)* and party leader together, and his intellect is not on a level with his ambition. He listens to too many mediocre men, especially to little politicians *(intrigants)*." There you have it—we shall come upon that word *moderator* again; La Fayette was at the head of revolutionary forces, put there by popular favor, and he wished to be the *moderator* between those forces and the old régime. I do not believe that any man in France could have accomplished that impossible task. A great human flood had overflowed its banks seeking a new channel; storm winds drove to the right, storm winds drove to the left, and La Fayette thought that the floods would follow the course he laid by his American compass. He thought that he was dealing with people disposed to act as a group of English-bred Americans, in comfortable circumstances, quiet and reasonable partisans of compromise, would have acted. He believed that the noise arose from rude malcontents but that there was a *vrai peuple* behind them, as steadfast in principle and creed as himself, whereas, in truth, the French people were passionate, imaginative, illogical, unreasonable, uncompromising, and as inconstant and volatile as Roman citizens in Shakespeare's *Julius Cæsar*. La Fayette was not an opportunist; he did not have what I may call a good political *seat,* he did not bend to the motions of the wild steed he was trying to ride, and so he was thrown. Of course there was something Quixotic in him, as several of his contemporaries, Colonel William North, the Marquis de Bouillé, Camille Desmoulins, as well as the Court, saw; but his conduct recalls the famous scene where Don Quixote enters the lists in behalf of Dulcinea, upon the condition that he who is vanquished shall confess the victor's lady to be the more beautiful. The Don and Rocinante were hurled to the ground. The triumphant Knight of the *Blanca Luna* stood over him with his lance and bade him confess or die. Don Quixote replied: "Dulcinea of Toboso is the most beautiful woman in the world, and it would not be right for my weakness to do dishonor to truth, thrust home your lance." But I have digressed too far and must return to La Fayette's dealings with Mirabeau.

La Fayette knew that popularity conferred immense power upon him, but also immense responsibility, a responsibility, as he says, "far above my talents." He, therefore, acted with a circumspection and hesitation that Mirabeau and others attributed to irresolution, or weakness of character, or to cunning, or fondness for intrigue. He had reason to hesitate before entering into an alliance with Mirabeau, for Mirabeau's character was far from admirable. Duquesnoy says of him: "One of the most detestable villains alive, no principles, no moral sense, except for his own interest at the moment, always for sale to the highest bidder" (February 10, 1790). Brissot called him "The most selfish and depraved of men." Madame de Staël compared him to Catiline. Gouverneur Morris says at this time, that "all the world knew him to be a rascal;" and when he died eighteen months later, Morris described him as, "Venal, shameless and yet greatly virtuous when pushed by a prevailing impulse; but never truly virtuous, because never under the steady control of reason nor the firm authority of principle."

Morris used to discuss with La Fayette the matter of putting Mirabeau and other men in the Cabinet. La Fayette declared that a minister should possess both talents and information. Morris notes (October 11, 1789), "unluckily, he does not reflect that he himself wants both talents and information. He again mentions that he will have Mirabeau, to which I reply that a man so profligate will disgrace any administration, and that one who has so little principle ought not to be trusted." Nevertheless, La Fayette believed that here was a great force that, if discreetly employed, could render most valuable service to the State. The chief obstacle was Mirabeau's character; La Fayette thought too meanly of it. He says that, in spite of his admiration *"pour de sublimes talents,"* he was shocked by Mirabeau's lack of principles, and that he could not avoid showing his want of esteem and so wounded Mirabeau's *amour propre.* "I do not like him," he said, "I do not esteem him, I do not fear him." But he was not unjust to him: "Mirabeau," he says, "was not inaccessible to money, but not for any amount of money would he have supported any opinion to the destruction of liberty or to the discredit of his intelligence."

The two men, however, in their efforts to cooperate, came together after the famous October days to agree between them, like duumvirs, on a change of ministry. Gouverneur Morris, as I have said, did not approve of La Fayette's acting with Mirabeau, and advised him not to (October sixteenth): "If you go into the Ministry with Mirabeau, or about the same time, every honest Frenchman will ask himself the cause of what he will call a very strange coalition. There are in this world men fit for certain employments, to whom one should not trust certain others. Virtue will always be sullied by an alliance with vice, and liberty will blush for shame at her entry into the world, if a polluted hand leads her." But the situation of affairs was very critical, it was very important to stay general disorganization, and the two men had almost daily interviews.

Mirabeau, cribbled with debts, wanted money; La Fayette offered a good sum. Mirabeau affected dignity, but he wrote to his friend La Marck: "I rejected very proudly all that concerned money. I admit to you, however, that that is the crux of affairs with me." He wished some important post that would carry with it large emoluments, and continued to make projects for a Ministry to which he should belong, while La Fayette was to be a marshal, and for a time commander-in-chief. La Fayette, who was ready to stretch a point in order to secure a union, wrote to him: "Reciprocal confidence and friendship is what I offer and expect."

The final difficulty lay there, "reciprocal confidence." Mirabeau had begun by making overtures to the Ministry in office; when they were rejected, he turned to the Duc d'Orléans and thereby became an enemy of the Queen. After the Duke submitted to banishment at La Fayette's command, Mirabeau entered into negotiations with La Fayette. The latter said that if Mirabeau desired to be on good terms with him, he must not persecute the Queen (October seventh). Mirabeau answered: "Certainly, M. le Général, if you say so, let her live. A queen humiliated may be of some use, but a queen with her throat cut is only fit for a plot in a bad tragedy." A year and more afterward, when Mirabeau was in the King's pay, he had a conference with La Fayette, in which he put himself forward as defending the Queen's interest. La Fayette laughed, and reminded him of what he had said on October 7, 1789.

The plan of forming a Ministry in which Mirabeau should have a place fell to the ground, because the Assembly passed a decree forbidding its members to enter the Cabinet. The two men continued to have intermittent relations, but they were not friendly; Mirabeau turned for advancement to the Court, and hobnobbed with Monsieur, the King's brother. La Fayette commented: "One of them is weak and in-

dolent, the other an enterprising and able rascal.''
Perhaps the Court made the first advances to Mirabeau, certainly it turned to him and not to La Fayette
for, as the Marquis de Bouillé said: ''We can count on
Mirabeau's cupidity and ambition, whereas La Fayette is a mad enthusiast.'' A little later Mirabeau
made his bargain: Mirabeau was to receive an em-
bassy, and in the meantime fifty thousand livres a
month, while, for his part, ''M. de Mirabeau binds
himself to aid the King with his knowledge, his capacity and his eloquence in whatever Monsieur shall think
for the good of the state and the interest of the King
two things which good citizens hold to be insepara
and if M. de Mirabeau is not convinced of the so
of the reasons that may be given him, he sha
his tongue.'' This agreement was afterward mo
by omitting the article of Mirabeau's holding
tongue, but I cite it to show that La Fayette's opini
of Mirabeau's integrity was really higher than that
integrity deserved. The Court having won Mirabeau
over to its side, then tried by means of Mirabeau to
win La Fayette. Mirabeau wrote on June 1, 1790, to
La Fayette urging him to play the part of Richelieu
and strengthen the monarchy for the good of the nation, and to permit him to play the part of a humble
assistant, Father Joseph (the Capuchin monk known
as *Son Éminence Grise*): ''Your great qualities need
stimulus from me, and my stimulus needs your great
qualities.'' But La Fayette was not told that, on the
same day, Mirabeau wrote to the King as to the best
way to destroy La Fayette's popularity and power.
The King lent himself to the disingenuous game and
wrote the following letter to La Fayette:

"June 1 (?) 1790

"We have entire confidence in you; but you are so much absorbed by your duties that it is impossible for you to do everything. It is necessary, therefore, to make use of a man of parts and energy to do what you for lack of time can not do. We are strongly persuaded that Mirabeau is a most suitable man, because of his force, his talents, and his familiarity with handling affairs in the Assembly. We therefore wish and exact of the zeal and attachment of M. de La Fayette that he should collaborate with Mirabeau on matters that concern the good of the state, of my service and myself."

But by this time La Fayette showed himself so cold toward any such collaboration, that the letter was never delivered; and the two men never got together. I have anticipated events in order to finish the story of La Fayette's relations with Mirabeau, and to explain why, as Morris says, Mirabeau became La Fayette's mortal enemy, for that takes the poison from the sting of Mirabeau's criticisms.

CHAPTER XIX

At the end of the year 1789 La Fayette, as I have said, swam in a sea of glory, and this immense popularity continued all through the first half of the year 1790, culminating in the great fête celebrated in Paris on July fourteenth, the anniversary of the fall of the Bastille. It was impossible that popularity of that character should endure longer in such a period of storm and stress; that it should have lasted so long is, I think, a great personal tribute to his character and charm. No more troublous world could present itself to a man whose heart was set on Washington's formula of liberty and order.

The people's triumph on October fifth and sixth had not led to peace and pleasantness. Bread was scarce and prices high. The national debt swelled to bursting. Little came into the treasury, for old taxes had been abolished, and the enfranchised people, regarding freedom as essentially freedom from doing disagreeable things, had destroyed all records of dues and obligations from them that they could lay hands on. The issues of assignats had sent prices higher and higher, and disordered business. In many parts of the country there were outbreaks of violence, political, religious and social. At Nîmes, for instance, revolutionary Protestants of the Cevennes, not averse to

220

wiping out old scores, massacred reactionary Catholics. The army was disaffected and insubordinate; as the officers were aristocrats and the men touched by the revolutionary spirit, there was constant ill will and often worse. In Paris the radical newspapers, edited by Marat, Camille Desmoulins and scores of others, demanded a freedom close upon anarchy. In the clubs and district gatherings, Jacobin orators poured forth denunciation and accusation.

In the foreground the National Assembly— *l'Assemblée constituante*—was at work building up a new political structure in place of that which had been swept away. It erected a new system of jurisprudence; it reformed the criminal procedure; it removed restrictions upon Protestants; it granted civil rights to Jews; it abolished primogeniture and titles; it declared for a constitutional monarchy with a single chamber. It accomplished so much, and, in many respects, so well, that the political edifice it erected, at least La Fayette thought so, was entitled to the loyal support of those who took an oath to maintain it.

Its policy, however, in three matters of surpassing importance in social life, produced unexpected and bewildering effects. First, it took royal domains, lands of the Church, and estates of emigrant nobles, and converted the whole into a national domain, and then sold it, for the most part to peasants, upon payments on long terms; with the consequence that, as the assignats were falling rapidly, the purchasers acquired the land for a song, and thereupon became violent opponents of the former owners, who, they feared, might in case of a counter-revolution reclaim the land. Second, the Assembly altered fundamentally the old ecclesiastical system: it cut the ties between the clergy and Rome, it made bishops elective, abolished tithes, suppressed monasteries, and obliged all priests to swear allegiance to these new laws. Here, too, grave consequences followed. The more religious priests— the nobler, the non-self-seeking, the purer-minded— refused to take the oath, and not only the peasantry, especially in Maine, Anjou and Brittany, but women everywhere including many in the aristocracy, approved and upheld them in their disobedience. Madame de La Fayette and her mother, the Duchesse d'Ayen, were among these pious people; and their insistance upon following conscience caused considerable embarrassment to La Fayette, who, though inclined to be agnostic and to sympathize with the purpose of the new legislation, disapproved highly of any attempt to interfere with liberty of conscience. His daughter says: "My father was far from disturbing my mother; but you can judge how painful it was for her to think that her conduct in this matter did him real harm and diminished a popularity that it was important to preserve." It was this outrage, as the more fervent Catholics believed, upon their conscience and their cult, that caused in the main the Chouan revolts, and civil war in la Vendée.

A third piece of legislation helped bring on immediate and still more serious consequences. The deputies belonged to the prosperous upper classes, to the comfortable *bourgeoisie* (to employ a word that now comes into use), people with property who set great store by property, and, honestly enough, believed that it was for the good of the State that they should carry on the government; they, therefore, imposed certain property qualifications for electors and for office-holders, with the result that those who had the right to vote, the *active citizens*, were not greatly in excess of the *passive citizens* who had no such right, and those with property enough to be qualified for office were of a distinctly limited number. The Assembly, in so doing, was but following existing precedents; England had imposed property qualifications, and so had the thirteen states of America. Nevertheless, this was class legislation, and inspired the democrats with horror. Robespierre argued that if all men are born free and equal, as the Declaration of Rights asserted, they all should possess the electoral franchise. Marat, too, advocated manhood suffrage and denounced this new class privilege; he warned the Assembly of the injustice, as he judged it: "Have a care lest you reduce us to despair, lest you leave us nothing but revenge, lest you force us to give ourselves over to all manner of excess. You still have the power to avert a revolution, the revolution that our despair will infallibly bring about."

This, then, was the general situation that confronted La Fayette: the King and Queen virtually prisoners in the Tuileries, hesitating and uncertain what to do; Orleanists and aristocrats plotting for a counter-revolution; *émigrés* collecting an army across the border, and knocking and bawling for help at every royal door in Europe; mysterious partisans of the old régime working underhand, no one knew just where or how, but enough to keep apprehension broad awake; the proletariat of Paris bent on obtaining a municipal government of its own choosing, and on having its own way generally; a peasantry still occupied in destroying records of undesirable obligations; and the division of citizens into two classes, the enfranchised and those not enfranchised. But there was no set scene;

events were moving fast, and the main aspect of the revolution was shifting from a struggle for liberty to a struggle for equality, while the privileged classes of Europe looked on, scandalized and indignant.

All this was not so plain at the time as it is in retrospect. La Fayette, encumbered one might say by his immense popularity, fearfully busy—with police duty, the National Guard, and all sorts of details— and well aware that he was not a man of great intellectual gifts but of a purer patriotism than most of the men struggling for power, turned over rather hesitatingly in his mind what he should do. Gouverneur Morris, inspired a little by a feeling, supposed to be common among competent Americans, that he knew what ought to be done, and vexed that La Fayette was not more pliant to his counsels, notes in his *Journal* (November 18, 1789): "La Fayette says: that Mirabeau has well described the Assemblée, which he calls the *Wild Ass;* that in a fortnight they will be obliged to give him [La Fayette] authority which he has hitherto declined. He shows clearly in his countenance that it is the wish of his heart. I ask him what authority. He says a kind of dictatorship, such as Generalissimo, he does not know exactly what will be the title. Upon this I tell him again that he ought to discipline his troops, and remind him of a former question, viz., whether they would obey him. He says they will but immediately turns round and talks to some other person. Here is a vaulting ambition which o'erleaps itself. This man's mind is so elated by power, already too great for the measure of his abilities, that he looks into the clouds and grasps at the supreme. From this moment every step in his ascent will, I think, accelerate his fall."

This is not quite just. In the first place, La Fayette was not under such illusions as to his power; he says: "I always have power to do harm but not enough to stop it." And he was pretty clear in his own mind as to what was best for France; his difficulty was to decide how to go about to procure that best. He may be described as a lover of ordered liberty, with the example of George Washington before his eyes—"He was always citing Washington," Brissot says—persuaded that the doctrines he had learned in America from Washington himself, from Jefferson, Madison, Hamilton and others, were true, that the suffrage should be limited to the educated, to taxpayers, to those (to employ an old phrase) who had a stake in the country, and that, given the French people, the executive should be a hereditary King vested with real power. Holding such doctrines he wished to tread a *via media,* shunning both the despotism of the old régime and the lawlessness of the Paris mob. He says in a letter to Washington, March 17, 1790: "We are attacked by two sorts of enemies: the aristocrats who hope for a counter-revolution, and the factious who wish to destroy all authority, perhaps even attempt the life of the reigning family. These two parties foment all our troubles."

In pursuing this *via media* he thought only of the good of his country with no personal ambition other than to have his name linked to her freedom and greatness. Proofs of this disinterestedness are abundant enough; one in particular may serve. It was obvious that a commander-in-chief of all the National Guards throughout France would be virtually dictator, a non-constitutional power superior to the King. La Fayette not only might have had such an office for the asking, but he would have had it, had he not prevented. For instance: in January, 1790, a motion was offered in the municipal council of Paris that the National Guards of all the Kingdom should be united under his command. He interrupted the speaker: "Stop," he cried, "that flattering motion! Let us wait and submit to whatever decrees the National Assembly shall enact for the organization of the National Guard; above all, let us offer neither example nor pretext, nor opportunity, to ambition. For my part, in the Assembly, when they take up this important article of the Constitution, I shall express my hope that no two departments shall be under one command." Of this speech Camille Desmoulins wrote in his paper: "M. de La Fayette then spoke, and not with the feeble gesture with which Cæsar pushed aside the crown that Antony offered him on his knees, but with just indignation, and in a tone that carried conviction he condemned the indiscreet motion." And, in June, when the National Assembly was discussing the project of an assemblage in Paris of the federated National Guards from all over France, La Fayette offered and carried the motion that he had promised.

There is every reason (in spite of Morris's doubts) to believe La Fayette's repeated assertion of his desire, following the example of George Washington, whom he revered as the greatest and best of men, to retire from political life when his work should be done and (to borrow Washington's words) "under the shadow of his own vine and his own fig-tree, free from the bustle of a camp and the busy scenes of public life . . . retired within himself, be able to view the solitary walk and tread the paths of private life with a heartfelt satisfaction." It was not only in private conversations with Gouverneur Morris, and others, and in his letters, that La Fayette expressed this wish, but also in public; in a speech in the Assembly he refers to himself as "a man, who, while promising the people not to flatter but to defend them, promised himself, on the termination of the revolution, to go back to the exact place he occupied when it began, and to be left with none but unspotted memories."

His belief was that, now that the nation had exercised "the sacred right of insurrection" to overthrow despotism, and had established a constitutional government with an elected legislature, it was the duty of every man, especially of the National Guard, "to shed the last drop of his blood to assure the execution of its decrees, the freedom of its deliberations, and to warrant the inviolability of every member." It was his unswerving loyalty to this conception of his duty that caused his downfall. Of course, he has been criticized by those out of sympathy with his *via media;* republicans blame him because he did not give rein to his early inclinations toward a republic, and the conservatives because he did not become a dictator, and stop the current of the Revolution in its early course before it became a devastating torrent. Of the first I shall speak later on. To the second, one may reply that to ask any man to stop the French Revolution in 1790 would be like asking Abraham Lincoln to stop the secession in 1860; and as to a dictatorship, La Fayette, moved perhaps in his unconscious depths by the knowledge that he had not the talents necessary to a dictator, would, in his conscious mind, have regarded any forcible assumption of a dictatorship as disloyal to his oath, to his ideals, and to the opinion of George Washington.

CHAPTER XX

THE *via media* was not the line of least resistance. Dealings with the King and Queen were difficult. La Fayette had a deep sense of personal loyalty to the King, and genuine respect for the kindness and goodness of his character, irresolute, hesitating, untrusting and untrustworthy though he was. He believed that it was best for France to have a King and that the King should have real power, and he tried to hold up the King's hands. And the King, though pulled this way and that by the superior will and energy of the Queen, and plastic also to a certain point in the fingers of his ministers, turned to La Fayette, as the most powerful man in the kingdom, for advice and assistance. Not long after the events of October fifth and sixth, he asked La Fayette to draw up a memorial as to what the National Assembly and the royal council ought to do in order to carry on the principles of the revolution while preserving to the Crown all the authority compatible with the nation's interests. This La Fayette did at some length. A few months later (I am merely giving instances) in April, 1790, the King, with an assurance of confidence and of a disposition to follow his advice, asked him for his ideas on the royal prerogative. La Fayette, accordingly, drew up a second memorial treating of the Declaration of Rights, the legislative power, the judiciary, the administration, the army and navy, the National Guard, public education, foreign affairs, and then, more particularly, the royal authority, curtailed, indeed, from what it had been: "It seems to me [he wrote] that in this situation, a King of the French . . . ought not, when he is as virtuous as your Majesty, to regret that opulence of power that used to be exercised in his name and which the nation looked at askance and disputed . . . I have already said to your Majesty, that before February 4th [the day the King accepted the Constitution] you merely risked your person and your throne; to-day you are bound in honor."

But the King was totally irresolute, and a few days later La Fayette writes to a friend: "I have nothing very satisfactory to tell you. The Queen pushes off our conversations; she flatters herself with chimeras and, by consequence, her husband whom she guides at will. . . . You have often preached to me to show deference to the King and the Queen; it was unnecessary, because my disposition inclines me to that course since their misfortunes; but they would have been better served and the public, too, by a hard man. They are big children who won't swallow wholesome medicine, unless you threaten them with hobgoblins." There are other letters of his that tell the King respectfully but clearly what he ought to do in certain minor matters for, as he says, "great consequences often flow from little acts." Giving advice to sovereigns, however, is a delicate matter. To the King he seemed dictatorial; Mirabeau called him the Mayor of the Palace, and the Queen frankly hated him with a *haine sans bornes*.

The King's two brothers shared these feelings.

Monsieur (twenty-five years later Louis XVIII) was "a weak and indolent" man, but with sufficient spite, it seems, to involve himself with a Marquis de Favras, in a plot to murder Necker, Bailly and La Fayette. One evening, two days after Christmas, La Fayette took Gouverneur Morris, who had been dining with him, into his study, told him of the plot, how Favras had been arrested, how he had found in his pocket a letter from Monsieur that proved the latter's complicity. La Fayette had taken the incriminating letter back to the Prince, and told him that nobody but himself and Bailly knew of it. Monsieur was delighted. And yet, bringing with him a troop of his friends, Monsieur (having the letter safe in his pocket) had come to La Fayette, and taking a haughty tone had spoken of some note put into circulation that had accused him of being in a conspiracy. Such was he.

The King's other brother, the Comte d'Artois, waiting with his fellow *émigrés* on the Rhine for a chance to invade their country, was pungently bitter against La Fayette. This ill will of the royal family became such that, a year later (March, 1791) without any change of attitude or infraction of loyalty on La Fayette's part, the King and Queen dictated a letter to the Comte d'Artois, in which they call La Fayette "*un scélérat et un factieux fanatique*" (a rascal, a fanatical malcontent) in whom they could put no trust. To this the Comte d'Artois answered, how thankful he was that the reports that their Majesties reposed confidence in La Fayette, and gave ear to his perfidious suggestions, were without foundation. On the whole, as you see, the Court was not easy to deal with.

As to La Fayette's dealings with the aristocrats, they depended on whether he regarded them as enemies or as reconcilable with the new régime. The Duc d'Orléans may serve as a specimen of the first category, the Marquis de Bouillé of the second. The Marquis was his cousin, and had acted as one of the witnesses to his marriage; he was known to be a man of courage and believed to possess military ability. Here is a letter from La Fayette to him:

"Paris, February 9, 1790

"My dear Cousin:

"We have been divided in our principles and our sentiments during the Revolution; but to-day we ought all to rally round the King and strengthen a constitution that you love less than I do, that may have some faults, but which assures public liberty and is so well established in the minds of the French people that its enemies can not attack it without overturning the monarchy. Now that we have reached this point, all good citizens constitute one party, and the King has taken his place at its head; this party, disconcerting both those that regret the old régime and those that entertain factious hopes, will tighten the bonds of public order and restore calm and union everywhere, and we shall all enjoy our liberty the better. . . . You, too, I hope, will feel that the best way to assure to the King the necessary constitutional authority is to satisfy the friends of liberty that perfect harmony exists between the King and constitutional principles and all those persons through whom he exercises his executive powers. I hear that you entertain an idea of leaving the country, as if your talents did not belong to her, as if wrongs done to you personally could give you the right to rob us of the battles that you shall win for us, in which I hope that you will permit me to fight under your orders. I flatter myself, my dear Cousin, that you know my character well enough to make it useless to say that the Revolution will put me back in exactly the same place from which it took me. . . . *Bonjour, mon cher cousin, agréez mon tendre attachment.*" And in a later letter: "I am touched, my dear Cousin, by the friendship you testify; our acting together in mutual confidence is the best means of security (September 15, 1790)."

The Marquis de Bouillé, however, did not hearken to this wise charming. He had no sympathy for "those people [as he says] so numerous in France, who have no property, who live by their industry, who are always ready to rebel and attach themselves to the man who will pay them for making a riot, in short, the populace." He maintained a double-faced attitude; he took the oath to support the Constitution but plotted with the King and Mirabeau.

This letter from La Fayette to the Marquis de Bouillé, that I have just quoted, speaks of the necessity to rally round the King. That had become the keystone of La Fayette's policy and is the explanation of his conduct when two years later he reached the crisis of this period of his life. In his ardent youth he had had a leaning toward republicanism. Plutarch's heroes had been republican, so was George Washington. But for France, with her monarchy of eight hundred years, with her debt to that monarchy, and with her proud and venerable traditions of loyalty all centering in the King, not only La Fayette but virtually all the members of the National Assembly held by the past, and it was enacted in the Constitution that "the French Government is monarchical."

And it was La Fayette's loyalty to the monarchical idea that brought him more and more into conflict with the lower and radical classes of society who first wished to clip and whittle down the royal authority and then do away with it completely. Already before this time Danton was denouncing him at the club of the Cordeliers, and Marat in *l'Ami du Peuple* railed at him and exhorted the people to cut the throats of the National Guards, of the municipal officers, and so on.

His first clashes with the populace came through his insistence upon law and order. I will cite an episode that he tells of in a letter of May 25, 1790:

"You ask me what happened yesterday; here's the story. A man accused of stealing a bag of oats was seized by the populace near Saint-Germain— l'Auxerrois. The police attempted to take him to the Châtelet [a prison], but a large crowd, consisting partly of vagabonds, gathered thicker and thicker about them, and were soon pushing in throngs along the quays. Neither the horse patrol nor the volunteers could manage them. Several men, armed with sticks, were beating the thief to death. I was coming back in my carriage by the little gate, when they told me. I was alone with Romeuf [an aide-de-camp], and in spite of the insistence of all the bystanders, we drove our way into the crowd as far as we could. Then we got out of the carriage and passing through the patrol, flung ourselves into the middle of the crowd. A man raised his club against Romeuf, who was trying to drag the corpse away from him. I straddled the dead man, and told the fellows that they were murderers, and said that, as I could not believe that everybody there was guilty, I called on them to point out those that were. Some National Guardsmen who had followed me pointed to a man; I seized him by the collar, and said to the crowd: 'I am going to show you that every action is honorable, when one executes the law.' I kept hold of my man by the collar, in spite of his cries, till we reached the Châtelet The patrol of National Guards followed us close, and did not wish to leave me alone; but, when I came out of the Châtelet, I bade them fall back, got up on the parapet, made all the people come round me, and then, right in the midst of them, I berated them most severely for their behavior. I told them that they were the dupes of factious men and of ruffians who wanted to force the National Assembly and the King to leave Paris and to set the city on fire, but that all the property in the capital, as well as its quiet, was in my care, and that I should crush down any one that dared disturb the public order; and that I should be upheld; but that even if I were all alone, I should resist crime and make the law respected to my last breath and that I did not believe that there were any men bold enough to attack me. In the meanwhile, at the other end of the quay a mob was proceeding to hang my thief, whom I had left because I thought that he was dead. Romeuf and I ran there. The National Guards joined us in a rush into the crowd, and we saved him: he will recover. I then began again my forensic discourse and commanded them to scatter, which they did, shouting *Vive La Fayette! . . .* That's yesterday's little adventure.''

I will cite another instance of an altercation between him and the mob, in order to make plain that, with the Court, the aristocrats and the counter-revolution on one side, and the proletariat, republicans, Danton,

Marat and other firebrands on the other, he was steering a course between Scylla and Charybdis. And remember that the power derived from popular favor, is not like that of a disciplined army at one's back or of an old, established, social order; it is like the wind that now blows strong and now dies away. He was in his office at the Hôtel de Ville, when a great crowd surged up, filling the *Place de Grève*, yelling for the head of Monsieur de la Salle. La Fayette put his head out of the window: "If I knew where he was, I should not give him up to you." The mob then shouted: "La Fayette is a traitor! We want La Fayette's head!" La Fayette ran down-stairs and walked out on the terrace in front of them. "Who wants my head?" he cried. "I will not deliver up another man's life; mine is my own. I offer that; who dares take it?" He had the gift of handling these men, as well as courage and *sangfroid;* and the crowd shouted: *"Vive La Fayette!* He's not afraid!"

La Fayette, though always imbued with Rousseau's theories of man's native goodness, and with the derivative belief that the "people" being naturally good would, now that they were freed from despotism, behave in a virtuous way, felt called upon to explain their less virtuous acts by attributing those acts to a few bad men who had been suborned by the Duc d'Orléans, by counter-revolutionists, by foreign governments, or by other ill wishers to the Revolution. For instance he explained to the Comte de Ségur,—who had married a very young half-sister of the Duchesse d'Ayen, and was therefore his uncle—in talking of the fifth and sixth days of October, that ruffians, hired by unknown hands, had mixed with *"le vrai peuple qui ne veut que justice et liberté"* (the real, true *people* who want only justice and liberty). And, during 1790, still with the same happy confidence in the virtue of the masses, he explains that violence and rioting is caused by "factious men." By this term, he refers to the Jacobins; that is, at first, to members of the Jacobin Club, then to their followers, inhabitants of the Faubourg Saint-Antoine, and so forth, and finally to all the proletariat.

The Jacobin Club, whose formal title is *Amis de la Constitution,* first held its meetings at Versailles, but when the Assembly followed the King to Paris, it followed, too, and took its seat in the monastery of the Jacobins, in the rue Saint-Honoré near the hall where the Assembly met. Already at Versailles many members of the Assembly, known or to become well known, belonged to it: Sieyès, Mirabeau, Bailly, Alexandre Lameth and a brother, Barnave, Beauharnais, famous through his wife Josephine, Duport, Robespierre, La Fayette and others. In Paris, David, the painter, Condorcet, the philosopher, Fabre d'Eglantine, the poet, Camille Desmoulins, and so on, joined. Naturally, with such members, the club enjoyed high authority. It discussed measures coming up in the Assembly, and prepared decrees, almost as if making drafts for that body to act upon. Branches were founded, first in the chief cities, and then in small towns, until, by August, 1790, there were one hundred and fifty, regularly corresponding with the mother society in Paris. In April, 1790, the moderate members, disagreeing with their radical fellow members yet without breaking with them, split off and founded *La Société de 1789* with rooms in the Palais Royal. Among these men was La Fayette, with Sieyès, Mailly, Mirabeau, Talleyrand, La Rochefoucauld, Condorcet, André Chénier, the poet, and others. But the new club accomplished virtually nothing.

As time went on the Jacobin Club became more and more radical; it wished to *silloner profond,* dig its furrows deep, looked askance at La Fayette as too restrained and moderate, and did what it could to diminish his influence with the National Guard and with the municipal authorities in the towns. La Fayette, on his part, regarded the club as an instrument of disorder, that labored by means of denunciation and vilification, to disorganize all forms and functions of the social frame, civil and military.

But I must not anticipate; the feud *à outrance* between La Fayette and the Jacobin Club did not rage at its fiercest until the spring and summer of 1792. At present I merely wish to indicate the pitfalls and gins that encompassed the *via media,* the American highway as he thought it, between tyranny on the one hand and mob government on the other. Both sides feared him as a possible Cromwell; both sides came to hate him. The royalists thought insurrection wicked; the Jacobins thought any interference with the mob wicked, and began to preach the necessity of a *saignée* (blood-letting). La Fayette constantly infuriated both parties; as, for instance, when in a speech he said: "Disorders were necessary for the Revolution, the old régime was servitude, and in such case *l'insurrection est le plus saint des devoirs;* but under our constitution . . . public authority must display force and energy." In this one sentence he attacked them both.

CHAPTER XXI

THE FÊTE OF FEDERATION AND THE MUTINY AT NANCY

As I said, I have been anticipating future events.
I now go back to July, 1790, when in spite of class
interests and divergences, the spirit of nationalism, of
the fraternity of all Frenchmen, was steadily growing.
The National Guards in the several provinces were
united by federal ties, and the idea was conceived that
there should be one great federation of all the National Guards throughout the kingdom and that a fête,
attended by delegates from this federation, should be
held in Paris on the first anniversary of the fall of the
Bastille, to celebrate the victory of the people, the triumph of the revolution. The Champ-de-Mars was selected for the fête; and as the municipality, being of a
frugal mind, had hired but few laborers to prepare this
field, which was then rough and shabby, the whole world
of Paris rolled up its sleeves and went to work. Not
since the building of the cathedral of Chartres had such
enthusiasm been evoked in honor of an idea. All
classes turned to, ladies of quality, women from *les
halles*, guardsmen, priests, coal-heavers, masons, wig-
makers, magistrates, tailors, schoolboys, "*la courti-
sane effrontée béchant auprès de la vierge au regard
timide*," everybody singing *Ça ira! Ça ira!*, helped
level the ground and clear away rubbish. So brotherly
were the Parisians in these brave days that "on ar-

238

riving at the Champ-de-Mars, every worker laid on the ground coat, cravat and watch, leaving them there at the mercy of public honesty, and went in all security to his labors. Nothing was lost, nothing taken. Patriotism furnished order, protection and restraint." Of this assemblage La Fayette was elected president.

Bliss was it in that dawn to be alive, and La Fayette, always expecting universal wisdom and happiness (as a contemporary says), floated buoyant on the flood of high romance. "Do not fear," he said, "that this holy enthusiasm may drag us beyond the limits that public order prescribes. The flag of liberty will never become the flag of license."

On the thirteenth of July La Fayette at the head of the federal delegates marched to the hall of the National Assembly "to offer the homage of the respect and gratitude of the National Guards of France." He addressed the Assembly: "May this great and solemn day be the signal of reconciliation between parties, of forgetting quarrels, of peace and public happiness." The delegates then marched on and paid their respects to the King: "Sire: . . . We delight to revere in your Majesty the noblest of all titles, that of chief of Frenchmen and King of a Free People. . . . Rejoice, Sire, in the reward of your virtues! May this pure homage, that despotism could not command, be the glory and recompense of a Citizen-King! You have desired us to have a constitution based on liberty and public order. All your wishes, Sire, shall be fulfilled; our liberty is assured; and public order is warranted by our zeal. The National Guards of France swear to your Majesty an obedience that shall know no bounds but the law, a love that shall end only with our lives."

Alas! The muse of history might indulge in an

ironical mood. The next day, July 14, 1790, the procession formed at seven o'clock in the morning. The electors of Paris, the municipal officers, a band of children, another of old men, sixty battalions of the National Guards, the National Assembly, soldiers and sailors, with flags, and tricolor cockades,

Jam redit et Virgo, redeunt Saturnia regna,
marched down the rue Saint-Denis, the rue Saint-Honoré, the Rue Royale, le Cours-la-Reine, across a bridge of boats to the Champ-de-Mars. La Fayette rode at the head. "See him," somebody cried, "gallop down the centuries to come." A soldier came up to him holding a bottle of wine and a glass. "Now, General," he said, "you are hot, take a drink," and poured out a bumper; La Fayette tossed it off amid great applause. Three hundred thousand spectators were gathered there, and in the center, on a platform twenty feet high, stood the altar de la Patrie, surrounded by clergy in surplices beribboned with the tricolor. The King and Queen sat in a covered gallery. The bishop of Autun, Talleyrand, attended by four hundred children robed in white, celebrated mass. Then La Fayette mounted the altar, laid his sword upon it and said: "We swear to be forever faithful to the nation and to the law and to the King; to uphold with all our might the constitution that the National Assembly has enacted and the King has accepted; to defend, according to the laws, the security of person and property; . . . to remain united to all Frenchmen in the indissoluble bands of brotherhood."

At one and the same instant, all arms were lifted and every voice cried, "I swear!" The King likewise took the oath. Then followed a delirium of enthusiasm, ten thousand of the confederate delegates rushed

forward shouting, *"Vive La Fayette!"* those near by
hugged him; they kissed his face, his hands, his coat,
and when he was again in the saddle, they kissed his
boots, his accouterments, his horse. The whole multitude were drunk with the new wine of joy and hope.
Few men have ever received such a tribute of homage.
On this day La Fayette reached his zenith.

It is said that, of old, great potentates in the East,
seated on their thrones and wrapped in glory, had at
their side a slave to remind them of Fortune's wheel;
I will put here some notes that Mirabeau wrote somewhat earlier, but still applicable:

"There is a man in the State who, by his position,
is the target for fortune, who can not compensate for
reverse by success, and who, in a way, is the bulwark
of order, one can even say, of public safety, of everything at once, of food, of finance, of obedience in the
army, of peace in the provinces.

"Who is this man? It is Monsieur de La Fayette.

"What are his means? A part of the military
force which he holds in his hand, and his influence
upon all the springs of executive power.

"This military force of which he disposes, is as
much of a hindrance as an advantage; if food fails, it
will be powerless, it will even turn against its chief.
Monsieur de La Fayette must therefore answer for the
supply of food.

"What are his means to provide food? The
municipality of Paris is not enough, his military force
is not enough. Unless he has a ministry of his own,
he can not count on wide enough authority.

"What are his means to manage the finances?
Here again he needs a ministry to carry out his will.

"Even the military power in his hands may be powerless, should the chiefs of the army refuse to obey, if the provinces fall asunder and go to loggerheads; and what means has Monsieur de La Fayette to prevent their falling asunder?

"So much for the military force as a prop. Monsieur de La Fayette's second means is his influence. But every influence is as nothing when food or finance is in question. Eloquence, virtues, public respect do not give bread, if there is no wheat, nor money without organized finance.

"Influence, as a means to keep the provinces quiet and friendly, is good, but not enough. Permanent faith in one man is a gift from heaven; not to be counted on. What good, then, is there in his influence? To procure ministers who will work for his patriotic purposes and for his glory, who will make no motion that is not in concord with the wheels of the machine, who will not discourage him by inaction, nor alarm him by opposing his views; who, in short, loyal to the people's interests and to the King's, to political union and personal friendship, will never separate their fate from his, whether to mount the dais of triumph or the scaffold? This is a *reductio ad absurdum*."

Mirabeau was right; and yet the cause of La Fayette's fall did not come in just the way he indicates. La Fayette, himself, pointed to the danger. At the close of the glorious fête, when it was time to take leave of the Guardsmen, he said: "Gentlemen, let the love of liberty be our guide. This says all: love of order, respect for law and good conduct. With that, property is inviolable, the lives of innocent men are sacred, and no man is guilty but by the law. By it,

everything is warranted, everything goes well. Let us
not forget, Gentlemen, that liberty is as much afraid
of license as of tyranny."

The spirit of fraternity—"*la plus tendre fra-
ternité*"—evoked with so great solemnity and enthusiasm at the Champ-de-Mars—showed itself shy and re-
tiring. On August third, La Fayette felt himself compelled to remind the National Guard that: "The
Commander-in-Chief regards every one that does not
hate license and anarchy as an enemy of liberty and of
the Constitution." And he had reason to speak out,
because the extreme radicals, the Jacobins, in pursuit
of their ideas of democracy, were gaining ground
everywhere. La Fayette, of course, seemed to them
reactionary; but Jefferson, who is regarded as
essentially a democrat and lover of the people, agreed
with him. He wrote to La Fayette at a later date, with
the knowledge of subsequent events: "They did not
understand their imprudence in abandoning an assured measure of liberty under a limited monarchy,
for the very uncertain chance of getting a little more
under republican forms. You did not share that
opinion; you thought they should stop there and
strengthen the constitution which the National Assembly had enacted; there you were right. This was a
fatal error of the republicans. Their secession, which
separated them from you and the constitution, caused
all the ills and all the crimes to which the French
Nation has been subject."

Now comes the affair of Nancy, like Belshazzar's
writing on the wall. The Jacobins contrived to imbue
the garrison at Nancy with their ideas of liberty and
the brotherhood of man, and started a Jacobin Club
among them. The officers, aristocrats and stern dis-

ciplinarians, were accused by the men of high-handed-
ness; according to the Jacobins, they were also guilty
of peculation, of falsifying the accounts of money due
the men, and of putting the money into their own
pockets. Much ill will was brewing. At this juncture,
a soldier disobeyed the military rules and was punished. His fellow soldiers mutinied. Disaffection in
the army, with foreign enemies, as well as the émigrés,
threatening France, was a serious matter. The
National Assembly passed a decree condemning the
ringleaders.

The Marquis de Bouillé, La Fayette's cousin, commander at Metz, was ordered to suppress the revolt.
He marched to Nancy and entered the town. According to his story, the mutineers, after apparent submission, fired point-blank on his men, and a battle began. Three hundred or more were killed or wounded.
The regiment mainly at fault was a Swiss regiment of
Châteauvieux that by the terms of hiring had jurisdiction over its own members. Its court-martial
sentenced thirty-three soldiers to be shot, and forty-
one to the galleys for thirty years; the Jacobin Club at
Nancy was dissolved, and Bouillé's soldiers lorded it
in the town. Bouillé, himself, was thanked and complimented; and La Fayette, as most men of military
experience would do, heartily approved his course.
But the populace of Paris was outraged; the club of
the Cordeliers shivered. Couthon, the *cul-de-jatte*,
destined to fame under the Reign of Terror, espoused
the cause of the mutineers. Marat wrote in the *Ami
du Peuple:* "Yes indeed, the soldiers of Châteauvieux
resisted a barbarous decree that would have delivered
them up to the sword of an army of assassins. . . .
Yes, indeed, the soldiers of Châteauvieux defended

themselves against the blind satellites who were marching up under the orders of a bloody conspirator to enslave or massacre them. Yes, indeed, the soldiers of Châteauvieux made fifteen hundred ferocious satellites, who were rushing on to murder them, bite the dust. For what do they blame them? For violating certain wicked decrees of a corrupt legislature? They did so for the sake of obedience to the most holy laws of nature and society, before which all authority must bow.''

An investigation was held by sympathetic members of the Assembly who reported in favor of the mutineers. One Jacobin deputy laid all the blame on the officers, accused the aristocrats of fomenting a counter-revolution, and demanded pardon for the condemned soldiers. The battle was dubbed a massacre; and the Jacobin Club at Nancy was reopened. Probably both officers and men were in fault. An army, possibly, is not a good place for liberty, equality and fraternity; and the consequences of Jacobin interference were that the bonds of discipline were still further relaxed, that soldiers learned to distrust their officers, and officers to distrust their men. Worst of all, the National Assembly, under guidance of the Jacobins, turned about and completely condemned the meeting. They blamed Bouillé and all who agreed with him. As for the subject of our story his approbation of the punishment meted to the mutineers cost him dear. Marat wrote: ''Soul of mud! Fortune had done everything for you, the gods were jealous of your destiny, but in place of the happiness of being the Savior of France you have preferred the dishonorable rôle of petty ambition, of greedy courtier, perfidious jobber, and to crown horror, the vile prop of a despot.''

Other symptoms of general unrest and disorder cropped up all over, for Jacobin doctrines had fallen on fertile ground. At Nîmes, as I have said, fighting and massacre were colored with a religious tinge; at Brest, and elsewhere, there were mutinies among the sailors, which patriotism attributed to British instigation. The peasants continued to burn and pillage. In Paris there were various disturbances. Nuns in convents, ladies in churches, were whipped for confessing to non-juring priests; three nuns died from their whippings. An aristocrat's house, the Hôtel de Castries, was sacked. Order was disturbed on one side by the populace, on the other by the aristocrats. Here are instances. The Commune of Paris, still in the hands of the moderate bourgeoisie, had directed repairs to be made upon the great donjon at the Château of Vincennes, a few miles out of the city. Rumors, started very likely in order to discredit La Fayette, flew about that it was to be converted into a new Bastille, and the patriotic multitude from the Faubourg Saint-Antoine, under the lead of the brewer Santerre, sallied forth to destroy it. La Fayette and a detachment of the National Guard arrived in time to save it. And while he was out of the city, a number of young nobles managed to get into the palace, perhaps to further the King's escape, probably because they thought the King might be in danger. The National Guards in charge of the Tuileries, excited by a report that La Fayette had been killed at Vincennes, were on the point of opening fire on the intruders, when La Fayette appeared. The King bade the rash nobles lay down their arms; and they were rudely pushed out, with jeers, insults and some rough handling. La Fayette, who, when he sup-

pressed a riot, was not only found fault with by the
Jacobins for violence offered to the sovereign people,
but also by the aristocrats because he had not been
harsh enough, was very indignant at this conspiracy.
In his order of the day, telling of it, he referred to the
great noblemen in attendance upon the King as *les
chefs de la domesticité,*—the head servants,—an expression that was meant to nettle them, and succeeded.
He was disheartened. He wrote to Monsieur de
Bouillé (February, 1791): "Paris is divided by factions, and the kingdom torn asunder by anarchy."

So long as the National Guard remained obedient,
however, he felt that he would be able to preserve
peace and order. But the leaven of Jacobin teaching
had also been at work in the Guard. On April eighteenth, the King proposed to go to Saint Cloud, a few
miles down the river, for Easter and attend mass
celebrated by a non-juring priest, for he was pious and
felt ill at ease in his conscience with priests who had
denied Rome. To have attended a non-juring priest
in Paris would have been dangerous. But the town
had been beset by rumors that the King meditated
escape, and the people were nervous. In this case
there may have been an intention to escape, but perhaps the excursion was merely meant to throw the
people off their guard. Mirabeau, indeed, as the first
step in his plan to stay the Revolution and secure the
throne, had proposed such an escape; but this plan
was a secret, and Mirabeau had died two weeks before
and his bones lay in the Pantheon, dedicated *aux
grands hommes par la Patrie reconnaissante.* The
Assembly, to whose ears these rumors of flight had
come, had decreed (without constitutional warrant),
that if the King left the kingdom, he should be liable

to deposition; and, only the day before, the extreme
Jacobins had placarded Paris with posters denouncing
the King for breaking the law against non-juring
priests. Excited by these placards and the rumors of
flight, a monstrous crowd collected around the
Tuileries. When the royal carriage drove out, starting on its way to Saint Cloud, the crowd seized the
reins and stopped the carriage. La Fayette ordered
the National Guards to clear the road; they refused.
Citoyen Danton, a National Guardsman, was there at
the head of a battalion. For an hour and more La
Fayette and Bailly harangued the Guards, in vain.
The King could not go on; so, with his usual impassive-
ness, he said that he would stay, and went back into
the palace. Afterward La Fayette succeeded in persuading a body of the Guards to clear the road, but
the King, after consultation with his courtiers, refused, saying that he would attend the church of a
constitutional priest and refrain from taking communion.

La Fayette, always prone to attribute riots and
lawlessness to plots of aristocrats rather than to the
newly liberated people, suspected that the mob had
been set on by counter-revolutionists in order to enable
the King to proclaim that he was a prisoner, and that
Danton, who had helped stop the carriage, had been
bribed by them. But the truth seems to be that the
people were afraid lest the King, their hostage, should
escape. La Fayette was bitterly chagrined and indignant; he had been used to an obedience from his
guards that bordered upon idolatry. He upbraided
them: "We are citizens, Gentlemen; we are free men;
but without obedience to the law there is nothing but
confusion, anarchy, despotism; if Paris, the cradle of

the revolution, instead of encompassing the national authorities with respect to the best of her ability, shall surround them with tumult and distress them with violence, she will cease to set an example and run the danger, rather, of becoming a terror to France." And he sent in his resignation. This awoke consternation among the constitutionalists. For them, at this critical juncture of public affairs, to get on without La Fayette was unthinkable. Indeed, it was virtually impossible for him to desert them; and on fresh promises of obedience from the Guards, he resumed command.

But, when the National Assembly, afraid of the Jacobins, approved of mutiny in the regular army, when the National Guard was only brought, not to obedience, but to promises of obedience, by a threat of La Fayette's resignation, it needed no prophet to foretell future woes, and that the day could not be far off when La Fayette must fall. Mirabeau, that clear-sighted man, had written, soon after the Nancy meeting, that the time would come when La Fayette must give the order to fire on the people and thereby would wound himself to death. So it happened, and La Fayette was grievously wounded; but the wound was not fatal, and at the end of forty years he rose a second time to the zenith.

CHAPTER XXII

JUNE 20 AND JULY 17, 1791

LA FAYETTE's popularity with the people of Paris, weakened by his approval of the suppression of the meeting at Nancy, and further weakened by suspicions, most unjust, of his complicity with partisans of the old régime, faced a crisis when the King actually attempted to escape. And for months before that, the Court on one side, the democrats on the other, had been working hard by underhand methods to ruin his political influence. All sorts of libels were published against him, some with indecent stories concerning Marie Antoinette. As he said in a letter to Washington (March 7, 1791): "It is my lot to be attacked with equal animosity on the one hand by all that is aristocratic and servile, in a word by all the adversaries of my principles of freedom and equality, and on the other, by the Orleanists and persons opposed to the monarchy, and all abettors of pillage and disorder."

The King's attempt to escape was made on June 20, 1791. Mirabeau had concocted the plan. After Mirabeau's death, the Marquis de Bouillé became the chief agent in it. Stationed at Metz, he was ready to receive the King, as well as to send detachments to protect the last stages of his journey. It was a good plan, and should have been successful; but poor Louis XVI botched all that he touched. Before leaving, the

King had drawn up his apology for flight, a manifesto setting forth the sacrifices he had made for his people, together with criticisms of the new legislation and his grievances and declaring that there was now complete anarchy. This document was to be published after his escape to safety. He then made ready to start with the Queen, their two children, Madame Elisabeth and some attendants. They had a false passport, made out for la Baronne de Korf, her two children, her valet and waiting-woman and three servants. The King, in a great chestnut colored coat and a round hat, was the valet.

That evening La Fayette on his way home dropped in to see Bailly, who had received, as frequently before, warnings which he did not credit that the King was planning an escape, and the two agreed that La Fayette should go to the Tuileries, and repeat these warnings to General Gouvion, the officer in charge. La Fayette did so, and bade Gouvion call together the principal officers of the Guard and make sure that they should patrol the courts of the Tuileries during the night. He then went to pay his respects to the King, and on his way into the palace passed close to Madame Elisabeth, who was about to get into a carriage, but did not see her. It was midnight. The King gave him solemn assurance that the rumors were untrue.

As soon as La Fayette was gone, the King got into bed, waited till all was quiet, got up and dressed as a valet. He sneaked out of the Palace and went to the little rue de l'Echelle hard by; the Queen followed, arriving late. There, awaiting them, was Count de Fersen, a young Swede, who had served in America and was devotedly loyal to the Queen, disguised as a cabman. They got into his cab and drove to the Porte

Saint Martin, where a great traveling coach with four horses was ready for them. The cabman said good-by respectfully, and the royal party started on their venturesome way. But time had been lost.

The flight was discovered early the next morning. La Fayette hurried to the Tuileries; he had pledged his life that the King should not escape. On the way he met Bailly and Beauharnais, husband of the more famous Josephine. Nobody knew anything; conjectures flew about. Was there to be a foreign invasion, would there be civil war? Then there was doubt as to the legal situation. Had they a right to arrest a citizen, even if he were the King, who had broken no law? La Fayette had but lately handed in his resignation because the National Guards would not protect that right. It strikes one as odd that after encircling the Tuileries with soldiers to prevent the King from leaving, there should be a doubt of the right to stop him; but La Fayette had a meticulous, a chivalric delicacy of respect for law, that amazed and annoyed less scrupulous men. He felt that the Revolution could only justify itself by strict observance of law, and that expediency could offer no excuse for any infringement. There is something Quixotic and high-minded in his hesitations and scruples, but, indeed, a revolution is an ill-chosen time for delicate scruples. He asked his two companions: "Do you think that the arrest of the King and his family is necessary to the public safety, that that alone can save us from civil war?" They were sure of that. "Then, I'll take the responsibility on myself," he said, and wrote out an order, saying that enemies of *la patrie* had carried off the King and his family—a formula that the constitutionalists afterward adopted—and that it was the duty of all citizens to arrest them. He dispatched copies of this order by all the roads out of the city.

In Paris, when the news spread abroad, excitement and indignation flamed up; even extreme royalists felt bitterly to have been abandoned unwarned. Crowds gathered in the streets, threatening the guards of the Tuileries, and denouncing La Fayette. Some cried that as La Fayette had pledged his head on the King's remaining, now that the King was gone, the pledged head should adorn a pike. If the King had not been caught, as the Marquis de Bouillé most truly said afterward, La Fayette would certainly have been murdered, and if he had been killed, all the royalists in Paris would have been massacred.

La Fayette was never accused, even by Mirabeau, or Marat, or Danton, of lacking courage. He walked through the streets to the Hôtel de Ville with a crowd at his heels; there he found a turbulent multitude who had seized the Duc d'Aumont, an officer who had been on duty at the Tuileries. His coolness quieted the mob, and at his command they loosed hold of their captive; he then harangued them, at first with some badinage, but seeing how in earnest they were, he spoke serious words. Fierce passion was ready to break out into violence, there were angry looks and angry hands; had La Fayette shown fear perhaps there would have been murder, but he finished his speech, and then, without escort, walked back calmly through the thick of the crowd. He went that night into the Jacobin Club. Danton mounted the tribune and shouted out: "And you, Monsieur La Fayette, who but just now said that you would answer for the King with your head, does your presence here discharge your debt? Either you have betrayed your

country or you were a fool to have answered for a
person for whom you could not answer. In the most
favorable interpretation, you have manifested yourself
incapable of commanding us. I prefer to believe that
we can reproach you only with mistakes. If it were
true that the nation's liberty depended on a single
man, she would deserve slavery; but France can be
free without you. Your fame has flown from pole to
pole; but do you wish to be truly great? Become a
private citizen again; and do not give more food to
the just suspicions of a great part of the people."

In *l'Ami du Peuple*, Marat called for La Fayette's
head, and even in the National Assembly, a member
began an attack upon him. "Stop," Barnave cried
out, "I stop the speaker from what he was going to
say. . . . Since the beginning of the revolution
Monsieur de La Fayette has held patriotic opinions
and has acted like a good citizen; he deserves our confidence; he has got it, and it is for the good of the
nation that he should continue to have it." There
was a burst of applause. And the Assembly, hearing
that La Fayette was in danger at the Hôtel de Ville,
sent a deputation to fetch him. When the deputation
arrived, they found him quite safe, and when they
asked him to take an escort of guards for the walk
back, he answered: "I will order one out of respect
for you; but I shall go by myself. The streets are full
of people and therefore I shall be perfectly safe."

The National Assembly as well as the city was
disturbed and anxious. It read the manifesto left by
the King, which La Fayette calls "pitiful, a complete
abdication of constitutional monarchy," and decreed
that the seal of state should now be affixed not by
order of the King but by the Assembly. The chief

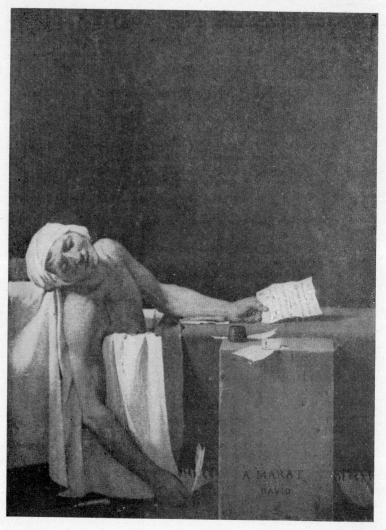

Marat Dying

From the painting by David (Musée de Bruxelles)

Robespierre

Bas-Relief in bronze done by François Théodore Ruhière, 1835

fear was of foreign invasion. Rochambeau was sent to take command on the frontier; La Fayette should be ready to march at the head of the National Guards. After long troubled hours of waiting a report came that a very large carriage had been seen driving in the direction of Châlons; and then that the King had been captured at Varennes. A few days later, on June twenty-fifth, the poor fugitives were brought back, prisoners, to the Tuileries.

La Fayette presented himself in the King's apartments: "Sire," he said, "your Majesty knows my attachment to you, but I have not left you in ignorance that if you separated your cause from that of the people, I should remain on the side of the people."

"That's true," the King replied, "you have followed your principles. It's a partisan matter . . . and here I am. I tell you frankly that till just now I had believed that I was merely in a group of people of your way of thinking, whom you had put about me; but on this trip, I learned clearly that I was mistaken, and that the general opinion is with you."

La Fayette asked: "Has your Majesty any orders to give me?"

The King laughed: "It seems to me that I am rather at your orders, than you at mine."

The Queen was less calm. In her irritation she offered La Fayette the keys of her boxes in the carriage. He declined to take them. She insisted, but he said that nobody would think of opening the boxes. And in fact, her papers were not examined.

As I have said, gross libels were circulated by angry members of the proletariat and its partisans against the Queen and La Fayette, but in reality there was no love lost between them. He regarded her as the King's evil genius, and she, brought up to regard royalty as hedged about by reverent obedience and adulation, found his plain speech hard to bear. "You ought, Madam," he said, "to have the more confidence in me from the very fact that I am free from royalist superstitions. If I thought that the destruction of royalty would be advantageous to my country, I should not hesitate, because what are called the rights of a family to the throne do not exist for me, but I hold it proved that under the present circumstances the abolition of royalty would be a public misfortune."

The immediate matter that pressed upon the National Assembly was what effect the flight to Varennes should have on the constitution of the government. Was the flight an abdication? Should the King be deposed, and the Dauphin set up in his place? Should the crown be given to the next branch of the family in the person of Philippe Égalité, Duc d'Orléans? The radicals demanded deposition, but they were in a small minority. Even Robespierre, when Pétion and Brissot said that they must prepare the people for a republic, bit his nails and asked with a smile, "What is a Republic?" The large majority believed in a monarchy, and that Louis XVI, if he could only be freed from evil counselors, was as good a King as they could get. Barnave, the famous orator, made an eloquent speech in support of this view. La Fayette seconded him: "I agree with the opinion of Monsieur Barnave, and ask that the debate be closed." All, except Robespierre, Pétion and a few others, voted aye.

La Fayette's daughter says: "There was no episode in my father's life for which my mother admired him as much as for this. She saw him, on the one hand, renounce his republican inclinations in order to unite with the majority, and on the other, how in all the painful dealings which his position forced upon him he assumed complete responsibility, and took all blame, in order to insure the safety of the royal family and spare it all the dolorous details possible." Hers was the opinion of a person in sympathy with La Fayette's ideals.

Of a contrary opinion are those who regard La Fayette's loyalty to his conception of duty as Quixotic, unpractical to the point of folly. Most famous of these dissentients is Bonaparte, who, when First Consul, said to him: "General La Fayette, you overthrew the strongest monarchy there was in Europe. Of all monarchies, in spite of its faults, ours was the most solidly established. Your action was fine, it was brave. But you made a great mistake to wish to maintain the old dynasty; for, if you refused it all power, the government could not work and if you gave it power, it would use that power against you. The difficulty was insuperable." Bonaparte set little store by the state of mind that longed for the good of France, with no benefit to self, beyond the honor of associating one's name with that good.

While the National Assembly was debating the King's fate, the radicals among the Cordeliers, the district club of which I have spoken, who met at the old convent near where the *École de Médicine* now stands, taking the position that the flight to Varennes was both a crime and an abdication, agitated for his deposition, and asked the Assembly to postpone a decision until all the districts of France could be heard from. This was in effect to propose a referendum, a procedure unknown to the constitution. The Assembly fobbed the petitioners off. Thereupon the malcontents went in crowds to the hall on purpose to overawe the deputies. This demonstration was also unsuccessful. Then Danton led a band of Cordeliers to the Jacobin Club, to urge them to cooperate in the preparation of a petition demanding the deposition of the King and "a substitution," and declaring that the petitioners would not recognize Louise XVI as King, unless the nation seemed to express such a wish. The petition carefully avoided the direct issue between a monarchy and a republic. To this the Jacobins agreed, and then Danton and others went to the altar dedicated to *la patrie* in the Champ-de-Mars, and read the petition to the crowd, who (probably not uninstructed) shouted out: "No more monarchy, no tyrant, no more kings!" By this time, however, the Assembly had passed their decree maintaining the monarchy. The Jacobins, therefore, acquiesced; but the Cordeliers persisted, except the leaders, who were uncertain what to do. Danton and Camille Desmoulins went out of town. The others continued. They drew up a new petition that declared the decree of the National Assembly null and void, demanded the trial of the guilty King and a new form of executive, marched off to the Champ-de-Mars, and laid it on the altar *de la patrie* with blank sheets for the public to sign.

The idea of a republic had come in haltingly. La Fayette from the time of his visit to America, had made fun of kings and had called himself a republican, but he had never seriously entertained the idea of overturning the French monarchy and setting up a republic. Camille Desmoulins had raised the cry, but he found scarce a handful of his way of thinking. A group of cultivated people advocated it, gentlemen and ladies, but so few, it is said, as to be almost able to sit together on one sofa in the salon of Madame Robert where they met. After the flight to Varennes, however, an increasing number of discontented democrats were working for a republic, the Cordeliers taking the lead. On the evening of July sixteenth, at the club of the Cordeliers, while the meeting on the Champ-de-Mars for the next day was under discussion, it was announced (so a witness testified) that the Mayor had orders to display the red flag and proclaim martial law and that La Fayette had *carte blanche* for calling out the National Guards; thereupon they voted to proceed to the Champ-de-Mars by different routes, carrying concealed weapons, and to repel by force any attempt to disperse them.

On the famous Sunday, seventeenth of July, 1791, the crisis came. It is hard to determine just what happened; contemporaries, chroniclers and historians recount the facts differently, according to their sympathies with the constitutionalists or with the populace. For the former, the affair is the enforcement of law and order, for the latter, as in the case of the meeting at Nancy, it is a massacre. The altar to *la patrie* in the Champ-de-Mars was a tall wooden structure, mounted by a flight of steps, and there the petition with blank copy-books attached was waiting for signatures. Two men, one a wig-maker—Michelet says that the wig-makers were the strongest partisans of the old régime, *les plus furieux royalistes,* and so he is quite ready to think ill of them—the other, a man with a wooden leg, *"poussés par une curiosité malsaine"* (pushed on by an unwholesome curiosity), hid themselves in the scaffolding; they were discovered, seized by a troop of indignant patriots, who probably believed them to be royalist spies, and murdered.

Their bodies were mutilated, their heads cut off and stuck on spikes. Rumors of riot and insurrection had been crowding in, and this news was disquieting. A battalion of National Guards was sent to preserve order. They were greeted with volleys of stones. You will notice, if you read the democratically minded chroniclers, that the people assembled on the Champ-de-Mars are spoken of as peaceable family parties, drinking lemonade and sauntering on the grass; whereas the conservative chroniclers speak differently. Madame Roland says that members of the Cordelier Club carried pikes on which were fastened declamatory handbills, and harangued those present and *"alimentaient l'indignation contre Louis XVI."* The leaders of the Cordeliers, in their turn becoming apprehensive, sent to the municipality to say that they were merely there, unarmed and orderly, to exercise the right of petition. The Mayor and Councilors were not persuaded.

La Fayette rode to the scene of action, at the head of more guards. They came upon a barricade made of carts; from behind it some fellow fired at La Fayette. He was identified and caught, but La Fayette bade him be released. Quiet seemed to be restored and La Fayette went back to the Hôtel de Ville; more rumors came in that fifty thousand ruffians were about to march on the Assembly. More alarm among the deputies, who urged the city government to take prompt action. This time the Mayor took the red flag and with La Fayette, at the head of cavalry and infantry, proceeded to the Champ-de-Mars. They were greeted by cries of: "Down with the red flag! Down with the bayonets!" by volleys of stones, and several shots. The Mayor started to read the riot act; some one fired a pistol at him, missed but hit a dragoon beside him. The National Guard fired in the air. The crowd, emboldened, hurled more stones; a number of soldiers were hurt, one knocked off his horse. Then the troops fired in earnest. A cannoneer was about to discharge his piece; La Fayette, not having time to speak, spurred his horse in front of the cannon, and stayed the man's hand. The crowd fled and the cavalry scattered the hindmost. One or two soldiers, caught apart from the troops, were killed. The National Assembly voted thanks to the Mayor and to the National Guard.

But Marat expressed contrary opinions, from which I take these quotations:

"My poor Citizens, it is not with staves that you will overcome the hordes of villains that conspire against your happiness. If they were the stronger, they would cut your throats without pity. You, therefore, must stab them without mercy. Shall not Duport, Bureau-de-Pusy, Barnave . . . Sieyès . . . Bailly, Mottié [La Fayette] be your first victims? Perhaps these bloody sacrifices will procure your safety." (L'Ami du Peuple, July 18, 1791.)

"Burning with impatience to begin the counterrevolution in the capital, and the massacre of the patriots, Mottié eagerly seized on the occasion of a meeting of citizens who had gone to the Champ-de-Mars to sign a petition against the decree that rehabilitates Louis the conspirator. . . . What does the infernal Mottié do? He suborns two officers of the invalides, gives them several barrels of powder, and the keys to the cellar under the altar of la patrie in order to blow up the Champ-de-Mars when the friends of liberty should be gathered together there. The villains were discovered in time; the people caught them in the act, and executed them on the spot. . . ." (*L'Ami du Peuple,* July 19, 1791.)

". . . The infernal Mottié assembles his paid ruffians, mounted police, etc., then his spies distribute money and liquor, telling them what to do. When all is ready for the bloody scene, the General, followed by the Mayor, marches to the massacre. But how are they to murder in cold blood peaceful citizens who go to express their opinions, while their wives and children are dancing on the grass? Some device is necessary. For that purpose, a lot of cut-throats, in Mottié's pay, had gone on ahead, and had mixed with the citizens in a corner of the Champ-de-Mars. On the arrival of the police and their armed satellites, these fellows throw stones, and fire some pistol shots. Mottié then orders the citizens to disperse, and has the troops fire in the air. The cut-throats throw more stones and fire more pistol shots. Mottié orders his men to fire, not on the rascals, but on the groups of patriots who had not had time to fly. O infamy! . . . Four hundred of these wretched victims were thrown by night into the Seine, etc." (*L'Ami du Peuple,* July 20, 1791.)

And summing up his feelings, Marat says: "To save the country he would go at their head to tear out the heart of the infernal Mottié in the midst of his battalions of slaves."

Marat has had many admirers, distinguished friends of the proletariat, Krapotkin and Jaurés for instance, who have or have had a right to be gratified by his testimony in favor of himself, "My heart is as pure as heaven's sunshine," but who ignore other testimony, whether of his own, (as, when a practising physician, he wrote, "I only care for cases where there is a good fee and little to do," or when in October, 1792, he demanded two hundred and seventy thousand heads), or that of others who adduce evidence that would convince an unprejudiced jury that he had robbed the Ashmolean Museum at Oxford. The moderate Monsieur Louis Madelin calls him: "A Mediterranean half-breed, deliberately sordid and evil-smelling . . . a man whose violence sometimes verged on insanity, as a rule quarrelsome, cynical and cunning." I mention these things as they render, in my judgment, his condemnation of La Fayette less derogatory.

Camille Desmoulins, who had fled to safety, says something of the same sort as Marat in an open letter addressed to La Fayette:

"Liberator of Two Worlds, Flower of High-Janissaries, Phœnix of Upper-Alguazils, Don Quixote of the Capet Family and of the Two Chambers, Constellation of the White Horse!" etc.

It was a fateful day, both for La Fayette and for France. The two contending classes, the proletariat and the bourgeoisie, had fired on each other. The number of killed and wounded has been very differently given. Bailly, the Mayor, in his report made soon afterward, says that at the time of writing, the numbers reported killed are eleven or twelve, with ten or twelve wounded: others, on the "people's" side run the figures up into scores, or hundreds. Robespierre said a thousand, and the more rhetorical raised the number to two thousand or so, according to their humor.

CHAPTER XXIII

BACK IN CHAVANIAC

THIS day, July 17, 1791, in momentous consequences does not lag far behind July 14 and October 5-6, 1789. Up to now the Revolution had been in the hands of moderate men, educated in the conventional sense that we attach to the word education, men who desired a constitutional monarchy, in which education and property should have a controlling voice. But now their power, already swaying in the balances, is soon to pass to the democratic masses, guided partly by ambitious men, partly by intellectual enthusiasts, all under the domination of the proletariat of Paris. This division into two parties, Constitutionalists and Jacobins, was virtually a class division, and the so-called "massacre" of the Champ-de-Mars was the opening fight between the two classes.

On the surface, the moderate party of law and order had won. Danton fled to England, Camille Desmoulins hid himself. Marat's printing press was seized and smashed, Robespierre showed fright (*effroi*) such as Madame Roland had never seen before. Deputies of the moderate party who had been members of the Jacobin Club, and almost all had belonged to it, withdrew—La Fayette, Barnave, two Lameths, La Rochefoucauld, and so on—with their friends, three or four hundred in all, and founded the *Club des Feu-*

illants; with the consequence that in the Jacobin Club the radicals became more and more dominant, and Robespierre the master spirit. The bourgeoisie acted as if they had really triumphed. They regarded their work as done, and themselves *functi officio.* They were sufficiently complacent and infatuated to enact a law that none of the members of the National Assembly, *l'Assemblée constituante,* as they are called from having made a constitution, should sit in the legislature, *l'Assemblée législative.* The King solemnly accepted the Constitution, and on September 30, 1791, the deputies disbanded. *"Sire,"* said one of them to the King: *"Votre Majesté a fini la Révolution."* Alas! irony plays a great part in human history.

La Fayette had foreseen the dangers of disorder. In a letter to Washington (March, 1791) he says: "Unfortunately the people have learned much better how to overthrow a despotism than they understand the duty of submission to the laws." But, in a sense, he was to be hoist with his own petard. He had solemnly announced that the right of insurrection against tyranny is sacred, and he had acted upon that principle. Now he had had as much insurrection as he judged good, and he held that, as tyranny had been overthrown, obedience to the new Constitution was an universal duty; the radicals agreed with him that insurrection is a sacred duty, but they held that a new tyranny had been substituted for the old, and that their present duty was to stir up a fresh insurrection.

For the moment, however, peace and order presented a sufficiently respectable exterior. La Fayette believed his task was over, and resigned as commander of the National Guard. I have said before that he had often repeated his purpose of returning to private life

when the Constitution should be finished; I quote, for
instance, from a letter to Washington (August 28,
1790): "I hope that our labors will finish this year;
then your friend this ambitious dictator, so blackened,
will enjoy with delight the happiness of laying down
all power, all political cares, and become a private
citizen in a free monarchy." Accordingly, he bade
the National Guard good-by: "Up to to-day, Gentlemen," he said, "to serve you has been a duty imposed
by sentiments that have animated all my life, and by
the devotion due to your confidence in me. But now, to
hand back to my country what power, what influence,
she has given me . . . is the duty due to my purpose
with which you are well acquainted, and the satisfaction of the only ambition that I entertain. . . .

"Nevertheless, take heed lest you think that all
kinds of despotism have been destroyed, or that
liberty, because we have set her up and love her, is
solidly established. She will not be, if political
opinions, personal feelings, or a perverted use of the
liberty of the press shall serve as a pretext for violence; if religious intolerance, cloaking itself under
some form of patriotism, shall permit a dominant cult
or proscribe a cult; if a man's house is not his castle;
or if all Frenchmen do not act together for the main-
tenance of civil liberty and a reverential observance of
law."

The men took leave of him with every expression
of affection and regret. Gouverneur Morris notes in a
letter: "Our friend La Fayette has no kind of influence.
He is about to retire into Auvergne, to spend the
winter on his estates. The King and Queen detest
him, and the nobles hold him in contempt and ab-
horrence, so that his sun seems to be set, unless he

should put himself at the head of the republican party who at present are much opposed to him."

Nevertheless, La Fayette's journey from Paris to Chavaniac was one long triumphant march. A letter describes some of the doings:

"Here I am at Chavaniac. My journey has been long; I have been obliged to stop everywhere, to go through towns and villages on foot, to receive carriagefuls of civic crowns. . . . I left Clermont at night; the city was illuminated. We were escorted by the National Guard and men carrying torches; it made really a charming sight. At Issoire, which you know well, everybody is very patriotic; you can imagine that I was well received there, and at Lempdes, too. Brioude made all the fêtes you can think of. . . . All the curés have been replaced by priests who have taken the oath but the latter are the under dogs here. Two of the non-jurors are to lodge in a house of mine that I keep for a chapel with the motto *Peace and Liberty*. The old curé of Chavaniac is there. The peasants, though released from their bonds, and paying but half what they used to, hardly dare to be glad of their freedom for fear of being damned. As for me I rejoice, like a lover of liberty and equality, in this complete change which has put all of us citizens on the same level, and respects only the legally constituted authorities. I can't tell you how much pleasure I get from bowing low before the village mayor. You have to be somewhat enthusiastic to enjoy all this as I do . . . and I get as much pleasure from absolute repose as I have done during fifteen years from action."

He stayed here two months with his aunt, Madame de Chavaniac, his mother-in-law, the Duchesse d'Ayen, his sister-in-law, wife of Vicomte de Noailles, and his own family. He deserved his absolute repose, for he had had not only his own cares to bear, but also those of his wife. Madame de La Fayette was a devout, high-minded, intense lady, hyper-sensitive to duty, a woman who might easily have entered a convent instead of marrying. Her character makes one think of "Moonlight shadows upon moonlit snow." I quote from their daughter:

"My father was elected, after the 14th of July, 1789, commandant of the National Guard of Paris. His life was bound up with all that happened at that time. You can judge in what anguish my mother passed the first three years of the Revolution. No prejudice had any empire over her. Moreover for a long time she had shared my father's opinions, which would naturally have been hers anyhow. She approved and admired his conduct. She identified herself with his sentiments, and supported herself in the midst of her anxieties by the thought that he was working for the success of right principles. The first misfortunes of the Revolution filled her soul with bitterness, to the point of making her insensible to any joy of pride for my father. Her only satisfaction was in seeing him often sacrifice his popularity in order to oppose some lawless movement or some arbitrary act. She had adopted and frankly professed liberal opinions, but she had a delicacy, of which it would be difficult to indicate the quality, that prevented her from being what you call a party woman. Her feelings led her not to fear the blame of certain societies; but she

trembled at the thought of the incalculable consequences of what was happening, and she was continually imploring God's mercy, while outwardly she
lived a very busy life.

"She accepted all the requests made to her by the
districts of Paris, sixty in number, to take up a collection at the blessing of flags, and other patriotic
ceremonies. My father kept open house. She did the
honors in a manner to charm his many guests; but
what she suffered at the bottom of her heart can not be
judged except by those that have heard her speak of
it. She watched my father at the head of a revolution,
the end of which it was impossible to foresee. . . .
Nevertheless she was always upheld by my father's
principles, and so convinced of the good that he was
able to do and of the evil that he was able to prevent,
that she endured with incredible strength the constant
dangers to which he was exposed. Never, she has told
us, did she see him go out of the house during this
time without the thought that she was bidding him
good-by for the last time. Nobody was more terrified
than she by the dangers to those she loved; but at that
time she was exalted above herself, devoted, as well as
my father, to the hope of stopping the crimes. . . .

"On July 17th the Jacobins stirred up a serious
riot. The ruffians began by murdering two men.
Martial law was proclaimed. It is difficult to imagine
my mother's state of anguish while my father was at
the Champ-de-Mars, exposed to the rage of a furious
mob who scattered shouting that my mother ought to
be killed and her head presented to him. I remember
the frightful cries that we heard, the alarm of every
one in the house, and above all my mother's lively
joy to think that the ruffians who went by were no

longer at the Champ-de-Mars. She kissed us crying
for joy, but took most calmly what precautions were
necessary in the pressing danger. The guard in front
of our house had been doubled and was drawn up
ready to fire, but the ruffians were on the point of
entering my mother's rooms by the garden that
fronted on the square du Palais Bourbon; they were
climbing over the little wall, when a body of cavalry,
riding through the square dispersed them.''

The other ladies of La Fayette's family encircled
him with love and admiration. The Duchesse d'Ayen
was a remarkable woman, high-minded, self-possessed,
generous; she was glad to be relieved of the responsibility of various seigniorial privileges, but ''she had a
horror of all excesses, an extreme aversion to all kinds
of disturbances, she feared the consequences of passion, and was alarmed by the symptoms of the
Revolution.'' Very fond of her son-in-law, she was
''full of disquietude of every sort at the active part
he took, nevertheless she judged him in all the details
of his conduct, with the illuminating good sense that
comes from the *application* of the heart. She saw him
always on the edge of the precipice, but always deserving esteem and love. She was with me [I am now
quoting Madame de La Fayette] at Versailles during
the various events that preceded and followed July
14th [1789]. . . . The King's acceptance of the Constitution put an end to her solicitudes, for it meant
the retirement of M. de La Fayette. She shared the
intoxication of my joy and decided to come and share
the first moments of it with us at Chavaniac. . . . It
was on the 4th of November [1791] that she arrived
at our retreat in Chavaniac, and we had the happiness
of keeping her there until the month of December.

M. de La Fayette, who felt deeply our happiness and
the value of such a mother, or our aunt, who felt this
almost as much as he, or my children, or anybody who
lived at Chavaniac and witnessed that day, would be
more capable than I of painting the picture that my
heart, blighted by grief, would vainly endeavor to
retrace. My mother was truly happier in my happiness than I myself. M. de La Fayette, after three
years passed in the midst of storms, remained just
what he had been, keeping his simplicity of manners,
preserving a flower of sentiment for his aunt and also
for the place of his birth, and happy in the midst of his
children, happy to find himself cherished by two
mothers [mother-in-law and aunt] whom he loved so
tenderly. This sweet sight renewed and rejuvenated
my mother's faculties. . . . It is easy to judge
whether I felt the value of her goodness and the happiness of possessing her. I never parted from her without a pang. But I expected to see her a little while
afterwards, and there was nothing violent in our parting, which however was to be our last."

La Fayette must have enjoyed his holiday; for
though he felt a true love of liberty, the path of that
true love had not been smooth. The *via media* was
beset with thorns; and apart from his own political
dissatisfactions and public cares, during these years
the ladies of his family had not only been at times
in physical danger, but they had also suffered in their
conscience from the legislation against the clergy.
Besides that many of his old friends had been
estranged by his democratic principles. For instance,
the family of his wife's sister, Madame de Montagu,
joined the *émigrés*. There is a fragment of a letter
that reveals how painful all this was to him.

"May, 1791.

"I can't describe to you to what a degree your letter afflicts me. . . . A revolution, much wished for by me, caused in part by my efforts, supported with all my might, makes all whom I love unhappy. I am devoted to that revolution to my last breath; but all its charms are poisoned for me by the effect it produces upon the objects dearest to my heart."

After three years of strain due to anxiety for the State, for his family, for his friends, La Fayette needed rest, but the time for rest was destined to be short and very much disturbed. The news from Paris was not satisfactory. A large majority in the *Assemblée législative* consisted of men who favored the Constitution, but they were hesitating and vacillating, while the Jacobin left was full of impetuous resolution. The orators of the *Gironde* declaimed glorious dithyrambs. Isnard said: "If the French people draw the sword and fling the scabbard far, they, by themselves, if provoked, blazing with the fire of freedom, armed with sword, pen, reason, eloquence, will change the face of the world and make tyrants tremble on their thrones of clay." The club of Cordeliers, with Danton roaring like a lion, demanded a republic; and the Jacobin Club, with Robespierre at its head, was nearly as radical.

The municipal government had become radical, too. Bailly had left the office of mayor. La Fayette and Pétion, a radical, were nominated to succeed him. The Jacobins worked hard for Pétion, and the Court out of hatred to La Fayette, did the same. The Queen said: "M. de La Fayette merely wishes to be mayor of Paris in order to be mayor of the Palace." The latter's friends were slack, some believed that he wished for a life of retirement, but it is plain that his popularity had greatly ebbed. Out of eighty thousand voters, not ten thousand voted, and of their votes Pétion received two-thirds (November 16, 1791). At about the same time Danton was elected an officer of the municipality.

Besides these happenings in Paris, the whole country was heaving under the revolutionary storm. In *la Vendée* and in Normandy, popular devotion to the non-juring priests and to the royalist cause was threatening civil war. Down by Avignon there was civil war, for the *Assemblée constituante* had annexed the province, which for centuries had belonged to the papacy, and those for and against were massacring one another. In Alsace, the *Assemblée constituante* had annulled seigniorial rights, but these rights belonged to German princes who shrieked robbery, and waving their shrunken purses before the Emperor's face, demanded help. The *émigrés* had collected an army at Coblentz. And beyond the *émigrés* loomed up the sovereigns of Austria and Prussia, menacing but hesitant, urging their fellow sovereigns of Europe to help them reestablish a government in France "equally advantageous to the rights of sovereigns and to the prosperity of the French nation." The sovereigns, of Russia, of Sweden, of Spain, had their own preoccupations but they were watchful, and England lay couchant biding her chance.

These thunders and rumblings were plainly audible on the banks of the Allier and the slopes of the Cevennes.

CHAPTER XXIV

LA FAYETTE's rest and retirement began in October and ended in December. He enjoyed his vacation. He wrote to Washington: "There, on a good estate, once a seigniory, now changed into a great farm and directed by an English farmer that I have had come to teach me, I was happy in the midst of my neighbors who are no longer vassals to anybody, and I was giving to my family the only quiet weeks they had enjoyed for a long time, when the mad preparations of the *émigrés* and the support that they had from neighboring potentates induced the Assembly and the King to adopt a very vigorous course of action."

One effect of that vigorous action was to pluck La Fayette from "the sweets of private life." The ministry at that time was composed of constitutionalists—a Feuillant Ministry—and the Comte de Narbonne had just come in as minister of war. When hostilities became likely, Narbonne selected Rochambeau, of Yorktown fame, Lückner, a German general who had entered the French service at the close of the Seven Years' War, and La Fayette, to command the three armies on the frontier. The King opposed La Fayette's nomination. Narbonne answered: "If your Majesty does not appoint him to-day, the people will compel you to appoint him to-morrow."

La Fayette was summoned to Paris toward the end of December, "covered all the way with testimonies of affection." From Paris he went to his headquarters at Metz. There the three generals were to meet and confer. It was inevitable that sooner or later the antagonism and irritation between revolutionary France and the privileged classes of Europe would burst into war. The Feuillant Ministry was inclined toward peace, but both the Court and the great majority of the Jacobins were for war. The Court seems to have thought that the allies would be triumphant and restore the old régime, or, at least, that danger would rally the nation to the King, while the Jacobins believed that they could tumble down all the thrones in Europe with the headlong impetus of freedom and equality. The orators of the Gironde let loose their passionate southern eloquence. Vergniaud called on the Assembly to take up the burden of Europe: *"Soyez à l'avenir une nouvelle Providence; associez-vous à la Justice éternelle qui protège les Français. En meritant le titre de bienfaiteurs de votre patrie, vous mériterez aussi celui de bienfaiteurs du genre human."* (Be in the future a new Providence; join with Eternal Justice that protects the French. By deserving the title of benefactors of your country, you will also deserve that of benefactors of the human race.) And on January 25, 1792, the Assembly passed a bellicose resolution, asking the Emperor of Austria what his intentions were, did he mean to live at peace with the French nation and take no part in any enterprise against the sovereignty, the independence, or the safety, of France, and threatening him that, if he should not render a satisfactory answer, without evasion, before March first, such reticence would be regarded as a declaration of war. The Emperor, confronted with this demand, denied any evil intent against France, or any purpose inconsistent with friendly relations, but in his reply he denounced the Jacobins as a "pernicious sect," as enemies of Louis XVI and of the fundamental principles of the French Constitution. This petulant denunciation, which both angered and flattered the Jacobins, emphasized the separation between privilege and democracy.

Meanwhile, domestic politics were evolving. The Jacobins, who were subsequently divided into Girondins and a more radical wing, known as the Mountain, were solidly united against the Constitutionalists. They alleged, and probably believed, that the latter were hand in glove with the royalists, and they uttered all sorts of accusations, as, for instance, that there was a committee working in the interest of Austria, *la comté autrichienne,* in which they included La Fayette, who knew nothing of such a conspiracy if there was one, and Rochambeau, who never meddled with politics at all. They turned for reinforcement more and more to the populace. Their orators rose to the occasion. Isnard burst into Biblical phrases: *"La France poussera un grand cri, tous les peuples répondront. La terre se couvrira de combattants, et les ennemies de la liberté seront effacés de la liste des hommes."* (France will cry a great cry, and all peoples will answer. The earth will cover herself with warriors, and the enemies of liberty will be stricken from the lists of men.) An empty treasury, and scarcity of food became powerful allies; for the people attributed all such evils to plots by counter-revolutionists or by foreign potentates, and it was not long before the Jacobins, borne onward by a rising tide of popular fear and anger, overthrew the Feuillant Ministry.

Monsieur de Narbonne, the Minister of War, was an aristocrat, but, (so La Fayette says) a constitutionalist *plein d'ardeur et d'activité*. According to Monsieur Mortimer-Ternaux, who wrote *Histoire de la Terreur*, he and Turgot were the only two men who might have been able to turn the Revolution from its path, *conjurer la tempête*. Narbonne was not only attacked by the Jacobins but was also at odds with his colleagues, and in danger of losing his post. La Fayette and the other two generals believed it to be very important for the public weal to keep him in office, but La Fayette—though Gouverneur Morris, always a little vexed because his advice is neglected, says that he had a "great deal of the *intrigant* in his character," and, when still more vexed, that "La Fayette is as cunning as anybody"—La Fayette was prudent and shrewd, but naif and a poor politician, as he proves by his behavior on this occasion. He and the two other generals, who no doubt followed his advice, wrote letters to Narbonne saying how necessary he was in the present military circumstances. These letters were published, with or without Narbonne's connivance. As any real *intrigant* would know, these letters produced an effect quite the contrary of that intended. Some say that Narbonne's fellow ministers seized upon this meddling by the generals as a ground for obliging the King to dismiss him; others say that the King wanted to get rid of him. He was promptly dismissed (March ninth).

The Girondins knew that their time had come. They pressed on to the attack of the Prime Minister, de Lessart, accused him of neglect in his dealings with

Austria, of treason, and what not, and succeeded in procuring his arrest. With de Lessart the whole Ministry fell, and the Girondins compelled the King to appoint a ministry from their party. The famous Dumouriez, who according to La Fayette was "an intriguer, both as a soldier and as a politician—but intelligent, brave, fertile in resources and gifted with great military talents," received the portfolio of foreign affairs, and Roland, a *"Quaker endimanché"* (a Quaker dressed up in Sunday clothes), husband of the more celebrated Madame Roland, received that of the interior. With power now in the hands of the Gironde, the threats of their orator Vergniaud ring with an ominous clang: "In old times Dread and Terror have often issued forth from the palace of the Tuileries in the name of Tyranny, now let them go back into that palace in the name of the Law. Let all that dwell therein know that the person of the King alone is inviolate, and that the Law will lay hold of the guilty and not a single guilty head shall escape the sword." But for the time being the Girondins recognized the fact that they were in office under a constitutional King.

La Fayette, I think, did not hate the Jacobins, he despised them. He regarded them as sly, mean, untruthful, untrustworthy, unpatriotic men, either in the pay, or under the influence, of royalist agitators, and he treated them *en grand seigneur,* consciously, as his moral inferiors, and, unconsciously, as his social inferiors. This mixture of arrogance and contempt, which he looked upon as a debt to honesty, was not conciliatory. It was as if he said, "I will not soil my own white hands by taking yours." He learned afterward to respect Dumouriez's abilities, but now he regarded him as an aristocrat in disguise, working for the counter-revolution; but let it be remembered in La Fayette's excuse that Dumouriez, after his tortuous, counter-revolutionary plots had failed, joined his country's enemies and took English pay. At this time, his offense was that he was a Jacobin.

As general in the field La Fayette was in close relations with Dumouriez; and to make his position clear, he wrote him with naive frankness, what he himself calls "*une espèce de traité.*" It is a lecture to the Ministry on their duties. The business of the government, he says, is to make the law respected, the royal dignity respected, religious liberty respected, to oppose aristocratic plots, to see that prisoners of war are not maltreated, and so forth, and that then, if the government does these things, he for his part will recognize it and act under it. The Ministry must have wished to dismiss La Fayette on the spot; this they could not do, because there were no Jacobin generals of sufficient experience as yet, and La Fayette's popularity, though waning fast, was still too strong in the country as well as with his army to be disregarded. But the Jacobins could afford to wait, for they were rapidly winning the whole of the lower classes in Paris. Of this there was striking proof. The mutineers of Nancy condemned to the galleys, now set free, were received in Paris with acclamations, welcomed at the bar of the *Assemblée législative,* hailed by an ode from André Chénier,—"*Salut! divin Triomphe!* This glorious day will not have its like till La Fayette mounts the scaffold"—rewarded with alms to which the King contributed, escorted in triumph through the streets, and complimented with a fête organized in their honor by the Jacobin Club.

La Fayette was now stationed at Metz. His command lay between that of Rochambeau to the north and that of Lückner to the south. He agreed with the other Constitutionalists in not wanting war. He did not think that the army was ready to take the field, for the troops lacked many essentials, the older officers being aristocrats were on bad terms with the humbler born officers who had replaced the *émigrés*, and he was full of distrust of the Ministry and apprehensive of what they might do. This situation was not good, as it was obvious that war was close at hand. He wrote to his wife:

"Metz, April 15, 1792

". . . I can not hide from myself that war is likely. There is still hope, but I should bet far more on war. We shall go into camp about May 10. Parties are divided at present in this fashion. Robespierre, Danton, Desmoulins *et al* make up the Jacobin rabble. These marionettes are moved from behind the scenes, shouting out that we [the Constitutionalists] are hopelessly beaten, and they attack me. They say that I have deceived the people and the Court, that I led astray M. de Bouillé, a far less guilty man than myself, and that I am much more dangerous than the aristocracy.

"The other party [the Gironde] known as the *Hauts Jacobins,* that supports the present Ministry, is composed of Bordelais, the abbé Sieyès, Condorcet, Roederer *et al.* They fear and hate Robespierre, but they don't dare risk losing popularity. They deem war inevitable. They appreciate Lückner, think that Rochambeau will leave, and they are agreed, for some time now, that though they hate me personally, they must have full confidence in me, as a steadfast friend of liberty and equality, and an incorruptible defender of the Constitution.

"I have made, through friends, an avowal to the two ministers with whom I have had to do and this will be passed on to the principal members of the Assembly. . . . Here is my position. I have, as I told them, no other party than the French nation. My friends and I will aid any one, who wishes to do right, to defend liberty and equality and to maintain the Constitution, we will reject whatever tends to make it either aristocratic or republican, and when the national will (expressed by its duly elected representatives and by the King) shall say that war is inevitable, I will do all I can for its success to the best of my ability.

"Good-by, I kiss you all very affectionately."

Two days after this letter was written war was declared. The old Emperor Leopold, Marie Antoinette's brother, had died, and his son Francis II, who was more willing to fight, had come to the throne. He demanded that the provinces which had belonged to the papacy (Avignon and the Comtat Venaissin), be given back, and that the German princes be restored to their seigniorial rights in Alsace. The Girondins did not hesitate, though Robespierre, Danton and others of the extreme left were for peace. The declaration of war was very popular, and the general enthusiasm for the cause of liberty against tyranny found appropriate expression in a battle hymn that a young officer of the engineer corps, a nephew of Bailly, Rouget de Lisle, stationed at Strasbourg, wrote at the time. It begins:

Allons, enfants de la patrie,
Le jour de gloire est arrivé!

In prevision of hostilities a plan of joint action had been made out by the three generals, and it had been agreed with the Minister of War that no order for an advance should be given until they were ready; but Dumouriez, doubtless for political or personal reasons, did not keep to the agreement, he not only changed the plans and ordered an advance before the generals were ready, but he divulged his new plans to third persons before communicating them to the generals. La Fayette was in high dudgeon. He wrote to Dumouriez:

"Metz, April 25, 1792

"When I besought you, Sir, if war was necessary, not to declare it till we were ready, I foresaw that this declaration would confront us with the alternative, either to leave the enemy to make the first move, or to make it ourselves with insufficient means. . . .

"Permit me also, Sir, to observe to you that your secrets are immediately divulged, I do not know how. Two weeks ago my movements and those of the other generals were announced in the societies at Metz, and the details of my instructions arrived by letter from several of my friends at the same time as by your aide-de-camp."

This disaccord between a general at the front and the Minister of War was not an auspicious beginning for a campaign. Everything was at sixes and sevens. Dumouriez ordered an advance ten days ahead of possible preparations, and wrote direct to Rochambeau's subordinates, Biron and Théobald Dillon, over his head. Nevertheless an advance into Belgium was attempted at three points, at Mons, Tournai and Givet. I will not go into nice geographical details. Biron advancing toward Mons was driven back in disorder. Théobald Dillon, advancing toward Tournai, was routed and chased to Lille, where the soldiers, whether from shame or worked upon by Jacobin agents, seized their unlucky commander, hacked him to bits, and then threw the bloody bits into the fire. Not content with this, the mutineers made common cause with the rabble in Lille and murdered six Austrian prisoners, a non-juring priest and one of their own officers.

In the meantime La Fayette had been ordered to be at Givet, which lies on the Meuse southeast of Mons, on April thirtieth, and Biron and Dillon with their detachments from Rochambeau's army were told to rely on his being there. But in spite of the vital importance of his arrival on time, the war bureau had provided no means of transportation for his artillery. La Fayette believed that this omission was part of a deliberate plan to wreck the campaign and throw the blame on him. But, thanks to his popularity, the people of the neighborhood supplied him with horses, and his infantry displayed the swiftness of foot that was to become famous in Napoleon's campaigns, and he arrived at Givet on time, as ordered. There he learned of the rout of the two French armies, and of the mutiny and barbarities at Lille. Of course, he attributed these misdeeds to Jacobin influence; boiling with anger he wrote to Dumouriez:

"Sir, The infamous conduct toward prisoners of war demands exemplary punishment; it is not the enemy, but the French army that demands this. The indignation that we all feel authorizes me to say that brave soldiers would be loth to fight if the fate of their conquered enemies was to be given up to cowardly cannibals.''

Rochambeau resigned. To those that remonstrated with him he said: ''How do you expect me to stand up against Dumouriez and the Jacobins, when La Fayette who has many titles to the people's confidence can hardly protect himself from them.'' On his resignation, Lückner and La Fayette were left in divided command of the forces at the front.

CHAPTER XXV

LA FAYETTE DEFIES THE JACOBINS

THESE are signs of perilous days: soldiers that murder commander and prisoners, generals who rate and scold the Minister of War, while the enemy is at the gates and there are fierce factional quarrels within. One hears the hissing of Medusa's snakes. At Paris there was great excitement and anger, not over mutiny and massacre, but because the French army had been defeated and the country might lie open to invasion. Robespierre declared that the army had been defeated because the King and his generals conducted the campaign. This was an attack upon the Court but still more upon the Ministry and marks the widening breach between the Girondins, Brissot, Vergniaud, Dumouriez and their associates, and the *Montagne*. It was the *Montagne*, the extreme radicals both in and out of the Assembly, that had organized the fête for the mutineers of Nancy, when the populace shouted, "Hang La Fayette!" and made pitiful lamentations over the martyrs shot at the Champ-de-Mars by his command. The Gironde and the *Montagne* had acted together to defeat the Feuillants, and now like comrades in a desperate venture were quarreling over possession of power. The Gironde was in office, but its situation was precarious. No government could tolerate mutiny in its army, but in order to be able

to enforce even elementary discipline they were obliged
to ask help of the Feuillants; while, on the other hand,
in order to cope with the conservative right, they
needed the support of the *Montagne.*

The natural sequence of events must have been
plain to a prophetic eye: first, concerted action against
the conservative party, next a struggle for mastery between the Gironde and the *Montagne,* and finally a
harvest of dragon's teeth, every man's hand for himself. Some sympathy is due to the Gironde who were
attempting to steer the ship of State. They were suspicious of the Court, rightly enough, for the Queen
was sending to the allies notice of Dumouriez's plans
of campaign. They were suspicious of the regular
soldiers, and discharged six thousand of the King's
guard. They were suspicious of La Fayette, and
turned a deaf ear to his demands for supplies and
more troops. And La Fayette, for his part, as I have
said, distrusted the government, and surmised that
they were wilfully playing into the hands of the
counter-revolutionaries. Besides, his troops were
really in need. Gouverneur Morris notes on May 12,
1792, that La Fayette's army was without necessaries
of every kind, the horses were dead, the soldiers sick
and weary, and officers apprehensive and discontented.
Even strangers could see this. Erich Bollmann, a German visitor, wrote home: "The ministry is disorganizing the army, for the Jacobins are trying to get the
upper hand in it. They favor only their own creatures,
so La Fayette and his army are in great need. The
Jacobins hate La Fayette because he is the only man
that can withstand them. They preach his murder in
the streets." La Fayette sent two officers to ask for
some battalions stationed near Paris to reinforce his

lines. Roland, the minister to whom the officers were referred, instead of listening to the request, complained to La Fayette that these officers had said that the French were cowards and, therefore, must have a large numerical superiority. The officers declared that they had only spoken of those that ran away under Biron and Dillon. La Fayette, irate over what he believed a purpose to deliver his army into the hands of the enemy, wrote back with what, even more than in his letters to Dumouriez, seems a touch of the *grand seigneur* dealing with a social inferior.

"Camp at Rancennes, May 30, 1792. "Sir: I do not inquire with what purpose your letter was written, but I can not believe that my aide-de-camp went to a man, of whose existence he was ignorant until he learned by the Gazette that he was a minister, and who even to-day he hardly knows by name, for the express purpose of slandering the French nation and his general's army. As for my army, as it is constituted to-day, I rely on it as it relies on me; our mutual confidence is based on a love of liberty, respect of law, hate of faction, and contempt of their chiefs. "P. S. I dispense, Sir, with pointing out your military errors, they have been already refuted . . ."

As Roland believed La Fayette to be still an aristocrat and was unwilling to make him more powerful by further reinforcements, and La Fayette believed Roland and all the Jacobins rascally, unpatriotic knaves, the exchange of letters did little good. Brissot, I think, is right in saying that La Fayette shows "all the arrogance of an ex-noble who has not forgotten the haughty manners of the caste to which he had belonged." Gouverneur Morris had said three years before: "I am very much mistaken if he is not, without knowing it himself, a much greater aristocrat than those [of the noblemen] opposed to him."

The Gironde was hostile to the monarchy, but they were directing the policy of the government, they were responsible for the safety of France, and, squeezed as they were between counter-revolutionists to the right and the red radicals to the left, they dared not cashier a general, still strong in his popularity with his troops, who might march upon Paris, and besides, they were in sore need of the Feuillants to aid them against the *Montagne.* For these reasons the Gironde on the one hand put up with La Fayette and, uniting with the Feuillants, passed a decree against Marat, who, as usual, was stirring up anarchy, and ordered a court-martial to punish the soldiers who had murdered General Dillon. On the other hand, in fear of the royalists, they acted with the extreme left, and passed a decree banishing non juring priests, and another for the formation of a camp of twenty thousand men under the walls of Paris. The King's conscience forbade him to approve the first decree, and his instinct of self-preservation forbade him to approve the second. He vetoed both measures. Roland, therefore, wrote him an indigant, or as others think, an insolent letter. Dumouriez advised the King to dismiss Roland and two others of his colleagues, agreeing himself to remain, if the King would approve the two decrees. The King dismissed the three ministers, but still refused to approve the decrees. There was wild agitation in the revolutionary districts of Paris, and Dumouriez was forced to resign. He received a command at the front.

It was in the midst of the popular excitement and rage over the King's vetoes that La Fayette, convinced that the Jacobin Club was bringing the country to anarchy, and was as dangerous as foreign enemies, threw down his celebrated challenge. It needed no political perspicacity to see that the Constitution, and with it law and order, was in danger, and he felt that he was the one man, if any, who by his reputation, his popularity, his command of an army, might stay the ruin. In denouncing the club, he was within his right, for the *Assemblée constituante,* sharing his views, had decreed that clubs should keep out of politics, that they should not exercise influence, nor any surveillance, upon the duly constituted authorities. This decree had remained a dead letter; but it was there. He wrote to the Assembly this letter:

"At the entrenched camp at Mauberge
"June 16, 1792.

"Sirs:

"At the very time, too long deferred perhaps, when I was going to call your attention to great public interests and to designate among our dangers the conduct of a ministry [Roland *et al*] which I have attacked in my letters for a long time, I learn that, unmasked by its division, it has succumbed to its own intrigues. . . .

"It is not enough, nevertheless, that this branch of the government should be delivered of a baneful influence; the common weal is in danger; the fate of France rests principally upon its representatives. The nation expects its safety at their hands; but when it adopted a Constitution, it prescribed to them the only road by which they can save it.

"Sirs, convinced that just as the Rights of Man are the law for every constituent assembly, so a constitution becomes the law of the legislators that it has established, it is to you, yourselves, that I must denounce the violent efforts that have been made to turn aside from this rule that you have sworn to follow.

"Nothing shall prevent me from exercising this right of a free man, from fulfilling this duty of a citizen—not the momentary vagaries of public opinion, for that opinion deviates from principles; not my respect for the representatives of the people, for I respect the people still more, and the Constitution is the supreme act of their volition; not the kindness that you have always shown me, because I wish to keep it, as I obtained it, by an inflexible love of liberty.

"Your situation is difficult; France is threatened from without and tumultuous within. While foreign courts proclaim the unendurable purpose of attacking our national sovereignty and declare themselves the enemies of France, enemies within, drunk with fanaticism or pride, entertain chimerical hopes and vex us to boot with their insolent ill-will.

"Sirs, you ought to put them down, and you will have the power to do so according to the measure that you follow the Constitution and do what is right. You wish to do so, no doubt; but look at what is taking place in the midst of you, and all around you. Can you hide from yourselves that a faction (or, rather in order to avoid vague appellations) that the Jacobin Club, has caused all these disorders? . . . It is that club that I here accuse.

"Organized like a separate empire, with its headquarters and its branches, blindly directed by ambitious chiefs, that sect forms a separate and distinct corporation in the midst of the French people, and usurps the powers of the people, by subjugating their representatives and their servants. It is at that club, in its public sessions that love of law is called *aristocracy,* and breaking the law called *patriotism;* it is there that the murderers of Nancy are hailed in triumph; there, that the crimes of Jourdan [coup-tête, a cutthroat of Avignon] find their eulogists; there that the recital of the assassinations that polluted the city of Lille are still calling forth infernal acclamation. Do those sectaries expect to escape these reproaches by bragging of an Austrian manifesto, in which they are named? Have they become sacred, because the Emperor Leopold has named their name? And because we must fight foreigners who meddle in our disagreements, are we exonerated from delivering our country from domestic tyranny? . . . I denounce this sect to you, I, who without speaking of my past life, can reply to those that would make believe suspect me: Come hither in this moment of crisis when each man's character shall be known, and let us see which of us is the more inflexible in principles, more stubborn in resistance, and will better brave the obstacles and dangers which traitors hide from their country and which true citizens know how to estimate and to confront on her behalf.''

He assails Dumouriez and the Girondin Ministry; declaring that their letters to him were worthy of the Jacobin Club, full of false calculations, vain promises, deceiving or futile information, perfidious and contradictory advice, that they urged him to advance without the necessary precautions, to attack without means, and then told him that resistance was likely to be impossible. And he accused the Jacobins and the aristocrats of a singular conformity of conduct; both (he says) wished to overthrow the laws, both rejoiced in disorder, both rose up against the authority conferred by the people, both detested the National Guard, both preached insubordination in the army and sowed distrust and discouragement.

"Now, I come to-day, full of confidence in the justice of our cause, of scorn for the cowards that desert it, and of horror for the traitors who wish to pollute it, I come to assert that the French nation, if she is not the basest in the world, can and ought to resist the coalition of kings who have armed against her. It is not in the midst of my brave army that timid sentiments are allowed; patriotism, energy, discipline, patience, mutual confidence, all the virtues, civic and military, are there. Among them, the principles of liberty and equality are cherished, the laws respected, and property held sacred; among them there are neither calumnies nor factions, . . . and I ask to what degree of degradation a great people is reduced, . . . that the coward idea of sacrificing its sovereignty, of compounding with its liberty, of dickering with its Declaration of Rights, could have appeared as one of the possibilities of the future that is coming upon us so fast?"

He then demands that the army should be increased and properly supplied, that the Constitution should be respected, that criminal justice should take its lawful course, that civil equality and religious equality should prevail, that the royal power should remain intact, that the King, invested with the nation's majesty, should be independent and respected.

Caricature of the Constitution of France. Monsieur, the Marquis de La Fayette, and Monsieur the Duc d'Orleans supporting Monsieur Necker

Caricature of the Minister, solemn Director of the Performance. La Fayette is represented standing on the top rung of a ladder balancing a pole on the end of his nose; Rochambeau is sitting in the supports of a tight rope; Luckner is performing a dance, etc.

"And finally I demand that you shall destroy the régime of the clubs, that they make place to the reign of law, that their usurped authority give way to that of a noble, independent, constitutional authority, their disintegrating ideas to true principles of liberty, their raving fury to the calm and steadfast courage of a nation that knows its rights and defends them, and their sectary politics to the real interests of the country which, in this hour of peril, should unite together all those for whom its servitude and ruin are not objects of atrocious joy and infamous calculation. . . ."

"LA FAYETTE."

At this denunciation the Assembly did not know what to do; some speaker doubted if La Fayette was really the author. The Jacobin Club foamed at the mouth. Robespierre cried: *"Frappez La Fayette et la nation est sauvée!"* (Strike La Fayette down, and the nation is saved.)   Danton followed him: "There is no doubt but that La Fayette is chief of the noblesse that is in league with all the tyrants of Europe." Camille Desmoulins repeated: "I have been telling you for two years that La Fayette is a great rascal." Brissot innocently asked: *"Pourquoi cet acharne-ment contre les clubs?"* (Why this ferocity against the clubs?)   Lasource said: "What Monsieur de La Fayette calls the Jacobite faction is the imposing multi-tude of Friends of Freedom who have never cast a vote except for her." And all worked upon the populace which was already furious that the King had vetoed the two measures for which it clamored, and whose anger flared up the more at a threat from the army, especially from the man who had ordered the *massacre* of the Champ-de-Mars.   On June seventeenth Morris wrote to Jefferson: "We stand on a volcano, we feel it tremble, we hear it roar, but how and when and where it will burst, and who may be destroyed by its eruption, is beyond the ken of mortal foresight to discover."

Four days were spent in preparations. Then, out from the poorer districts of the city a great mob swarmed, armed with pikes, hammers, swords, axes and bludgeons; they fraternized with the National Guards and persuaded many of them to join. The municipal officers read the riot act, but there was no one to enforce it, and the mob did not obey. They marched into the assembly hall, drunk and disorderly, dancing to the tune *Ça ira!* with shouts *"Vivent les patriotes! Vivent les sansculottes!* Down with the veto!" One man carried an old pair of breeches, another a calf's heart with the words, *"cœur d'aristocrate."* Nobody had the courage to bar their way. One of them harangued the deputies: "The people are up [he said] ready to employ great means to avenge their outraged majesty," and then stating their demands, ended with, " . . . they await in silence an answer worthy of their sovereignty." The President answered that the Assembly would baffle all conspiracies, and invited the people to assist at its session. The mob then marched to the Tuileries. The soldiers on guard showed sympathy; no officer dared oppose them. Dragging a cannon, the manifestants burst into the palace. They swarmed into the King's chamber, they made him stand up on a bench, put a *bonnet rouge* on his head, and yelled: "Down with Monsieur Veto! Down with Madame Veto!" A butcher shouted out at him: "You are a traitor; you have always deceived us, you are still deceiving us. But look out for yourself."

The King, always wrapped in his passive courage, said that he should do what the Constitution commanded. Pétion, the radical Mayor, came at last, and tried to calm the people: *"Vous avez agi* [he said to them] *avec la fierté et la dignité des hommes libres."* (You have acted with the just pride and dignity of free men.) At last the rabble went, parading through the Queen's room, insolent and defiant, and tramped out of the palace, dragging the cannon. The King had behaved courageously and well, but the throne was tottering.

CHAPTER XXVI

FLIGHT

THE riot of June twentieth was not the effect that La Fayette had hoped for, but it justified his letter. The Jacobin Club, with its head at Paris and branches all over, proved stronger than he knew. There was one other effort he could make; his presence might succeed where his letter had failed. He asked Marshal Lückner if his going to Paris would be prejudicial to the military defense. The old Marshal disapproved of his going "because the sans-culottes will cut off your head." That being the only objection, La Fayette started out with one aide-de-camp. At Soissons, also, the local authorities begged him not to go. He arrived in Paris quite unexpectedly, and went to the house of his dear friend, the Duc de La Rochefoucauld (June 28, 1792). His own family was at Chavaniac.

The same day he went to the Assembly, avowed his letter, and stated that he had not written it because he had been under the protection of his soldiers, that he entertained the same sentiments now, and had come to express his indignation, and that of the soldiers, at the brutal events of June twentieth. He demanded that the instigators and ringleaders of those riots should be prosecuted for the crime of *lèse-nation*, that the Jacobin faction be put down under foot, and that the Assembly should take measures to have the duly constituted authorities respected. The Jacobin deputies ventured no further than to ask if he had received official leave of absence from the front; and the President feebly responded: "The National Assembly has sworn to maintain the Constitution; faithful to our oaths we will protect it from all attacks." It was plain enough that the Assembly was cowed by the Jacobins, and that his stroke had failed. At the Jacobin Club that night he was called a traitor, an impostor, a rascal, an enemy to his country, the greatest of criminals and so on.

He went to Court to have an interview with the King. There the King's counselors held a hurried discussion as to what attitude they should take toward him. Madame Elisabeth, the King's sister, said that they must forget the past and throw themselves with confidence into the arms of the only man that could save them; but the Queen spoke up: "It is better to perish than to be saved by La Fayette and the Constitutionalists." All that he accomplished here was to convince the Court that he had wished to make his peace with them. One hope still remained. It happened that the King was going to hold a review of the National Guard, four thousand in number, the next day; La Fayette asked permission to attend and to address them. The Queen (it is said) sent word to Santerre, one of the ringleaders on June twentieth, and also to Mayor Pétion that La Fayette meant to take advantage of the occasion to stir up the Guard. Pétion countermanded the review. There was nothing further to be done. La Fayette gathered together a few friends in the Guard and once again rehearsed the coming dangers, and then went back in dejection to the army. It is plain enough to us now that La Fayette could only have suppressed the Jacobin Clubs, if he had had an army at his back. But such use of military force was out of the question for him; it would have been an offense against the Constitution as grave as those which he was combating, and he could not, consistent with his duty to his country, withdraw his army from the frontier in the face of the enemy.

He had nothing to hope for from the Assembly; it was under the control of the Jacobins. The directory of the department, with La Rochefoucauld at its head, suspended Mayor Pétion for his conduct on June twentieth, and the King confirmed the directory's act; Pétion shook with indignation. But the pusillanimous Assembly quashed it and reinstated Pétion. The Feuillants had become, as an adversary said, *des feuilles mortes*. La Fayette, however, still commanded an army, loyal, so he believed, to the Constitution and to himself. He would not use it to march on Paris, but it might be used to protect the King, and not contravene the law. He reverted to an old plan of Mirabeau, somewhat modified. The King possessed the right, while the legislature was in session, to reside within twenty leagues of Paris; he, therefore, might lawfully go to Compiègne, a royal residence within that distance on the road to the Belgian frontier; La Fayette would not be far away in case the King's personal safety was threatened. At Compiègne the King should issue an order forbidding the *émigrés*, especially his brothers, to advance, declare himself ready to march at the head of his troops, and also that he was unequivocally devoted to the Constitution. La Fayette thought that these explicit declarations would reassure good citizens who were apprehensive of the *émigrés*, disconcert the Jacobins, and liberate the King both from his counter-revolutionary counselors and from the Parisian mob.

But the Court hoped for a victory by the allied sovereigns, and was not inclined to accept safety at La Fayette's hands, *"Nous savons bien,"* they said to themselves, *"que M. de La Fayette sauvera le roi, mais il ne sauvera pas la royauté."* (We know very well that La Fayette will save the King, but he will not save royalty.) The King, too, did not dare to be severe to his brothers, for he expected them to come back in triumph, and he feared their animosity. The Queen, likewise, was opposed to the plan: "It would be too unendurable to owe our lives to him twice," and she recalled Mirabeau's remark: "In case of war, La Fayette will wish to keep the King a prisoner in his tent." She hated him; and, at least so he states, part of the libels that were published against him day by day were paid for out of the King's purse.

La Fayette had hit as hard as he could legally against the Jacobins, and they were not slow to strike back. They continually worked upon the populace, preaching that La Fayette should be removed and the King deposed; and they won over most of the National Guard of Paris. With the ground prepared, and the mob to back them, the Jacobin leaders denounced him at the bar of the Assembly, while Robespierre assailed him in the Jacobin Club: "Liberty will be in danger," he said, "so long as La Fayette is at the head of our armies; he is meditating a crime which he means to impute to the friends of liberty . . . for no other way to pursue his ambitious career is left to him." Brissot and five other deputies swore that General Lückner, who had come to Paris for official duties, and had dined with the Archbishop of Paris, and apparently drunk too much wine on that occasion, had said that he and La Fayette had agreed to march jointly upon the capital. But Lückner denied the story. Among other letters one from Lückner to La Fayette was produced, but instead of containing treason, the Marshal had written *"Paris est affreux à mes yeux."* La Fayette merely said, "The story is not true."

But the Jacobins were fearful of La Fayette, lest he should turn his army against them, and told tales of La Fayette and his wicked ambitions so successfully through the length and breadth of France that when a detachment of volunteers from the department of the Gironde passed through Chavaniac, some of them suggested burning the château, and only Madame de La Fayette's tact and hospitality prevented any outrage. They, also, kept directing the Minister of War to give specific orders to do this and to do that, and so keep hold upon the army. La Fayette's position as a responsible commander was becoming impossible. He wrote:

"To M. A. M. d'Abancourt, Minister of War
        "Camp at Moreton, August 8, 1792.
"Sir:
    It is contrary to my principles and to my character to make complaints or shirk responsibility, but it is due to the public welfare and to myself, to make myself clear on one point. You have taken from M. de Lückner general officers whom he needs and put them in my army; you assign to me M. Dumouriez, as to whom everybody knows my opinion, after he had been rejected by M. de Lückner as insubordinate, and who will certainly be less obedient to my orders than

to his. You are carrying on a direct correspondence with M. Arthur Dillon as to the disposition of troops to the left of my command from Dunkirk as far as Mauberge, and the orders I send him are often contradicted by orders from you. . . . In the business of war there must be unity of command."

The Minister of War excused himself by *"l'inquiétude de l'Assemblée."* But the *inquiétude de l'Assemblée,* in other words, the hostility of the Jacobins, did not stop there. On August eighth an impeachment was moved; Brissot supported it, but it was rejected by a vote of four hundred and forty-six against two hundred and twenty-four. The left was applauded by the rabble, and on leaving the hall some of the Constitutionalist members were assaulted with sticks and stones. Gouverneur Morris wrote to Jefferson that if La Fayette were to go to Paris without his army he would be cut to pieces.

La Fayette's acquittal was the last success of the moderate party. Already the republican tide had been mounting. On July twenty-ninth a fiery troop of Jacobins from Marseilles tramped into Paris, singing Rouget de Lisle's battle hymn:

Aux armes, citoyens! formez vos bataillons!

Then came the news of the Duke of Brunswick's manifesto:

"The city of Paris and all its inhabitants must make immediate submission to the King, and give him complete liberty. And their allied Majesties declare, on the word of an Emperor and of a King that, if the

Château of the Tuileries is forced or insulted, if the
least violence, the least outrage, is done to their
Majesties, the King and the Queen, or royal family . . . they will take exemplary vengeance,
memorable for ever, delivering up the city of Paris
to military execution and total overthrow.''

La Fayette's acquittal, following upon this proclamation, poured oil on the flames. The proletariat of
Paris gave warning that if the Assembly should not
have granted to the people justice and their rights,
that is, if it should not have done what the Jacobin
Club wished, by midnight on August ninth, that the
tocsin would sound, drums beat, and patriots appear in
arms. The Assembly lacked spirit, and did nothing.
On August tenth, a memorable day, the people assembled at various places, the bells were rung, a
revolutionary committee took possession of the Hôtel
de Ville ousting the lawful government, they tricked
the chief officer of the King's guard at the Tuileries
from his post and murdered him. They seduced the
National Guard. Then the people attacked the Palace.
The King's guards, chiefly Switzers, defended it. For
two to three hours the battle raged. The King slunk
away to the Assembly for safety, and sent orders to
his guards to lay down their arms. Those that did
were massacred on the spot, or tried later for treason
in shooting the sovereign people. A number of the
French Guards, the Duc d'Ayen, La Fayette's father-
in-law, among them, escaped. The Switzers were almost all killed. The palace was sacked; the King sent,
a prisoner, to the Temple. Mathieu Dumas, crossing
the Place Vendôme, found young lads and children
playing with heads on sticks.

By this insurrection of the people, by this second revolution rather, the Jacobins came into complete power. The King's authority was suspended, and a law passed providing for the election of a convention to draw up a new constitution. The Assembly, now a mere rump, for the right and the center dared not speak, elected an Executive Council of six, of whom Danton, now minister of justice, became the chief. The Commune of Paris became the tyrant of France.

La Fayette was stationed near Sedan in the department of Ardennes, when the news of August tenth reached him. Curiously enough, as it appears to us as we look back, he seems at first, so besetting was his suspicion and fear of the royalists and of a counter-revolution, to have supposed that the outbreak was the work of the allied sovereigns. He wrote to the Minister of War (August twelfth): "The disorders in the capital are without doubt paid for by the foreign powers in order to boost the counter-revolution. This supposition finds confirmation in the conjunction of the mob's movements, and the time chosen, with the movements of the foreign powers." This theory of his shows his extraordinary naïveté and guilelessness, and his belief in the natural goodness and law-abidingness of the people; one notices in his correspondence, and in his speeches, throughout the Revolution, that he attributes outrages and insurrections to foreigners, to royalists, to *agents provocateurs,* who have cozened and misled the people. But his acceptance of this could hardly have lasted long after August tenth; and now if he was to act, he must act quickly.

It is said in Taoist philosophy "that the practise of enlightened virtue will not succeed in establishing good government." There are times when a man must choose between what he has been taught to consider virtue, coupled with failure, and what he has been taught to consider unrighteousness, coupled with success. Mirabeau had said that politics and morality did not go together. La Fayette has been much criticized for his conduct during this eventful summer. The substance of that criticism has been expressed by a man who looked on matters from an opposite point of view. "La Fayette," this critic said, "committed a great error, not that he declared against the tenth of August, but because he did not the year before overthrow the Assembly, seize the government and reestablish the monarchy." Of this critic (Fouché), who, as I say, was the complete opposite to La Fayette, it has been said: *"Il ne manqua rien en habileté, peu en bon sens, tout en vertu."* (In cleverness he lacks nothing, in common sense but little, in virtue all.) La Fayette, at this crisis, did not act with cleverness, and hardly, I think, with good sense, but he did what he thought right.

The situation was compassed about with difficulties. La Fayette clutched at any plank in this shipwreck of law and order, in his wish to save the King, and through the King the monarchy. His last hope was to unite the neighboring political departments in the support of King and Constitution and make them the base of a league of law and order. Beginning with the municipal government of Sedan, he told the officials that as two of the powers of the State, the executive and the legislative, had been lawlessly suppressed, he must turn to them for legal sanction. But, in fact, it was he that gave commands and the municipal authorities carried them out. The Jacobins sent down three commissioners to administer a new oath of liberty and equality to the soldiers, and with power to suspend or depose the generals. These commissioners were arrested by the municipality of Sedan as envoys of a rebellious faction; they then endeavored to procure an interview with La Fayette; and told his aide-de-camp that it only depended on him to become the first man in France. But blandishments had no more power than threats.

For a moment La Fayette thought of marching on Paris, taking the loyal regiments, that were few, and the loyal officers who were many, and raising the standard of the Constitution. The idea could not be carried out. Dumouriez refused to obey his orders, Arthur Dillon hesitated, Biron although an aristocrat, accepted Jacobin authority, even La Fayette's own troops wavered, some refused to take the oath of loyalty to the King. On August seventeenth the Executive Council decreed that La Fayette should transfer his command to Dumouriez and repair at once to Paris to give an account of his conduct. On the nineteenth they charged him with rebellion and treason. A price was set on his head, and pledges given to bring him alive or dead. His troops, however reluctantly, drifted with the popular stream, they obeyed the rump of the Assembly, as the only source of law. There was no safety left him, nor opportunity for public service for country or King in France, so he decided to escape to America. He exercised great care to make such a disposition of his troops that the enemy could not profit by the interim between his flight and Dumouriez's assumption of command. Nor would he take with him, as he might have done, a considerable number of soldiers and officers. As he wrote to a friend: "I did not wish the most fastidious scrupulousness to have anything to reproach me with." On the nineteenth, accompanied by twenty-one officers of his staff who shared his principles, he left Bouillon and rode to the border, where Alexandre Lameth, also threatened with arrest, joined him. That night they crossed into the enemy's territory. The Jacobins cried out that he was a traitor, a deserter, an *émigré*, that he had carried off army friends, etc. But among the King's papers that were seized by the Jacobins was found a correspondence with La Fayette. Morris says: "It breathes from beginning to end the purest sentiments of freedom. It is therefore kept secret, while he stands accused of designs in conjunction with the dethroned monarch to enslave his country."

This is sometimes called the crisis of La Fayette's life, and men will judge it according to their preconceived notions concerning political values in France at the time; the right and the left, royalists and socialists, conservatives and radicals, disagreed fundamentally on the issue. La Fayette had done what he could to obey the oath that he had taken to uphold the constitutional monarchy, he would not bow to the Jacobins within, nor march with the Austrians who assailed his country from without. I will leave the reader to look up adverse criticisms, and confine myself to one authority. Bonaparte, in after years, said to La Fayette: "*Tenez, mon cher, une belle conduite c'est la vôtre!* (My dear fellow, your conduct was admirable.) To guide the affairs of one's country, and in case of shipwreck to have nothing to do with its enemies, that is the way to act." To this I will add La Fayette's own statement written to a stranger:

"To Monsieur d'Archenholtz,

"Magdebourg, March 27, 1793.

". . . My situation is really peculiar. I had sacrificed my republican inclinations to circumstances and to the will of the nation. I was obedient to its sovereignty according to the constitution that it had adopted. My popularity was great. The Legislative Assembly defended me better on August eighth than it defended itself on August tenth. But I had displeased the Jacobins by blaming their new aristocracy that had usurped illegal powers; I had displeased the priests of all categories, by demanding, in opposition to them all, real religious liberty; I had displeased the anarchists, by putting them down, and the conspirators, by refusing their offers. Such are the enemies that joined those whom the foreign powers and the anti-revolutionists, together with the French Court itself, hired to act against me.

"Remember, dear Sir, the premeditated attack of August tenth; how the guards stationed in the name of the law were butchered in the name of the people; how citizens, without distinction of age or sex, were massacred in the streets—some burned in fiery brasiers, some put in prison to be murdered in cold blood; how the King's life was only saved by an illegal suspension of his office, how the National Guard was disarmed; how the oldest and most faithful friends of liberty and equality, a La Rochefoucauld, were pointed out to assassins; how observance of the Constitution became a mark for proscription; how the press was muzzled; how liberty of thought was punished with death; how private letters were broken open and falsified; how jurors were replaced by cut-throats, and their chief [Danton] made minister of justice; how the municipal and administrative bodies in Paris were quashed and reconstructed by rioters; how the National Assembly with a knife at its throat was forced to sanction the mob's furious acts; how, in a word, natural, civil, religious and political liberty, was smothered in blood. . . . What was a man to do, what was he to think, who had never breathed or thought, except for liberty, who, the first in Europe, had proclaimed a Declaration of Rights; who had pronounced, on the altar of Federation, in the name of all Frenchmen, the civic oath, and who looked upon the Constitution, in spite of its defects, as the best rallying point against our enemies? Although the National Sovereignty was violated in the persons of its representatives; as well as by the new delegation of powers, I did not wish the military forces to cease their obedience, so I asked for orders from the civil authorities within reach of the camp. Of course, I earnestly hoped that political liberty, and the constitutional authorities, would be reestablished by a general demand; and, if after the independence of election and deliberation had been assured, the nation had wished to revise the Constitution, do you think that I would have protested, I the first and most obstinate defender of constitutional conventions? Of course, I was too averse to any connection with the crimes committed and with the crimes that I foresaw, not to encourage resistance to oppression. I regard resistance as a duty; and I venture to say that my conduct, hard as it was to decide, will pass the severest scrutiny."

And I will supplement this declaration with a statement that La Fayette made concerning his notions of what republican principles are in a letter to Mr. Pinckney, July 4, 1793: "May all the real republican traits, liberty, equality, honest industry, moderation, purity in morals, candor, liberality of mind, obedience to the laws and firmness against all usurpation, continue to prove that American freedom has its root not only in the head but in the very heart. . . ."

It was a satisfaction to La Fayette to learn afterwards that Bonaparte agreed with him in thinking that, if the early leaders of the Revolution as well as their ideas had not been trampled down and proscribed in 1792 and thereafter, the revolutionary movement would have spread far and wide and that all Europe within ten years would have adopted the principles of the Declaration of Rights.

CHAPTER XXVII

ARREST

THE little band of fugitives hoped to make their way between the Austrian lines to their right and the French troops to their left, northward into Holland; from there La Fayette intended to cross the channel to England, where his family should join him and all emigrate together to America. After riding twenty miles they came to a place called Rochefort in the Bishopric of Liége, nominally a neutral country, where there was an Austrian army of occupation. La Fayette stayed behind, hoping to escape notice, and sent his aide-de-camp ahead to explain that they were French officers, who had resigned their places in the French army for political reasons, that they were not *émigrés* but neutrals bound for a neutral country, and asked for permission to proceed. La Fayette, however, was recognized. The commandant sent to Namur for instructions. While waiting for the expected passports, La Fayette wrote to his wife at Chavaniac.

"Rochefort, August 21, 1792
"Dear Heart,
"Whatever the vicissitudes of fortune, you know that my spirit is not of a temper to be cast down; but you know it well enough to pity the wrench it cost me to leave my country, for which I have devoted all my

310

efforts. She would have been free and worthy to be free if personal interests had not worked together to disorganize our means of resistance without and of liberty and safety within. So it comes that for having served my country with courage I am an outlaw and forced to cross into enemy's land. . . .

"An Austrian post barred our road. The Commandant deemed it his duty to stop us, and we are to go to Namur, but I do not believe that they are treacherous enough to detain strangers who are going on to a neutral country, Holland or England. . . .

"You know that my inclination was to be republican, if reason had not forced me to be royalist to a certain point, if fidelity to my oath and to the nation's will had not obliged me to defend the King's constitutional rights. The less others resisted, the louder has been my voice. I have become the object of all attacks. The mathematical demonstration that I was powerless to prevent crime, induced me to save my life when it was evident that I should be put to death without any advantage. I don't know how much my journey will be retarded but I am going to England where I desire all my family to join me. Would that my aunt could come too. I know that they detain families of _émigrés_,—but those are _émigrés_ in arms against their country—but me, Good Lord, what beast would dare put me into that category. . . .

"LA FAYETTE."

His expectation that the Austrians would let him pass by and continue his journey to England, is further evidence of the guilelessness, the naïveté, that were such conspicuous traits in his character. Madame de La Tour du Pin calls it _"une niaiserie de_

confiance" (in the silliest confidence). He held his
head high —*mens conscia recti*—and expected sympathy and approval. Really no one less simple-
minded than La Fayette would have imagined that an
absolute monarch, the nephew of Marie Antoinette,
could have looked upon the revolutionists of '89 as
other than malefactors.

In fact when word of the capture reached the
general in command at Namur, he cried out: "La Fayette! La Fayette! Hurry, hurry! Go tell M. le Duc
de Bourbon! La Fayette! La Fayette!" dispatched
a courier post haste to Brussels, and, instead of granting passports, ordered the fugitives to be brought
prisoners to Namur. At Namur La Fayette was received very politely by le Marquis de Chastelar, who
informed him, with a certain significance of emphasis,
that Prince Charles of Lorraine was coming from
Brussels to talk to him about the situation of affairs
as he had left them in France. La Fayette answered
brusquely: "I do not suppose that any one will permit
himself to ask questions which it would not be proper
for me to answer." And though Prince Charles was
very polite, La Fayette received him very coldly. The
interview, "too brief and formal to be called a conversation," was soon over. Nevertheless, the Marquis
de Chastelar, in writing out his report, showed La
Fayette how he had sought to attenuate La Fayette's
torts révolutionnaires, among others *son amour de
l'égalité.* At this, La Fayette reviewed the part he
had taken in abolishing privileges, and begged the
Marquis to cut out all that tended to disavow his conduct or his principles.

From Namur they were conducted to Nivelle. Here
an order came from the government to seize the

trésor—the military funds of the army—that (as they assumed) La Fayette had brought. La Fayette observed: "No doubt their Royal Highnesses, if they had been in my place, would have taken it." At Nivelle, La Fayette, and three others, La Tour-Maubourg, Bureaux de Pusy and Alexandre Lameth, all formerly members of the *Assemblée constituante,* were separated from the others and sent to Luxembourg. At Nivelle La Fayette wrote to his dear friend the Duc de La Rochefoucauld a letter that tells some of his difficulties in the army during the last weeks:

"And while threats of murder and pillage frightened all civilians, they [the Jacobins] took the most efficacious means of disorganizing the army. You know that no army can resist the combined efforts of the executive and legislature branch, . . . especially when no offence is punished, but all offences are rewarded or applauded, when confidence in the chiefs and attachment to the Constitution is treated as lack of patriotism, and when a crowd of disorganizing agents are sent to every army corps under the guise of recruits. . . .

"All my last thoughts were devoted to the safety of the army. . . . You know that, as I am popular with the soldiers I could have brought a good many with me. But such an idea was as far from my heart as from my principles, and I sent back all down to the lowest orderly. . . ."

This letter was never delivered; for the Duc de La Rochefoucauld had been murdered. The Jacobins, for their part, did not hesitate over scruples. They deposed the King, overturned the Constitution, adopted severe measures against *émigrés* and non-juring priests, proclaimed *la patrie en danger,* sent emissaries to preach their doctrines to the undecided, dismissed those officers from the army who would not accept the new régime, and created revolutionary tribunals to judge those guilty of the crimes of August tenth, that is those who had defended the King and opposed armed resistance to the will of the people. The Assembly, however, had become but the registrar of another's will. Above the Executive Council of the Assembly, above the Assembly itself, rose the Commune of Paris, full of energy and purpose, animated like the first disciples of Islam, with faith and fury. Taine has analyzed the Jacobin spirit: *Provocation à l'utopie, débordement de la parole, dérangement des idées . . . domination des formules et suppression des faits, perte du sens commun et perversion du sens moral.* (Incitement to Utopias, floods of words, ideas deranged . . . the domination of formulas and suppression of facts, loss of common sense and perversion of moral sense.) They howled for vengeance against the enemies without and the aristocrats within.

At this juncture the Prussians crossed the border, captured Longwy, and advanced on Verdun. Fear and anger rose higher and higher. The Gironde was alarmed and wished the government to withdraw to Blois, but Danton breathed his own courage into them and persuaded them to stay. Volunteers crowded to the army. Robespierre, more and more dominant, denounced a plot to make the Duke of Brunswick king of France, and pointed to members of the Gironde, Brissot and Roland, as the plotters in this likely plot. Suspicion was broad awake, listening to rumor with her hundred tongues. The Commune named a *comité de surveillance,* including **Marat,** *l'ami du peuple.* This committee cast its eyes on the improvised prisons—the Abbaye, the Châlelet, the Grande Force, the Petite Force, Bicêtre—for the ordinary jails could not contain the suspected aristocrats, non-juring priests and Swiss guards, nearly three thousand, but first they saw to it that petty criminals should be discharged.

On September 2, 1792, news arrived that the Prussians had invested Verdun. The bells rang. Danton shouted out his famous phrase: *"Il nous faut de l'audace, encore de l'audace, toujours de l'audace, et la France est sauvée."* (We must be bold, be bold, be bold and bold, and France is saved.) According to an opinion common among French historians, popular fury was the only revolutionary force capable of arousing patriotic enthusiasm to the pitch necessary to save France. This notion, alien to us, makes it easier to understand why La Fayette, a disciple of George Washington, had been crushed beneath the burden of his respect for law and order. On this very day, a Sunday, La Fayette, La Tour-Maubourg, Bureaux de Pusy and Alexandre Lameth, who as ancient members of the *Assemblée constituante,* and therefore worse offenders, had been separated from their fellow fugitives, were traveling south from Nivelle toward Luxembourg. It was as well for them. In Paris several carriages of non-juring priests, who had been sentenced to deportation, had started for the city barriers but had been stopped, brought back to the Hôtel de Ville and thence back to the Abbaye and to the Carmes. The municipal district known as *la section Poissonnière* had already passed this vote: "The section considering the imminent dangers to the *patrie* and the infernal machination of the priests, decrees that all priests and suspected persons in the prisons of Paris, Orléans and elsewhere, shall be put to death.'' But it is idle to consider who was primarily responsible, whether Danton or Marat or the Executive Council, or merely the furious mob. When the priests were getting out of the carriages, they were attacked, and the September massacres began. That evening Maillard, one of the heroes of July fourteenth, who had led the procession of women to Versailles on October 5, 1789, sat as president of the improvised tribunal at l'Abbaye. Those condemned were taken out and murdered, to shouts of *"Vive la patrie."* The judges ate and drank to refresh themselves for their work. One hundred and twenty-two were killed at the Abbaye, two hundred and forty-four at the Carmes. An official notification was sent out: ''The Commune of Paris hastens to inform the communes of all the departments that a number of the ferocious conspirators held in prison have been put to death by the people, an act of justice that the people judged indispensable in order to terrify the thousands of traitors hidden within the walls and keep them quiet while the people marched against the enemy.'' Couthon said: ''The people exercised their sovereign justice.'' I venture to suggest that these doings seem to offer some justification for La Fayette's letter of June sixteenth, but as I say, it is idle to allot responsibility. Danton stopped Marat from arresting Brissot, Roland and other members of the Gironde, as inopportune while the enemy were invading France. But nobody stopped the massacres. In four days one thousand one hundred perished. With these dead bodies lying before our eyes, it seems a little senti-

mental in Mr. Hilaire Belloc to find fault with La
Fayette's passion for a constitution of law and order,
"so singular and unnational an intellectual weakness."

Lafayette who knew nothing of what he had
escaped, reached the borders of Belgium on September
thirtieth. We can follow his course by some letters
written to a kind friend of his and his family in
England, Madame de Hénin, a lady ten years his senior
described by her niece by marriage, Madame de La
Tour du Pin, as very handsome, "handsome hair,
charming eyes, teeth like pearls, superb carriage, and
a very noble air."

"Arlon, September 3d, 1792

". . . It is strange enough that La Rochefoucauld
and Barnave should be in a Jacobin jail, and I and my
companions in Austrian chains. The friends of liberty
are proscribed on both sides; my place, therefore, is in
a prison, and I prefer to suffer under the despotism
that I have fought against, than under the people
whose cause is dear to my heart, and whose name is
now profaned by ruffians."

From Arlon the four captives proceeded to Luxembourg where some *émigrés* wanted to assassinate La
Fayette, and where he received an answer from Monsieur de Saxe Teschen refusing his request for a passport and insinuating that his head might go to the
block.

The next letter that has been preserved is from
Coblenz, dated September sixteenth:

". . . I have promised you the journal of my
captivity, and at the same time it is for my wife, my

children and my friends that I write. You know where the objects of my affection are [he didn't, he thought that they were on their way to England]. You will pass on my news, they know my affection.

"When I wrote you from Luxembourg I was passing from Austrian to Prussian control. . . . We proceeded in the middle of a detachment of cavalry. The officer in charge of us sat in my carriage; some under officers rode in the other three carriages while I had others on the box at the back of mine. We arrived at Trèves, where we were put in four cells with a little bed and a table, I had a petty officer with a pistol in his hand." He mentions the interest aroused among the people they passed, most of them sympathetic. . . . "I can't help telling you how insupportable it is to have the eyes of a petty officer fixed on you for every second of the twenty-four hours. . . . I don't know what is going to happen to us, and I submit to necessity as best I can. I don't write to my friends, because a letter would compromise them, nor to Madame de La Fayette, who is probably on her way to rejoin me. Give all of them my news. Tell the American Minister, too. He will be astonished, as well as the English people, at what has happened to me, especially if they know the circumstances."

CHAPTER XXVIII

IMPRISONMENT

In the meantime Madame de La Fayette was far from reaching England. While stationed at the front her husband had tried to persuade her to join him, but she was fearful lest she should hamper his movements or lest it be said that he was trying to put his family in safety, and therefore decided to stay at Chavaniac. Then she heard of the tenth of August, and was in an agony of apprehension. Newspapers told her of her husband's efforts to set up resistance at Sedan, and on the twenty-fourth she learned that he was out of France. Then she experienced an *"ivresse de joie."* But fearing a visit from the patriots, she burned some papers, hid others, and was in doubt as to what to do with the children. The girls stayed with her, the boy was housed by a priest, who had taken the oath, somewhere off on a mountain. True to her principles, she herself heard mass celebrated by a non-juring priest. On September tenth at eight o'clock in the morning the château was surrounded by armed men, and a commissioner with some soldiers, led by a patriot from the neighboring town of le Puy, who was suspected of having taken part in the recent murder of a prisoner, came in. The commissioner, whose reputation also was bad, presented her with an order from the Committee of

Public Safety, dated August nineteenth (the very day that La Fayette left France) commanding the commissioner to bring her and her children to Paris; he also produced a letter from Roland, who had been reinstated in the Ministry, directing him to execute the order. One of the soldiers boasted to Madame de La Fayette that he had killed his officer who was an aristocrat. She judged it prudent to obey without protest, bade the horses be harnessed at once and made ready to go. The commissioner opened her desk to take out La Fayette's letters. "You will discover, Monsieur," she said, "that if there had been any legal tribunal in France, Monsieur de La Fayette would have appeared, confident that not an act in his life could compromise him in the eyes of any true patriots."

The older daughter Anastasie accompanied her mother; the younger daughter was hidden. The old aunt, aged seventy-three, who had never been induced to leave Chavaniac, said that she should go, too, and several servants, hoping to make friends with the soldiers, also went along. They were taken to le Puy. A prisoner had been murdered there a few days before. Madame de La Fayette said to Anastasie, then fifteen years old: "If your father knew of this he would be very much disturbed, but also he would be very contented with you." But nothing happened beyond some yells and a few stones thrown at the carriage. Madame de La Fayette asked the authorities of the department to give her copies of La Fayette's letters that had been seized, before they were sent to Paris, remarking that in the Assembly there was a good deal of lying. She also asked leave to read them aloud; somebody suggested that it might be painful for her. "Oh, no," she answered, "on the contrary, Monsieur,

the sentiments they express uphold and console me."
The letters produced a sympathetic response in the
audience. She kept her head completely, and when
the Mayor, an old friend, showed his kindly feelings,
fearing lest he might be compromised, she sought to
show how little intimate they were by reproaching him
for not having come to Chavaniac for a long time.
Then she asked that permission be granted her not
to go to Paris but to stay at Chavaniac upon parole.
She wrote a letter to Brissot, one of the leaders of the
Gironde, in support of her request, ending: "I consent
to owe you this service." Brissot showed her letter to
Roland, who granted the request, but wrote an answer
full of insulting references to La Fayette and ending
by saying that the expression she had used, *"de con-
senter à lui devoir une service,"* belonged to the
superannuated pride of those who had been known as
the *noblesse*. But no sooner had she given her parole
than learning of La Fayette's imprisonment in Germany, she wished to withdraw it and to have leave to
join her husband. She bent her pride to beg this of
Roland himself:

"It is on my knees, if I must, that I ask this favor;
judge of the state I am in.   NOAILLES LA FAYETTE."

Brissot, for the Gironde was then entering into
a death-struggle with the *Montagne,* evaded an answer,
but Roland said to wait, that it would be imprudent
for Madame de La Fayette to travel then, and that
he would see what might be done. Roland fulfilled his
promise and obtained her release from her parole,
but the regulations that fettered the movements of
former nobles prevented her from traveling.

Meantime La Fayette and his three fellow prisoners had been transported to Wesel, on the Rhine, for they were now prisoners of the King of Prussia. Here La Fayette passed three months, seeing nobody but his servant who waited on him at table, the officer on guard who was forbidden to answer any questions, and the soldiers outside the window who watched him day and night. The cell swarmed with rats and vermin. Under the severe confinement La Fayette fell ill, so ill that La Tour-Maubourg asked permission to hear his last wishes, but the request was denied. Any change in his régime was also refused. But one day the commandant came in with a letter from the King of Prussia, who proposed a betterment in La Fayette's treatment, provided that for the benefit of their common cause, he would give information about the French plans. La Fayette remarked that the King was very impertinent to mix his name with any such proposals.

From Wesel he was removed to Magdebourg on the Elbe. At Magdebourg he was locked in an underground cell, five and a half paces long by three paces broad, entered through four doors in sequence, bolted and barred, and furnished with one small grated window, through which light came but no sunshine. The cell had been dug beside the rampart of the citadel, and its vault and the wall next the moat were damp and moldy; outside it was defended by all sorts of "walls, ramparts, ditches, and soldiers." He was allowed no paper, ink, pen or pencil, nor to receive letters. Books in French, English and Latin were permitted but not until all the blank pages had been torn out. By a miracle, as he said, he managed to get a piece of paper, vinegar mixed with soot for ink, and a toothpick for a pen. Much later, when at last he was allowed to write, it was merely to say that he was well, for if he said that he was ill or employed the word liberty, the letter would be returned for correction, once, twice, or three times, if the officials thought necessary.

La Fayette's valet was allowed to pass through the four doors and enter his cell in the morning, but his secretary, Félix Pontonnier, a lad of sixteen, was locked up in a separate cell, and there was no communication between La Fayette and his three friends. For eight months he had no news of his family, and then, at least so he thought, only in consequence of the interposition of Mr. Pinckney, the American Minister at Hamburg. But he learned of the French victories at Valmy and Jemappes, of the King's death, and subsequently some gazettes were admitted. The reason for this severity toward La Fayette was communicated to him indirectly a year later. It appeared that at a conference held to decide upon his fate it was stated, that "Monsieur de La Fayette is not only the promoter of the French revolution but of world-wide liberty . . . the existence of Monsieur de La Fayette is inconsistent with the safety of the governments of Europe."

The health of the prisoners was at first bad; Alexandre Lameth nearly died and Pusy and La Tour-Maubourg were very ill. La Fayette himself was miserable. But after months, when the doctor informed the authorities that Lameth would die without better conditions, the captives were allowed an hour, each by himself, under guard, to walk in a little garden. The United States sent ten thousand florins to provide for La Fayette's necessities, so he was not reduced to the bread and water of prison fare. His one resource was to write surreptitiously a very occasional letter;

he does not say, for fear of being discovered, how he smuggled these letters out. There is one that I have already quoted in part, to a Mr. d'Archenholtz, editor of a paper at Hamburg, who had published some references to La Fayette, which displays the pleasant naïveté and Latin unself-consciousness, as well as a touch of picturesque emphasis, that add a childlike charm to La Fayette's character:

"Ah! Monsieur, how grateful I am to you for your sympathy with my inexpressible grief, when my soul is on fire for the cause of humanity, and greedy for glory, and cherishes my country, my family, my friends. Alas! after sixteen years of work, fate has torn from me the happiness of fighting for all the principles and sentiments for which I have lived. But what was there left for me to try? . . . You can imagine, Sir, what pains this coalition has made us suffer; but what are such sufferings compared to those that an unjust people have thrust into my unenslaved soul? Here the triple tyranny of power, despotic, aristocratic, superstitious, takes its vengeance; but the monster is wounded to death. All the ingenuities of inquisition and prison cell are exercised upon us, but these cruelties do us honor. And whether we are reserved to adorn a triumph, or whether they prefer to poison us gradually by the unhealthiness of our underground cells, by depriving us of air, by not letting us walk out, and by every moral torment,—I hope that compassion and indignation over our fate, will be so many seeds that will raise up defenders for liberty. It is for those future defenders, Sir, that in the sincerity of my heart, I bequeath to you this consoling truth, that there is more joy in a single service ren-

dered to the cause of humanity, than the wrath of
all its enemies, than even the ingratitude of the people,
can cause of pain."

But what for us, an inarticulate race, hedged about
with shyness and traditions of restraint, is hard to
understand, is that he was saying exactly what he
felt. His letters to Madame d'Hénin have the same
quality:

"I admit it, my dear Princess, I am given over to
the most violent of passions—Liberty, that had my first
prayers, that has so tossed all my life, is here the
perpetual subject of my solitary meditation. It is
what one of our friends calls my holy madness; and
whether a miracle shall deliver me from this place, or
whether I mount the scaffold, *Liberty Equality* will be
my first and last words! . . . 'My manners,' you say,
'irritate the powers.' . . . Rather than be silent before crime, rather than connive at injustice, I that had
no royalist superstition, I whom the Court continually
betrayed, I, democrat to excess perhaps, I pushed
aside, I do not speak of offers that meant nothing to
me, but the immense perspective of glory, worked for
during sixteen years, of which I felt sure. I abandoned
family, friends, country, and the one possession that I
prided myself on, my popularity. And yet should I
not have had excuses—the defense of the country, the
wish to stop the evil—and above all, should I not have
had success, after attaining which all except my conscience would have absolved me? And now dead to
the world, responsible only for myself, after having
denounced popular tyranny with horror in my soul,
shall I light-heartedly make up to the tyranny of kings?

No, my dear Princess, when I disdained the rôle of a great usurper, in order that I might remain faithful to liberty and to duty, I acquired the right, for the rest of my life (which my present régime is shortening) to continue not to flatter men or vices that I hate."

So, for five years—hated by the kings of Europe, hated by the Jacobins, who toppled down his bust, the gift of the state of Virginia, from its pedestal in the Hôtel de Ville, who broke by the hands of the executioner the medal cast in his honor, who proposed to raze his house to the ground and erect a column there to commemorate what they called his crimes, who covered him with opprobrious names, coward, hypocrite, charlatan, and confiscated his property,—so, for five years, the man, who had done more for the good of his fellow men than all but very few, who had tasted and had valued *la délicieuse sensation du sourire de la multitude*, dragged out his life in a cell fit only for the basest criminal. His places of imprisonment were changed, but the captivity was much the same. From Magdebourg, in January, 1794, after a sojourn there of nearly a year, he was taken to another underground prison in Neisse, in Silesia, close to the Austrian frontier. His friend, La Tour-Maubourg, had been transferred to a prison at Glatz, where he was joined by his sister, Madame de Maisonneuve. La Fayette, without a touch of envy, was delighted that his friend had the comfort of his sister's company. He writes to her:

"They shall not prevent me, at least, from enjoying the happiness that you and he will have at seeing one another again, and if I were not a little embarrassed by the barricades of the jail, by my three sentinels by day and my five by night, by my great guard and my little guard, by the fortifications over my head and all round me, you should see me most speedily with you, to share a society so acceptable to my heart. . . . I do not write to Monsieur de Maubourg to-day in order not to multiply labors of inspection, translation and copying, for little as you would suspect the liking they have in this country for my writings, I must tell you that this little letter before arriving at Glatz will have already reached its third or fourth edition."

At Neisse the keepers were more polite than at Magdebourg, and he was allowed to learn that his wife was safe in a house belonging to her at Brioude, the little town near Chavaniac. He dared not write direct to her for fear that his letters would be opened in France, and so had to depend upon his friends to give her indirect news of him. Meanwhile the Revolution had been galloping on in Paris. The new Convention met in September, 1792, and abolished the monarchy; then, cleft into two warring factions, the Gironde and the *Montagne,* it began the internecine battle that ended in the destruction of the Gironde. The King was put to death in January, 1793, and in February the Convention declared that the *République Française* was at war with King George III and with the Stadtholder of Holland, affecting to believe that while kings were its enemies, all peoples were its friends. But democracy did not find the path smooth before it. There were reverses at the front, bringing forth cries of treachery. La Vendée blazed out in counter-revolution. In Paris prices rose, causing louder cries of treachery. Dumouriez was caught playing false and declared *hors la loi.* By the end of May the *Montagne* had given the *coup de grâce* to the Gironde, and the harvest of dragon's teeth, fallen on rich ground, sprouted up an hundredfold. Marat rose to the zenith, to die in his bath, and Charlotte Corday suffered the penalty, bidding her father not to grieve, *"la cause était si belle."* Terror leaped to its feet. William Pitt was pronounced *"l'ennemi du genre humain."* The revolutionary tribunal burned with a red glow, while Fouquier-Tinville, the public prosecutor, fed the furnace. Marie Antoinette mounted the scaffold, then the Girondins, Brissot, Vergniaud, Madame Roland and their associates, and after them Danton, Camille Desmoulins and so on. The master spirits of the storm, Robespierre, Couthon, Saint Just, ranted and raged.

CHAPTER XXIX

CHAVANIAC is far from Paris, and for a time Madame de La Fayette's life was suffered to run on calmly. In the morning she would take her children out for a walk, and sitting beside a brook, their faces toward the mountains, read aloud to them. But the ferreting out of aristocrats was not long delayed. November 12, 1793, the local authorities came to search the house for papers *entachés de féodalité*—(with feudal stains). They carried off what sealed documents, grants, warrants, concessions and so forth they could find, together with busts of the King, or Mirabeau, to make a bonfire for patriots to dance around; but at Chavaniac the people would have nothing to do with such merriment, so the dancing patriots had to go on to Aurat. That evening a commissioner, on his rounds empounding all the *ci-devant aristocrates* (former aristocrats), said that next day Madame de La Fayette must go to Brioude a few miles away.

At Brioude she found herself in company with the aristocratic ladies of the neighborhood, who, having had nothing to do with her since the breaking out of the Revolution, were at first very uncivil. In fact society in the house of detention was divided into groups that cordially detested one another, but Madame de La Fayette was a saintly lady as well as a

329

member of a very aristocratic family and the wife of a very distinguished man, and the ladies, though quarreling among themselves, soon professed respect and liking for her. Even the Jacobins behaved with greater consideration to her than to the others, except on occasion when she ventured to beg a favor for a sick lady, "that drew down on her insults impossible to repeat." She continued to keep in close relation with her children, who were left at Chavaniac with the aunt, too old to be worth arresting. Sometimes by ingenious methods she contrived to see them, one by one, at night; sometimes the laundry list, pinned to the clean clothes that came once a week, contained a few words on the back. But dolorous news came from Paris, Madame de La Fayette's mother, the Duchesse d'Ayen, her grandmother, la Maréchale de Noailles, and her sister, the Vicomtesse de Noailles, had been placed under arrest, although permitted to remain in their house, l'Hôtel de Noailles. Then came a notice that La Fayette's confiscated property was to be sold and Madame de La Fayette asked leave to be present at the sale. A devoted friend, Monsieur Frestel, carried her petition to the official at le Puy; this person greeted him with a flood of insults against La Fayette, whose bowels, he was pleased to say, he would like to tear out, and against Madame de La Fayette, "the personification of the pride of the Noailles," and against their children, "vipers that the Republic nourished at its breast." The petition was not granted.

Clouds continued to gather. In April, 1794, news came that the three ladies in Paris had been transferred from the Hôtel de Noailles to the Luxembourg; this was followed on May twenty-eighth by an order

that Madame de La Fayette should be transported
from the house of detention at Brioude to the prison
of la Force in Paris. The good Monsieur Frestel obtained for her the respite of a day. This she employed
in confessing to the non-juring priest, imprisoned
overhead, and in a parting interview with her children.
They said their prayers together and recited *Veni,
Sancte Spiritus.* Anastasie, the eldest daughter, now
sixteen years old, was beside herself with a passion of
grief, and persuaded her mother to let her follow her
to Paris. But official permission was also necessary.
For this she went to le Puy. While she pleaded with
all her heart, the official, Citoyen Guyardin, continued
writing at his desk, refused to read the letter that
Madame de La Fayette had written to him, and denied
the request with very coarse jokes. The poor girl returned in a state of violent rage and despair, crushed
at the thought of being separated from her mother.
Madame de La Fayette then was taken to Paris, followed by good Monsieur Frestel, who went to beg for
help from their very kind friend, Gouverneur Morris.
It was the nineteenth of Prairial (June eighth) a week
after the decree of arrest against the Girondins. The
work of salvation, as French historians say, was proceeding. "France was saved . . . because a small
group of resolute men, in days of danger and
emergency, imposed their authority by terrible
means." So, this resolute little group proceeded "to
the disarmament, arrest and condemnation of all
suspects." There were sixty victims a day. Madame
de La Fayette was taken to la Petite Force; her former
femme de chambre went there every other day, then
wrote what news there was to her children. Monsieur
de Saron, her uncle by marriage, had been executed on

Easter day and *"on avait commencé d'immoler des femmes."* Her mother, from the prison in the Luxembourg contrived to send her counsels of prudence. After a fortnight she was transferred to Plessis, the old school which La Fayette had attended as a boy, now turned into a prison; there she found a cousin, la Duchesse de Duras. On June twenty-seventh, Maréchal de Mouchy, father-in-law of her sister, Louise de Noailles, and his wife were guillotined. Part of the evidence against them was that a *ci-devant Christ* had been found in his room. The Maréchal said: "At seventeen I mounted the breach for my King; at seventy-seven I mount the scaffold for my God; my friends, I am not unhappy." Their daughter was in the prison with Madame de La Fayette, who was charged to give her the news. Every morning twenty prisoners were taken from Plessis to the Conciergerie to receive sentence of death. "The thought that one will soon be of the number," she wrote, "makes one stronger for such a sight." She composed a little testament, half farewell: "I forgive my enemies, if I have any, with all my heart, whoever they are, even those that persecute the man I love. I pray God to lavish good things upon them, and to forgive them as I forgive them."

But much went on of which mercifully she did not hear. On the twenty-first of July, 1794, *les citoyennes Noailles, la ci-devant Maréchale de Noailles, la Duchesse d'Ayen, la Vicomtesse de Noailles,* the last a charming lady of thirty-five who looked but twenty-four, were taken to the Conciergerie.

Lasciate ogni speranza voi ch'entrate.
(Leave hope behind, all ye that enter here!)

They had been despoiled at the Luxembourg, and because they did not have more than forty-five francs left, the turnkeys refused to give them beds. At nine o'clock the next morning the attendants came and conducted them before the revolutionary Tribunal. It was raining hard, with thunder and lightning. The trial was brief. They drove across the Pont-au-change, up the rue Saint-Antoine, the Maréchale in the first tumbril, the Duchesse d'Ayen and her daughter in the second. A devoted priest hurried along on foot by the tumbrils, as best he could, pushing his way through the crowd, trying to catch their attention. He missed a chance here, then there; at last they saw him. The storm grew more furious, but the populace shouted insults the louder. The tumbrils reached the square that opens out just before you come to the Faubourg Saint-Antoine. The priest turned toward them. Madame de Noailles saw him. He lifted his cap, raised his hand, pronounced the formula of absolution and the succeeding words of the service very distinctly. The storm, having as it seemed, served its purpose of screening this pious act, died down. The tumbrils reached the Place du Trône. There, in the midst of an amused and laughing crowd, la Vicomtesse de Noailles, as she stepped down from the cart, fixed on the priest "those looks so full of animation, so sweet, so expressive, so heavenly"; and the grandmother, the daughter-in-law and her daughter each in turn laid her head upon the block. "How abundantly and with how deep a red the blood flowed from her head and neck." Six days later, on the tenth Thermidor (July twenty-eighth) Robespierre's head fell under the guillotine.

Robespierre's death stopped the murders and relaxed the severity of imprisonment. Madame de La Fayette was allowed to write to the Luxembourg prison to ask for news of her mother, grandmother and sister. She never expected to be comforted again. She had a Latin copy of the psalms which she had heard so often in church that she could read them: "In them," she wrote to her children, "I sometimes find the sentiments of those for whom I weep, sometimes the sentiments that I desire for you, and also those that I ask God to implant in my heart, and sometimes have received." The other prisoners were discharged, but one of the committee in power held back Madame de La Fayette's release. James Monroe, at that time our minister to France, did what he could but in vain. After another winter of imprisonment she was discharged on January 22, 1795.

In the meantime La Fayette had been taken from Neisse, handed back to the Austrians and lodged in the prison at Olmütz, in the western part of Moravia, not very far from the field of Austerlitz (May, 1794). There the jailers took from the prisoners what the Prussians had left, their watches and buckles, taking leave of each with this information: They should see nothing but the four walls; they should have no news of anything, or of anybody; there names had been suppressed and they were to be designated by numbers; they should receive no assurances concerning their families or concerning one another; and, to prevent danger of suicide, they should have no knives or forks. La Fayette remarked that he was not going to be so accommodating as to put an end to himself.

Once safely locked in, La Fayette turned his thoughts upon the question of how he could get out. He wrote to his friends that there were three possible means of securing his liberation: (1) An aroused and indignant public opinion; (2) The instance of eminent friends; (3) Escape. As to the first he admitted difficulties: The people of Austria and Prussia might be slow to stir in favor of a soldier but lately in arms against them; the people of England might not be unmindful that he had contributed in no little measure to cut the bonds between them and their revolted colonies; the United States were far away; in France the Jacobins had taught the people to hate him; and Spain hardly possessed a public opinion. On the whole this plan seemed impracticable. Of course, it was visionary, but the naïveté in La Fayette's character, added to his lover-like passion for liberty, that as in the case of other lovers blinded him to the fact that others did not share his passion, appears here in its childlike and charming simplicity. He had an intense hatred of despotism and oppression, scarcely greater now that he was a sufferer from them than before, and believed it was a common human passion. Otherwise he could hardly have entertained the thought of an outraged popular opinion forcing the Emperor of Austria to liberate him. Besides, it might be asked, did the fact that La Fayette and his friends tore off their epaulets on crossing the border wholly deprive the governments which they had just been fighting of the right to treat them as prisoners?

The second method had been tried and failed. George Washington and various eminent Americans had done what they could. Charles James Fox, Sheridan and others, including, to his honor, General Tarleton, raised the question in the House of Commons, but the government of England sided with the governments of Prussia and Austria. Madame de La Fayette begged and entreated; the Emperor said that it was the King of Prussia that was obdurate, the King said it was the Emperor.

The third method was the most satisfactory to La Fayette; and now, by one of the friends that La Fayette's character and conduct had raised up to him in foreign lands, it was to be tried. A young German doctor from Hanover, Erich Bollmann, on taking his degree in 1791, had gone to Paris where he attended lectures at one of the hospitals, and incidentally conceived a great admiration for La Fayette. He had wandered about the scenes of slaughter on the night of August tenth, and was out of sympathy with the Jacobins. Somehow his adventurous disposition brought him into relation with persons of distinction. At the request of Madame de Staël he contrived to get the Comte de Narbonne, ex-Minister of War, safely out of Paris to England. News of the exploit passed about among the French refugees in London, and Lally Tollendal asked him to carry a petition to Berlin in behalf of La Fayette. This was while La Fayette was in Magdebourg. No answer was granted to the petition, and La Fayette disappeared. Bollmann, who had found a congenial task, set out to find where he had been taken to. He went as "a traveler in pursuit of knowledge," searched through Saxony and Silesia, and discovered that La Fayette had been handed over by Prussia to Austria, and that Austrian soldiers had escorted him from the border in the direction of Olmütz. Bollmann affected interest in mining lead, and established himself near Tarnowitz in Silesia, not far across the border from Olmütz, but being a physician he made visits to the hospital at Olmütz, and got into friendly relations with the chief surgeon there. Bollmann turned the conversation between them on the effects of mind upon the body, and maintaining the affirmative he suggested that the surgeon should make the experiment on La Fayette, in the state prison, by showing him a pamphlet that Bollmann produced, and telling him that all the people named in it were well and as much attached to him as ever, and that this news came from a traveler just back from London, and that the surgeon would find a greater beneficial effect from this good news than from any medicine.

The surgeon, who could not read French, took the pamphlet and gave it to La Fayette. Bollmann, also, by the doctor, an unwitting intermediary, sent a letter written on a scrap of paper in lemon juice with a few innocent visible words ending with, "When you have read this note, put it in the fire." La Fayette took the hint, held the paper to the fire, and from this time on they corresponded, writing on the margins of pamphlets and books in lemon juice. The first letter said that Bollmann was working for his rescue, and would send him a file to cut the bars. La Fayette answered that the authorities now permitted him, on account of his feeble health, to drive out every other day in the afternoon, that he could be distinguished by his plain frock coat and round hat, while his keeper wore a corporal's uniform. Here is one of La Fayette's letters written in his rusty English:

"Olmütz—19 October 1798

"It is impracticable, my dear friend, now to enter into the particulars of my situation, which however I will do against the time the shaking doctor can come back, provided you persuade him to give me your answer, and to smuggle another book to me. Let me only say that the usual means of evasion have been so well provided against that nothing is left for us but the uncommon ones. It is true that if the lieutenant or the corporal provost were to fetch me the evening in the general's name, I think I could get out. . . . The scheme could not fail unless we were betrayed.

"Which to avoid, I have a plan equally easy; you may depend on an undoubted success. The lieutenant is an old slavish hardened fool, the corporal a more sensible covetous, but most cowardly rogue. He may be bribed; but his cowardice is such that he may prefer a little reward and no danger, to a fortune with some risk. It is a thousand times better to go off in spite of him when we ride together.

"We are in a phaeton; nobody with me but the corporal, who, by the by, is afflicted with a rupture, and a clumsy driver who sometimes, as to-day, is left at home, and then the corporal drives the phaeton. We go different roads, sometimes through bye-roads, and do not always return the same way we came. But we always go a half German mile (one league), and sometimes a whole mile (two leagues) from town. But suppose it is half a mile; you can overtake us on horseback, as we generally drive slowly. Have a trusty man with you. Stop the driver. I engage to work to frighten the little cowardly corporal with his own sword, that I will not have the least difficulty to jump on a led horse of your man who can ride to some distance behind me. If the driver is not there, so much the better; if he is, he will do nothing but save himself.

"Depend upon it, my dear Sir, (as you may choose your time and place, and have one or two sets of

horses on the road) that nobody will think, dare, or
wish, to hinder us, and before the slow German general
knows what we did or what to do, we shall be safe.
My friends, La Tour-Maubourg. and Pusy, think it
beyond doubt. It is for this that I have asked to ride,
and they have not asked it for themselves, in order
that I may go out every other day. The bolder it
seems, the more unexpected it is, the better it shall
succeed; and we may say with the poet that

> Presence of mind and courage in distress
> Are more than armies to procure success.

Take care not to mistake Beurnonville or Bancal for
me. They ride on the day I do not, the one at 1½, the
other at 4. I wish you may have pocket-pistols for
me when I am on horseback. Till then I want them
not, and the corporal's own sword will be more than
sufficient. I ardently hope for a farewell answer, my
dear friend, and will be ready every day for the execution.

"I am going to owe you a thousand times more
than life—but do not miss this excellent opportunity.
Every other way has dangers. This is certainly *im-
manquable*. Adieu, my dear friend."

Bollmann, in order to provide for details of the
plot, went to Vienna, where he met young Huger, son
to that American Major Huger who had taken La
Fayette into his house on the coast of South Carolina
seventeen years before. Young Huger had gone to
Vienna to study surgery, but was delighted to help.
They bought saddle horses with money provided by
Lally Tollendal and his friends, and returned to

Olmütz. Bollmann told his friend, the doctor, that they were going back to England and should start on November eighth, a day that they knew was one of La Fayette's days for driving. He sent a groom to a town named Hoff, twenty-five miles away and bade him have fresh horses ready at four o'clock in the afternoon, as they wished to cross the Prussian border the same night. At two o'clock, the hour of La Fayette's drive, their horses were saddled and Huger went to watch for the carriage; when he saw it driving slowly he ran back to their inn. The carriage drove out into open fields some two or three miles, then stopped, and La Fayette and the keeper got out and walked arm-in-arm. The coachman with the soldier at the back of the carriage drove on to a tavern, where La Fayette and the corporal were to overtake them. The two rescuers galloped up, Bollmann dismounted, La Fayette seized the keeper's sword. A scuffle followed; La Fayette sprained his back and the keeper bit one of his fingers. Bollmann laid hands on the keeper, too, and the three fell. Bollmann held the keeper down while La Fayette mounted one of the horses. Bollmann shouted: "Go to Hoff." La Fayette understood "Go off," and galloped off. The second horse balked at the double load, reared and threw both riders. Bollmann was hurt; Huger said: "The Marquis needs you, push on, I'll take my chance on foot." Bollmann galloped off in pursuit of La Fayette, taking the road to Hoff. At Hoff he found the carriage but no La Fayette. Thinking it better to try to attract pursuit to himself, he got in and drove off and at midnight crossed the border into Prussia. Huger ran till he fell from exhaustion; he was then picked up by peasants and handed over to the author-

La Fayette shortly before his death

From *France and New England*. Photograph by Giraudon, Paris

Napoleon Crossing the Alps

From the painting by David (Versailles)

ities. La Fayette had taken the wrong fork of the road. Troubled as to what was happening to his rescuers he turned back, found that he was pursued, turned again and galloped on. His clothes were foul with blood and mud, so when, after riding twenty miles, he reached a village and offered money for a fresh horse, he was suspected, arrested and in due course taken back to the prison.

Bollmann also was arrested in Prussia and handed over to Austria; he and Huger were kept in prison for eight months. La Fayette, whether or not in consequence of his physical efforts on the day of his attempted escape, became very ill, even the keepers admitted that he was in a dangerous condition, but he was left without assistance, even without a candle, that is without possibility of help all night long, for the keys were carried to the other end of the city. He had but two shirts and was unable to change after his night sweats; and the surgeon, who came to dress his finger, was hurried away by the officer in charge, and hardly allowed to say a word. The keepers were very rude. He had no news of his wife and children, nor of his friends, and he felt great anxiety over the fate of Bollmann and Huger, who, he was told, were to be hanged in front of his window. Maubourg said that La Fayette was almost dying from this cruel uncertainty.

Maubourg, however, was at last allowed to receive letters, and hearing that Madame de La Fayette was alive, he asked the commandant to tell La Fayette. The commandant replied: "That is expressly forbidden." And thereafter any letters for Maubourg, in which she was mentioned, were not delivered. But he gave his friends a hint to speak of her by another name. Then Félix, the young secretary, invented an ingenious method of conveying information by the lilt and notes of popular airs, whistling, or playing them on a little pipe. In this way he got news from Maubourg's servant and passed it on to La Fayette. But the range of this information was narrow.

CHAPTER XXX

The saintly Madame de La Fayette was let go from prison on the 2 Pluviose (22 January), 1795. Her feelings were terribly tense and her purpose clear. She went at once to the kind James Monroe, thanked him for what he had done and endeavored to do, and asked him to help her get a passport. Her one thought was to join her husband. She saw her boy, George, then fourteen, for the first time after the perils they had gone through: "I feel," she said, "consolation so deep, so far beyond all my hopes, that I feel it more strongly perhaps than any other that I may hereafter hope for." Then she sent him with an American gentleman, a Mr. Russell of Boston, to Havre where he went aboard a small ship. The good Monsieur Frestel, in order not to awake suspicion, sailed separately. George Washington Lafayette on landing was received with kindness, and plans were made for his education. Having bidden good-by to her son, Madame de La Fayette set out for Auvergne; her two girls met her at the village of Veyre near Clermont-Ferrand. "You will understand the intoxication of our joy." The next day they went to a hamlet in the mountains, for revolutionary dangers were not yet past, to hear mass. And, continuing her journey, she met her sister at Brioude, Madame de Grammont, with

343

her husband, who, too poor to take a private chaise, too prudent to ride by public coach, had traveled on foot from Franche-Comté to Paris to see Madame de La Fayette, and missing her there had continued on foot to Auvergne.

After Madame de La Fayette had seen her family, she set her face toward Olmütz. But there was a delay in preparations. The revolutionary Jacobins had stirred the proletariat to riots in Paris and it was uncertain whether they, or the party that had won on the ninth of Thermidor, would finally triumph. But the red radicals were beaten; and, as a definite sign of this, the buildings at Rue Saint-Honoré formerly occupied by the Jacobin Club were pulled down to make place for a market, which still stands there to-day. At last a passport was got, and Madame de La Fayette and her two daughters left Dunkirk for Hamburg. There they met *émigrés* eager for news of France. Madame de La Fayette's daughter says: "The behaviour of the *émigrés* toward my father might well have inspired my mother with bitterness; but there was never a trace of resentment in her. It was marvelous to love with an exaltation so great, and never, under any circumstances, feel the shadow of bitterness against those that had slandered and persecuted the object of all her affection." From Hamburg, they went by the help of an American passport, under the name of Madame Motier, resident of Hartford, Connecticut (for La Fayette had received the gift of citizenship there), which Mr. Parish the United States Consul secured for them, as no French citizens were allowed to enter Austria.

At length they reached Vienna. There Madame de La Fayette had an interview with the Emperor, of

whom she asked permission to share her husband's
captivity. "That I grant," he answered; "as to his
liberty, that I can not give, my hands are tied." Then
she spoke of the vexations that had been practised in
the Prussian dungeons, and asked, if in case she
wished to make any request, she might apply direct
to him. He answered: "I consent. But you will find
Monsieur de La Fayette well taken care of, well
treated. I hope that you will do me justice. Your
presence will be one more comfort. Besides you will
like the Commandant." She took leave of the Emperor *dans l'ivresse de la joie.* The Minister, Monsieur
de Thugut, whom she saw afterwards, was cold; every
sentence revealed a hatred of La Fayette that he was
unable or careless to conceal. Still some red tape, and
then on the twenty-ninth of September, 1795, they left
Vienna. I will quote the daughter's narrative:

"We arrived at Olmütz the next day but one, at
eleven o'clock in the morning, in one of those open
carriages that one finds at all post houses, for ours had
broken down. I shall always remember the moment
when the postillion pointed out to us the far-away
steeples. My mother's emotion is still visible before
me. For some time she was suffocated by sobs, but
when she could speak, she blessed God in the words
of the canticle of Tobias: 'Blessed be God that liveth
forever, and blessed be his Kingdom. For he doth
scourge and hath mercy: he leadeth down to hell and
bringeth up again: neither is there any that can avoid
his hand; confess him before the gentiles, ye children
of Israel.'

"We got out at the house of the commandant of
the city. We did not see him. He sent the officer who

was charged with keeping the prison, to conduct us. After we had gone through the first gate we passed down long corridors to two padlocked doors that opened into my father's room. 'I don't know,' my mother said the night before, 'how I can support what we are going to feel.'

"My father had not been notified of our coming. He had been given no letter at all from my mother. Three years of imprisonment, the last passed in complete solitude (for since his attempt at escape he had not seen his servant), anxiety for all he loved, sufferings of all kinds, had deeply affected his health. The change in his looks was frightening. My mother was hard hit by it; but nothing could diminish the delirium of her joy except the bitterness of her irreparable losses. My father, after the first happiness of reunion, did not dare to ask any questions. He knew of the reign of terror in France, but he did not know the names of the victims. The day passed without his daring to question her concerning his fears or her being able to muster strength to tell him. Only in the evening, after my sister and I had been shut into the next room, not connected, did she tell my father that she had lost on the scaffold, her grandmother, her mother and her sister.

"You know the details of prison life at Olmütz. My mother shared its hardship. All communication with M. de Maubourg and M. de Pusy was forbidden. We were not allowed to hear mass, though it was said in a church that adjoined the building in which we were. We had no communication with the outside. The doors were opened when food was brought. We were refused the services of a charwoman. When we arrived they asked for our purses and took the three forks that were in our bundles. They refused to give others, and we always ate with our fingers. My mother made some requests that she thought proper; they were all refused.

"My mother was greatly pained to be unable to mitigate the lot of our friends in captivity. But as for her, I can't describe her happiness. You will get some idea, if you will remember the love that had animated her life since she was fourteen. She had always suffered by frequent separations and the incessant business that took my father from the house, or by the great dangers to which he was exposed. The last three horrible years she had passed almost without the hope of seeing him again. Now she had the happiness that, all her life, had been the object of her prayers. Every day she saw how her presence benefitted my father's health, and all the comfort she brought to him. She was amazed to recover the faculty of being happy and reproached herself with being content with her situation, while my father was a prisoner. She was refused permission to write to her son, for they did not wish any news concerning the prison to reach the United States. But she learned by my Aunt Montagu that George was with General Washington.

"The deprivation of religious worship was very painful to her; but she felt that God had guided her to the prison. . . . She joined herself in spiritual communion, with all the ardor of her faith and the vigor of her love, to those already in possession of heavenly rewards. She put herself in their presence; she lived in her memories of them and decided to gather those memories together for us. She wrote the life of my grandmother with a toothpick and a few drops of Chinese ink on the margins of the illustrations in a volume of Buffon. . . .''

She was ill and on La Fayette's insistence she asked permission to visit Vienna to consult a physician there. This was refused except upon the condition that if she left the prison she should not go back. This condition she declined to accept.

"My mother's illness made rapid headway. The doctor saw her for a moment during the officer's visit. He could not talk to her as he did not know French, but he expressed his anxiety to my father in Latin. She had a violent eruption, first on her arms that swelled so much that she could not use them nor even lift them, then on her legs; and fever all the time. This condition lasted eleven months, from October, 1796, to September, 1797. During these eleven months of illness, there was no relaxation of prison conditions. She had no armchair. But her sufferings did not alter her serenity one whit. As we saw her always equable, always enjoying the happiness she had got back, and the comfort she had brought, we were all less anxious than we should have been. . . .

"My sister made up by her work for the lack of service from outside; she even made shoes for my father; but her principal occupation was to write, at my father's dictation, on the margins of a book. My mother occupied herself with teaching me, she read with me; but the margins of a book, toothpicks and the scrap of Chinese ink, were too precious for me to use. In the evenings, my father used to read something delightful. I still recall all the pleasure of it.

"A few months after our arrival at Olmütz, some

patriotic Germans succeeded, in spite of difficulties
and dangers, in getting into relations with my father.
One of them, the Rector of the University of Olmütz,
is entitled to our deep gratitude. He got some news
to us; and arranged a secret correspondence which
allowed my mother to write letters that a friend
carried across the Austrian frontier, and to get
answers that were not subjected to the inspection of
the keepers. And inside the prison we had effected
relations with our companions in captivity. Already
before our arrival, my father's secretary had communicated with them through the window by the aid
of a Pan's pipe for which he had contrived a cipher
known to M. de Maubourg's servant. But this means,
which was used for a long time, did not permit exten-
sive communications. We procured better through
the help of soldiers whom we bribed by a good meal.
At night, through the double bars, we lowered part
of our supper by a cord to the sentinel on guard under
our windows, who in the same fashion transmitted a
packet, which had been fastened to the food, to M. M.
de Maubourg et de Pusy, who were locked up separately in the same prison.

"M. le Marquis de Chastelar, an Austrian general,
was sent to Olmütz by the Emperor in the month of
July, 1797, on a mission from the Emperor to offer the
prisoners their liberty, on condition that they would
bind themselves never to enter his dominions."

[I interpose here a paragraph from La Fayette's
Memoirs.] General Chastelar said very plainly to M.
de La Fayette "that he was regarded in Europe as the
chief of the new doctrine, and that as the principles
he professed were incompatible with the tranquillity

of the Austrian monarchy, his Majesty the Emperor, for reasons of state, was obliged to refuse him liberty until he had promised not to enter upon Austrian soil, without express permission from the Emperor." To this notification La Fayette responded, a little haughtily, that he had no desire to set foot in the Emperor's Court, or in his country, even upon urgent invitation, nevertheless his duty to his country prevented him from binding himself not to obey her possible commands (July 25, 1797). The other two prisoners made the same answer; they would agree "saving the rights of my country over my person." This restriction [I now return to the daughter's narrative] shut the gates of their prison.

"My mother prized this worthy behavior highly. In spite of all her sufferings, she would have bought most delightedly, at the price of many months of captivity, the satisfaction that she got from my father's answer to the demand of the Austrian government."

The Marquis of Chastelar had not gone to Olmütz from any of the motives that La Fayette and La Tour-Maubourg imagined, but under impulse from a new power, not any eminent lover of liberal government, a new power that spoke with a voice of authority, for it could speak with cannon.

The war originally waged to defend French soil from foreign invaders had altered during La Fayette's captivity. The French had been victorious and had overrun the territory on the left bank of the Rhine, and Belgium and also Holland (1794), and they were fighting now to force Austria to consent to various changes in the map of Europe. Peace had been agreed upon with Prussia, the princes of North Germany, and Spain (1795); but Austria kept the field. The Directory, a body of five that formed the executive under the new Constitution, appointed General Bonaparte to the command of the army that was to invade Italy. Bonaparte issued his famous proclamation: "Soldiers, you are naked and ill fed; I will lead you into the most fertile plains in the world, etc." He pushed the little Kingdom of Sardinia out of his way, descended into Lombardy, crossed the River Adda at Lodi (May 11, 1796), drove the Austrians headlong, entered Milan (May 15, 1796), fought various battles, compelled the surrender of the fortress of Mantua (January, 1797), and advanced into Austria toward Vienna. He crossed mountain range after mountain range, and had reached Leoben, two-thirds of the distance from Venice to Vienna, when Austria acceded to his proposals for preliminaries of peace (April 18, 1797).

By this time there was a reaction in public opinion in Paris in favor of La Fayette. His most violent enemies had been guillotined or silenced, and men remembered that he was one of the first advocates of liberty, and had organized the National Guards, who, as General FitzPatrick said in the House of Commons, "gave to France the power to maintain her independence and establish a government of her choice against the efforts of confederate Europe." His friends, too, took up the matter of his release. Talleyrand, Benjamin Constant, went to Barras, one of the directors, (whom La Fayette nevertheless describes as possessing a mixture of pseudo airs of a grand seigneur, behavior suitable to the Reign of Terror and scandalous morals), to ask for his help. Madame de Staël also wrote to

him: "Dear Barras, you are not made of ice, you have
a soul of Provence . . . we must give La Fayette
back to France, back to the Republic." Barras, thus
solicited, wrote to Bonaparte. And Carnot, also a
director, wrote to General Clarke, whom the Directory
had associated as plenipotentiary with Bonaparte.
"Obtain, if you can, the liberty of La Fayette,
Bureaux-Pusy and La Tour-Maubourg. The national
honor is concerned with the deliverance from the
prison, in which they are confined solely because they
began the Revolution" (May 5, 1797). The two chambers of the new legislature, the Council of Elders and
the Council of Five Hundred, supported the Directory.
In obedience to these requests the plenipotentiaries
asked for the prisoners' release, but they met more
objections, hindrances and subterfuges on this demand
than on any other. The Directory stood firm, and enjoined upon Bonaparte to insist that the terms of
agreement should include the liberation of the three
captives:

"Paris August 1st 1797

"Citoyen Général,

"In consequence of fresh appeals made to the
Directory with regard to the prisoners of Olmütz, the
Directory reminds you of its wish (that it has already
expressed to you) to see their captivity end as soon as
possible. It feels sure that you share the interest that
it takes in their unfortunate situation.

"The President of the Executive Directory
"CARNOT."

The Citoyen Général had ideas of his own concerning
the future that might lie before him. "In our days,"
he had already said, "no one has conceived anything

great; it falls to me to give the example.'' The Directory might direct, but he would do as he pleased. He did not wish to disobey them openly, and he probably thought that he would gain popularity by procuring La Fayette's release; but he did not propose to put a man, whose popularity and potential influence could not easily be estimated, whose loyalty to liberty was absolute, in a position to thwart his personal ambitions. He and his associate Clarke, *ministres plénipotentiares de la République française* sent the following note to the Austrian plenipotentiaries:

''The undersigned, ministers plenipotentiary of the French Republic, have the honor to inform the Marquis de Gallo, minister plenipotentiary of his Majesty the Emperor, of the interest which the Executive Directory of the Republic takes in the fate of the prisoners at Olmütz, La Fayette, La Tour-Maubourg and Bureaux-Pusy.

''They have already had the honor of talking to him on that subject at Leoben, and after the request which they make to-day in the name of their Government, they hope that the Marquis de Gallo will be kind enough to use his good offices with His Majesty so that the prisoners may be set at liberty and be allowed to go to America or anywhere else, *without however being allowed for the present to go to France.*''

This restriction, La Fayette always believed, was written in by Bonaparte himself. Others say that the Directory was responsible for it. Gouverneur Morris believed that the Emperor had granted La Fayette's release in consequence of American solicitation, and indeed the Emperor accepted that convenient excuse, but I think that there can be but little doubt that Napoleon was the *causa causans*. At any rate, the prison doors opened at last on condition that La Fayette should go direct to Hamburg. The rest of the story I let his daughter tell:

"We left for Hamburg on September 19th, 1797. It was five years and one month since my father's arrest and twenty-three months since we joined him. The prisoners were accompanied by an Austrian major till they arrived at Hamburg, who usually drove in a carriage ahead. . . . Our road, particularly at Dresden, Leipsic, Halle, and Hamburg, was one continual triumph. Throngs gathered to see my father and his companions. The prisoners, who at first could not bear outdoors, grew stronger every day, but my mother's health prevented any real joy. The fatigue of the journey was too great in her state of exhaustion and illness; nevertheless, she made efforts to take part in the general joy and to respond to the numerous marks of respect shown to her."

On reaching Hamburg La Fayette was welcomed like a conqueror. Gouverneur Morris and John Parish were there to meet him. Parish says, "An immense crowd of people announced their arrival. The streets were lined, and my house was soon filled with them. A lane was formed to let the prisoners pass to my room. La Fayette led the way and was followed by his infirm lady and two daughters. He flew into my arms, his wife and daughters clung to me. A silence— an expressive silence, took place. It was broken by the exclamations of 'My friend! My dearest friend, my deliverer! See the work of your generosity! My poor,

poor wife hardly able to support herself!' And indeed
she was not standing, but hanging on my arm imbued
with tears, while her two lovely girls had hold of each
other. The scene was extremely affecting and I was
very much agitated. Again the Marquis came to my
arms, his heart overflowing with gratitude. I never
saw a man in such complete ecstasy of body and mind.
He is a very handsome man, in the prime of life, and
seemed to have suffered but little from his
confinement.''

CHAPTER XXXI

EXILE

THE first matter in hand was to write letters of thanks. He wrote to Talleyrand, Minister of Foreign Affairs, to Barras, recommending for permission to return to France the little group of officers who had accompanied him across the border, and, to Bonaparte whose victories for France had given him the liveliest joy:

"October 6, 1797

"Citoyen Général,

"The prisoners of Olmütz are happy to owe their deliverance to the good will of their country and to your irresistible arms. They rejoiced in captivity to think that their liberty and lives were bound up with the triumphs of the Republic and with your personal glory. They rejoice now in rendering grateful homage to their liberator. It would have been a pleasure to offer in person the expression of their gratitude, to see the theatre of so many victories, the army that won them, and the hero that has added our resurrection to the number of his marvellous achievements. But you know that the journey to Hamburg was not left to our choice. . . .

"In the lonely retreat, on Danish soil in Holstein, where we are going to try to restore health to those lives that you have saved, we shall mingle with our patriotic wishes for the Republic, the most vivid inter-

est in the illustrious general to whom we are attached
more because of the services that he has rendered to
the cause of liberty and to our country than for the
personal obligations that we are proud to owe to him,
or than for the very lively gratitude forever imprinted
on our hearts.

"*Salut et respect.*

"LA FAYETTE, LA TOUR-MAUBOURG, BUREAUX DE PUSY"

At Hamburg La Fayette saw a good many Americans and various other persons who warmly welcomed
him. Kind letters also came. He was most touched
by one from Madame de Staël, Necker's daughter,
written when she heard that he was likely to be set
free.

"June 20, 1797

"I hope that this letter will reach you. I should
like to be one of the first to tell you all the indignation,
sorrow, hope, fear, anxiety and discouragement over
your fate that has filled the soul of one who loves you.
I do not know that it is possible to render your cruel
memories endurable. However I venture to say to
you that while calumny has undone all reputations
(while factions, unable to triumph over our cause, have
turned upon man after man), your misfortune has
preserved your glory, and if your health can be restored, you issue forth undiminished from that
sepulchre where your name has gained new lustre.

"Come straight to France! There can be no other
country for you. You will find there the republic
that your judgment approved when your conscience
bound you to the monarchy. You will find her glorified
by victory and delivered from the crimes that sullied
her beginning. You will uphold her; because only

through a republic can liberty exist in France, and because you, both as hero and as martyr, are so united to liberty that I use indifferently your name or hers to express what I desire for the honor and prosperity of France.

"Come to France! You will find there friends devoted to you, and let me hope that my constant concern for you and my vain efforts to serve you give me some claim to a little interest from you."

It was all very well for Madame de Staël to urge La Fayette to come directly to France. She did not know of Bonaparte's opposition; and now a new obstacle presented itself, the eighteenth Fructidor (September 4, 1797). La Fayette's constancy and simplicity show themselves once again in capital letters. The incident is so characteristic, that I must recount it. In the government many of the deputies and two directors favored the royalist cause, and had organized, so it was said, a vast conspiracy with the intention of overthrowing the republic. It is unnecessary to go into the facts, to determine how far this party was prepared to violate the existing Constitution. The majority of the directors, Barras and two others, and their adherents did not wait to find out. They came to an understanding with Bonaparte, who sent General Augereau to help them; and with the aid of Augereau's troops they arrested the alleged conspirators, purged the legislature, and deported fifty deputies or more. As soon as La Fayette heard of this violent and high-handed act, he at once denounced it with his usual vigor, and rightly enough (as it seems to us), for it opened the door to Bonaparte's military dictatorship. La Fayette expounded his horror to the French Minister at Hamburg; he said that the eighteenth Fructidor was as bad as the tenth of August, 1792, and that he entertained a high regard for the good citizens who on both these occasions had become martyrs to their ideals. He could hardly have closed the door into France more effectually. His own brief comment is: "The Directory was displeased. They sold what little property I had left in Brittany." In his *Souvenirs en sortant de prison* he was still of the same mind. He describes what happened and says: "That was the crime of the 18 Fructidor. The next day the victorious party crowned its outrages. The proscribed deputies, the Director Barthélemy and other personal enemies, after being shut up in cages, subjected to cruel and insulting treatment, were sent to perish in the pestilential deserts of Guiana. A crowd of priests and other victims of their infamous vengeance and tyrannical fear, were also deported thither in successive batches. Such was the political situation, in which we had to take a position."

La Fayette was not worldly-wise. Had he approved the eighteenth Fructidor he might well have had again high political position. Maréchal Lefebvre, better known to us as the husband of Madame Sans-Gêne, said afterwards: "If La Fayette had listened to our advice he could have been in the Emperor's place." He simply shut the door in his own face. A friend, who had worked for his deliverance, said: "They write me from Paris that our friend has flung down his gauntlet against the eighteenth Fructidor, which means that he has issued a decree of ostracism against himself. I told Talleyrand who thinks as I do, that such a lack of discretion can't but ruin everything." It is to such judgments as that of Talleyrand that La Fayette refers when, years afterwards, he makes this general reflection: "I observe that men, who during the Revolution were stopped by scruples, who although they had influence obtained neither power nor money, inspire certain people with a sentiment of contempt that to me seems humorous." Talleyrand, for his part, spoke of La Fayette as a "ninny"; Talleyrand, who at a later period was also irritated by Lord Castlereagh's integrity, and who when in office told the American envoys that if they wished to do business with the French Government they must first pay him twelve hundred thousand livres.

La Fayette might, indeed, have prudently withheld his judgment as to the rights and wrongs of the eighteenth Fructidor, he might have pleaded ignorance due to his captivity. That was not his way. His position as to the sacred right of rebellion, and the sacred duty to obey the established Constitution, may seem illogical, and his stickling for legality when a nation was still heaving in the throes of a great convulsion may have been quixotic, but it can not be said that he was illogical in his own interest or quixotic to secure honors or safety for himself.

After a few days at Hamburg, La Fayette and his family moved to Wittmold, a little place in Holstein near Ploën. America was out of the question on account of Madame de La Fayette's ill health. They stayed with their beloved aunt, Madame de Tessé, who owned a farm on a tongue of land running out into Lake Ploën. She is said to have been a delightful person, with her bright eyes and her expressive lips which a slight nervous trick twisted a little as she spoke, only to add to the *esprit* that marked her conversation. She was a great talker, and kept the ball of conversation rolling. Madame de Montagu, Madame

de La Fayette's sister who was somewhat of an aristocrat, was there. Later the lovely Comtesse de Simiane,
who had escaped from France by means of a false
passport, came also to stay at Madame de Tessé's.
Madame de Staël had already made one attempt to
rescue her, but she had refused to leave her brother.
As for La Fayette, he had not changed, keeping that
simplicity of behavior that his wife speaks of on his
retirement from public life in 1791. Madame de Montagu writing to another sister, Madame de Grammont,
says: "Gilbert is just as good, just as simple in his
behavior, just as affectionate in his loving ways, as
you have always known him. He loves his children
tenderly, and in spite of his cold exterior is very sweet
to his wife. His manners are gracious, with a phlegmatic bearing that does not deceive me, and with a
secret desire to be in a position to take part in things.
I avoid as much as possible talking to him on anything
that concerns the Revolution, both as to what he up-
holds and what he condemns. I am afraid to burst
out, and I am afraid to hurt his feelings. I am glad
to see that my reserve is approved by the others. To
be patient and to evade are my rules for behavior
toward him. Poor Gilbert! May God keep him from
going back on the stage!" And again: "He is so little
changed that one turns young in listening to him. He
takes one straight back to the rights of man and the
dawn of the Revolution. What followed was only an
accident, deplorable of course, but not more discourag-
ing (in his opinion) than a tale of shipwreck to stout
mariners. *Son aveuglement et sa frénésie morale
pour la liberté sont une croix pour moi.*" He was all
ready, as Madame de Montagu said, to reembark on the
ill-jointed raft of 1791, and risk his fortune, and that
of others, in the enterprise.

A little later the La Fayettes and the La Tour-Maubourgs took a good-sized château at Lhemkulen near by (November 17, 1797), where Madame de Maisonneuve, La Tour-Maubourg's sister, lived with them. There La Fayette meditated and discoursed upon the events in France during his imprisonment, and upon his own part in the preceding revolution, the *via media* that he had chosen, that "funambulatory track and narrow path of goodness" which took its straight and self-consistent way between the privilege of the old régime on the one hand and the lawlessness of the revolutionary Jacobins on the other. He says in a letter to Washington: "I have served the cause of the friends of liberty in Europe. Imbued with your teachings, my dear General, and with those of your friends, during three years on the great stormy stage of the French Revolution, I proclaimed and upheld, with some boldness and not without public approval, the principles for which you fought with so much glory and led us with so much success." But he could see that by pursuing the *via media* he pleased neither party, royalist or republican. "The consequence must be," he says, "that, unless there should be some very great occasion to serve liberty and my country after my own fashion, my political life is over. For my friends I shall be full of life, but for the public a sort of museum piece, or a book of reference. As for liberty, I find motives in all this to love it more; but as almost all hearts are too cabined and confined, too timid, too apathetic for the complete development of truth, liberty and justice, my reason tells me that there will never be anything more for me to do, and that even for my reputation's sake I should terminate my political life."

CHAPTER XXXII

UNCERTAINTY

Here in Holstein, La Fayette busied himself with literary labors upon past politics. His son George came back from America, where General Washington and Alexander Hamilton had been very kind to him. Charles La Tour-Maubourg, younger brother to La Fayette's old friend, fell in love with Anastasie. Neither had a penny. Madame de Tessé said that there had been no such marriage since Adam's to Eve. But poor Madame de La Fayette was in very bad health, in consequence of her sufferings in prison. She had to be carried to the wedding. "In spite of her sufferings (I quote her daughter again) she enjoyed deep happiness. 'When I think,' she said, 'of the horrible situation that my children were in a little while ago, and that now all three are with me, and that I am about to acquire a fourth child, after my own heart, I am unable to render due thanks to God.'"

Disregarding her ill-health she was obliged to go to France to look after the remnants of her husband's fortune and the settlement of her mother's estate. Her daughter Virginie went with her. While in Paris they tried in vain to persuade the president of the directors, Lerevellière, to let La Fayette return to France. This gentleman wrote in his memoirs a sentimental account of her visit. I think that he is certainly incorrect as to the number of children that were with her on that occasion. She was alone with Virginie. He says: "Madame de La Fayette, this woman who has become immortal by her most generous devotion and her most beautiful example of conjugal piety, did me the honor to come to my house with her three children, George La Fayette and the two young ladies. I never felt a deeper emotion than at the sight of this interesting family. Beside the memory of their misfortunes, a feeling of admiration rose within me, and to my eyes my study became a temple, in which I saw the highest virtue surrounded by the most touching objects, most worthy to share with her the love and respect of good people." The law, however, was clear, forbidding emigrants to return, and nothing could be done.

La Fayette's life runs on now quietly enough. He moved to Holland; but the future was uncertain, there might well be an invasion of Holland. England was an enemy, America was nearly at war with France over privateering. He really longed to go back to his native land. He often repeats his old wish, derived perhaps from the example of the peerless Washington, to lead a tranquil life upon a farm among his own people: "Those who know my opinions and my wishes," he says, "may be very sure that the services that I should like to render to my country would be of a nature to conform to the mode of life that suits my position, my wife, my family and myself, that is to say, a tranquil and philosophical establishment on a good farm far enough from the capital not to be importuned in my solitude, and not to see anybody but my intimate friends. . . . I believe that I can be more useful by my opinions and my example in a retreat than by a more active part."

But France was closed to him. He was worried about money, and also very anxious about his wife's health. Before she joined him at Olmütz he wrote to a friend: "The conduct of my wife in every respect increases still more, if that be possible, my love, gratitude and veneration for her." And again: "I am waiting impatiently for a letter from my wife. . . . Tell her that I am alive, that I pity her with all my soul, that I think all the time of her misfortunes, of what she is feeling and of my inexpressible, eternal love." And now when she is away in France, he writes to her, giving her household news: "To-day is the anniversary of our arrival at Wittmold; Pauline [Madame de Montagu] came back for our dinner, and the day was celebrated without forgetting the absent. With what a joyous spirit I shall celebrate the day that shall bring you back to me. I need to see you, my dear Adrienne, I feel more than ever how necessary you are to me. Farewell, dear heart; what you say of your health gives me great pleasure, but do not forget that though you are better, you are not cured. Say over to yourself my recommendations without ceasing, and tell yourself, too, every minute that I am very happy because of you and that I love you a thousand times more than I can express."

Madame de La Fayette rejoined him in February, 1799. Two of her sisters, both much younger than she, were there, too. Madame de Montagu wrote: "Adrienne's faith, zeal and uprightness are admirable. She is a model. I am more impressed than ever by her good sense and her knowledge. *Elle écoute d'une manière ravissante.* (She listens in an enchanting manner.)" But within a few months she was obliged to go back to France upon business connected with La

Fayette's debts and with the succession of her mother's estate. In the division of this property she received the farm of La Grange, situated in the department of Seine-et-Marne, near Rozoy, about forty miles from Paris. There were eight hundred acres of land and a château, once a baronial castle with much of its ancient character still left, it stood three stories high, and had circular towers capped by conical roofs. La Fayette was very much interested.

[TO MADAME DE LA FAYETTE]

"May 29, 1799

"You will write me, won't you, full details about La Grange. First, as to the house, with answers to all our ideas as to how we shall settle ourselves; and then of the farm. I should like to know how many animals they have there, big and little, how much it all costs, how many hands they need to take care of them. Then a word about the park and the wood. Liancourt has lent me some books by Arthur Young; I am deeper than ever in the study of agriculture. . . . It seems to me that La Grange offers the possibility of a retired spot in the lap of French liberty."

But so long as the proscription against La Fayette remained in force, La Grange could be but a pleasing dream. Madame de La Fayette made occasion while in Paris (May 20, 1799) to see Sieyès, now a member of the Directory, and ask him what would happen if La Fayette came back. Sieyès said it would be too dangerous, that they could not disregard the law. Sieyès did not wish his own plans to be disturbed by any factor of such uncertain potential energy as La

Fayette, and his own policy was difficult to decide upon. On August tenth he was to make a speech in honor of the triumph of the republic, *"Je vous salue, jour de justice et de gloire!"* and on November ninth (eighteenth Brumaire) to help overthrow the Constitution.

La Fayette, finding no hope of entering France, turned his thoughts to America. He writes (August 5, 1799) to his wife:

"Since yesterday George and I have been arranging for a farm, either in the beautiful Shenandoah Valley in the further part of Virginia, not far from the Federal City [Washington] nor from Mount Vernon, or in the beautiful fields of New England, within reach of the city of Boston, for which you know my predilection. I do not disguise from myself, dear Adrienne, (since I am sorry over the serfs in Holstein as sad companions for a friend of liberty) that I shall find negro slaves in the Valley of the Shenandoah. . . . It is true, that with our experience at Cayenne we can get some comfort; still I should prefer New England. Nevertheless I appreciate all the reasons that should place us near Mount Vernon and the seat of the Federal Union. But we still need the first dollars toward buying our farm."

These speculations as to some safe abode were not idle imaginings. France, whether under the impetus of her first rush to defend herself from foreign tyrants and to spread the blessings of liberty, or from the consequences of personal ambitions, was now at odds with almost all Europe. She had incorporated Mulhause, also Geneva; she had forced Switzerland to

compliance; Belgium had been ceded to her; Holland
had been turned into the Batavian Republic, with the
privilege of paying for a French garrison of twenty-
five thousand men; the Kingdom of Naples had been
brought to book; the Pope had been turned out of
Rome; England was an enemy; and the United States
on the verge of becoming such. La Fayette, in Holland, was already unwelcome to the French army of
occupation, but what if the armies of Austria and
Russia should come in? It really seemed as if France,
even a French prison, might be safer than elsewhere;
although Sieyès had hinted at something worse than
prison. He was growing impatient, and turned over
many possible plans. In a very long disquisition to
La Tour-Maubourg he says: "The first means of success is to *dare,* and seeing that everybody is afraid of
compromising themselves, I have offered to arrive unexpectedly in Paris, (putting the men in power under
the alternative of taking action or of murdering me),
to ride on horseback with Beurnonville and Lefebvre,
proclaim liberty in the capital and consequently in
France, on behalf of all and against all. I was told
that I should lose my life and accomplish nothing."
La Fayette while still writing a long discourse to La
Tour-Maubourg—"this volume scribbled faster than
one talks"—suddenly adds (October 18, 1799):

"Here is great news, Bonaparte's arrival. . . .
You remember that his first words in Italy were that
I could not come back to France. But he has said
that he hoped to make my acquaintance . . . and
Madame Bonaparte said to George that it was necessary that her *husband and I should make common
cause.* Again, however, though Bonaparte spoke very

obligingly of me at Paris in talking to Louis
Romeuf . . . he finished by saying definitely that
'our political opinions were too divergent for him ever
to believe that I could be allowed to come back.' . . .
Bonaparte thinks only of his own ambition, and as yet
he has not put his glory to the service of liberty, perhaps he will do so now. . . . The time is very
favorable for him. He will not risk any personal advantage for liberty; he has shown that his soul could
look on calmly while it was violated, and even cooperate, nevertheless, if his glory and his ambition require
him to step forth for the good cause, he will do it. His
wish ought to be to establish the republic on a solid
base of freedom and justice. Perhaps he would like
to be president for life; I should like that arrangement
very much; it would be an interesting experiment.''

His wife, who was in Paris pulling what strings she
could, and consulting the political horoscope daily, to
further his deliverance, became troubled by his evident
desire to take some part in the restoration of his beloved freedom. He writes to comfort and reassure
her:

"Vianen, 30 October 1799
". . . As for me, dear Adrienne, whom you are
frightened to see so ready to return to a public career,
I assure you that I am no longer susceptible to many
pleasures which I used to rate too high. I am more
alienated than ever, invincibly so, from the idea of
taking permanent part in public affairs, I should only
join in for a shoulder push, as they say; and nothing,
nothing in the world—I swear to you by my honor, by
my love for you, by the spirits of those for whom we

weep—will persuade me to renounce the plan that I
have formed for retirement, in which we shall pass
quietly the rest of our life. . . . I am in a great
hurry, dear Adrienne, and I can't read over what I
have written you. But I must repeat, once more, that
I am completely happy and satisfied with what you do,
with all you say, and still more with all that you are. I
read in your heart, my dearly beloved Adrienne, and
none of its good, tender, generous throbs, escape me;
I am inexpressibly impatient to see you again, here,
or there, and to secure at last the blessed moment when
we shall part no more."

CHAPTER XXXIII

DEATH OF MADAME DE LA FAYETTE

A FEW days later, on the eighteenth Brumaire (November 9, 1799), Bonaparte, protesting that he restored the principles of eighty-nine, executed his *coup d'état*. He turned out the Directory, and became First Consul. Madame de La Fayette, who was in Paris, saw that her husband's chance had come. She sent him a passport under a false name. In two hours' time he was on the road. Arrived in Paris, he wrote at once to Bonaparte and Sieyès. Bonaparte was angry; Talleyrand said that violent measures were likely, and urged La Fayette to go back. La Fayette answered that his friends must not compromise themselves, but that, "as he had judged it suitable to return to France, it was now for Consul Bonaparte to judge whether it was suitable for him to remain there unmolested, that they ought to know him sufficiently well to know that this imperious and threatening tone was enough to make him hold firm to his first decision." And walking away with a friend he said: "It would be a humorous thing if I were to be arrested by the National Guard of Paris and put in the Temple by the restorer of the principles of eighty-nine."

The next day Madame de La Fayette went to see Bonaparte. He said: "I am enchanted to make your acquaintance, Madame, *vous avez beaucoup d'esprit;*

371

but you don't understand political affairs." He said that La Fayette's presence would hinder his progress toward the reestablishment of La Fayette's principles and would oblige him to clew tight. "You don't understand me, Madame, but General La Fayette will, and as he is no longer in the center of things, he will realize that I can judge better than he. I conjure him to avoid any *éclat;* I rely upon his patriotism." She answered that that had always been her husband's intention; and Bonaparte left her very politely to go to the council, where, it was said, he arrived in very bad temper. But before long, Bonaparte, feeling himself secure, spoke warmly of him: "There is no man in the world so hated by the enemies of liberty and of France; I, who negotiated for his release, know very well the price foreign powers set on his detention." And when La Fayette was presented to him, he said: "I don't know what the devil you did to them, but they were very loth to let you go." And afterward, for La Fayette went several times to see Bonaparte in the interest of various banished friends, he would revert to the same topic: "I am well hated, and others, too, by these princes and their suites, but, bah! All that is nothing compared to their hatred of you. I was near enough to see it, and I could not have believed that human hatred could go so far."

The relations between them became quite friendly, Bonaparte would admit him to interviews of two or three hours, and they talked *"avec une liberté mutuelle"* tête-à-tête. In one of these Bonaparte learned that George La Fayette was in the outposts of the army of Italy. "Diable!" he cried, "an only son!" And when he was told that George had received two wounds, he said in a most friendly fashion: "Good!

that's an admirable beginning for a young man; I rejoice with you." La Fayette also attended Madame Bonaparte's receptions, where one night he saw Moreau as well as Bonaparte and other heroes. "Your salon," he said, "is like a volume of Plutarch."

Nevertheless, La Fayette would not accept any post under the government. He preferred to live quietly in the country. He refused to become Ambassador to the United States because "he was too much of an American to act there as a foreigner"; he also refused to accept a seat in the Senate "because," as he laughingly told Talleyrand, the Minister of War, "the very next day he would be obliged to denounce both the administration and its chief." Bonaparte inquired indirectly as to La Fayette's attitude toward himself, saying: "No man likes to pass for a tyrant, and General La Fayette seems to designate me as such." "I answered," La Fayette says, "that my silent retreat was the maximum of my deference; that if Bonaparte had wished to serve liberty, I should have been devoted to him; but that I could not approve of an arbitrary government, nor associate myself with it." He never veiled his opinions from Bonaparte; and one gets the idea that Bonaparte at bottom respected and liked him for it. One day Bonaparte taxed him good-humoredly with having criticized to Lord Cornwallis, who had come to Paris as British plenipotentiary, the present arbitrary government of France. La Fayette replied that he did not think he had done so, not to an Englishman, but that if he had been asked whether the present régime meant liberty, he would have said no. Bonaparte then said seriously that he did not like to have La Fayette give to the enemies of the government the support of his name. "What more can I do," La

Fayette asked, "than live in the country in retirement? But whenever I am asked if your régime corresponds with my notion of liberty, I shall say no." And yet, in another place, he records how Bonaparte once said to him: "You may disapprove the government, you may think me a despot; but men will see, you shall one day see, whether I am working for myself or for posterity." And La Fayette adds: "His sentiments were so nobly expressed, he spoke so well of the glory of France, that I grasped his hand to show the pleasure he gave me." Even La Fayette's old enemies, the royalists, approved of his conduct toward Napoleon. Madame de La Tour du Pin says: "His character was gentle to the point of foolishness, but he was not weak, as his conduct under the Empire clearly proved. He resisted all Napoleon's advances, offers and cajolings."

The star of Napoleon rose with "new spangled or" and blazed in the zenith. He infused into the centralized government his own energy and enterprise, and bestowed upon France such prosperity as she had never known. The First Consul was the State. He issued the *Code Civile* that has made the tour of the world. He entered into a concordat with Pope Pius VII which brought the non-juring priests to his side, gave him appointment of bishops, and threw a halo of piety over his rule. He allowed the *émigrés* to return, and gilded his official state with the polite luster of the old régime. He organized, imposing unification and centralization, his system of education throughout France. He founded the Legion of Honor. In 1804 he assumed the imperial crown. At home he called out all the abilities; and abroad, whether from the fatal entanglements of circumstance, or the irrepressible conflict between a revolutionary and bully-

ing France and the old régime of reactionary
Europe, he fought from Cadiz to Moscow. He crushed
the Austrians at Austerlitz (1805); he overthrew
Prussia at Jéna (1806) and at Auerstadt; he defeated the Russians at Friedland (1807). But his
indomitable enemy, Great Britain, held the sea,
dominium maris, and like a great sea serpent wound
her toils round her terrestrial adversary. The tide of
fortune turned. Wellington drove the French from
Spain; the winter's snow drove Napoleon from Russia. Then followed Leipsig (1813) and the allied
invasion of France; and the vast imperial edifice came
tumbling down. On April 6, 1814, the Emperor abdi-
cated and was exiled to Elba

During these tumultuous times La Fayette lived
in retirement at La Grange; his family consisted of his
wife, his married daughter, Anastasie, his younger
daughter Virginie, afterward Madame de Lasteyrie,
George and his wife, and several grandchildren. La
Fayette occupied himself with his farm, with merino
sheep, Devonshire cattle, Maryland pigs, orchards,
fields of grain, and in writing to his old friends. As
time went on his admiration for Napoleon's talents,
and for the benefits that he had conferred upon
France, paled before his indignation at Napoleon's
despotism. He refused to join the Legion of Honor,
and fell into the master's bad graces. George, in spite
of his wounds, in spite of having saved General
Grouchy's life at the battle of Eylau (1807), was denied preferment in the army, and virtually forced to
resign. The only offer of public employment came
from America, where President Jefferson would have
made him governor of the newly acquired territory of
Louisiana, had La Fayette been able to be there.

I have anticipated and must go back to the year 1807. Peace had been made (Tilsit, June, 1807) and George had come home safe. He had married Émilie, daughter of the Comte de Tracy, and Virginie had married Monsieur de Lasteyrie, and all was well except Madame de La Fayette's health. She had never wholly recovered from the privations and illness in the dungeon at Olmütz. But, being a woman of high spirit and great piety, she made light of her ailments and much of her happiness. "It seemed," her daughter Virginie says, "as if God had accomplished all my mother's desires in this world. For me I can not conceive of greater happiness than that I enjoyed from the time of the peace, and the birth of my eldest daughter, till my mother's fatal illness." This illness was sad, for though Madame de La Fayette knew her family, she was often delirious and then talked, like Ophelia, in sentences more touching than in moments of complete sanity. She called Anastasie to ask: "Have you an idea of what a mother's love is? Do you enjoy it as I do? Is there anything sweeter, more intimate or stronger? Do you feel as much as I do the need of loving and of being loved?" And Virginie goes on to say: "God and my father occupied her last moments. What she was to him in the midst of this complete deliverance is inconceivable. The effect that he produced on her, her choice of expressions to describe her love with more abandonment than she had ever shown him, . . . the manner in which she used all this charm to speak to him of God and of religion, all this can not be described." Then she repeated in the midst of her delirium the canticle in the *Book of Tobit* that she had recited on seeing the city of Olmütz. She died at midnight on Christmas Eve, 1807. She said to them: "I wish you the peace of God," and to her husband, "I am all yours."

In January La Fayette wrote a very long letter to his dear old friend La Tour-Maubourg, from which I take these extracts:

"My dear Friend,

"I have not yet written you from the depths of the abyss of sorrow in which I am plunged. . . . During thirty-four years of a union in which her love, her goodness, the loftiness, the delicacy, the generosity of her soul charmed and beautified and honored my life, I felt myself so accustomed to all that she was to me that I did not regard her as apart from my own existence. She was fourteen, I sixteen, when her heart took into its very self all that could interest me.

". . . The day that she received the sacraments, she set great store by my being there. She then fell into a continuous ecstasy, the most extraordinary and the most touching that ever was seen. Imagine, my dear friend, a brain wholly deranged, believing itself in Egypt, in Syria, in the midst of the events of the reign of Athalie . . . confounding almost all ideas that did not concern her heart; in short, continual delirium, and at the same time an unalterable sweetness, and that obligingness that always sought to say something agreeable, that gratitude for the pains taken for her, the fear of tiring others. . . . There was also an elevation of thought, a nicety in her definitions, an accuracy and an elegance of expression that astonished all beholders. . . . But what above all was adorable was the tender love in her heart pouring increasingly on her six children and her sister . . . rejoicing to hear her friends spoken of, and all in the midst of the disorder of an imagination which was never fixed steadily except when by a miracle of sentiment it was turned upon me. It seemed that this impression was too deep to be touched, stronger than her illness, than death itself. . . . 'How happy I have been,' she said. 'What a possession to have been your wife. . . . If you do not find yourself loved enough, find fault with God because He did not give me greater faculty for loving. *Je vous aime,*' she said in the midst of her delirium, '*chrétiennement, mondainement, passionément.*' . . . She congratulated herself on the noble courage, the disinterestedness, the loftiness of soul in her son and her sons-in-law, and said that if there were to be a persecution against Christians, if there were to be martyrs, she counted on me to protect the oppressed. 'It seems to me,' she said, 'as if the world were beginning again unending experiments. When will the world run on two wheels, as you wish?' They humored her mad fancies, and then, recovering herself, she would say: 'What! I, married to the sincerest of men, and shall I not know the truth?' . . . She was only mistaken about me for a moment or two, persuading herself that I had become a fervent Christian. But the thought was very fleeting and accompanied by doubts and questions that showed a wish as much as an illusion. 'Are you not a Christian?' she said to me one day. And, as I did not answer, 'Ah! I know what you are, you are a Fayettiste.' 'You attribute great conceit to me,' I answered, 'but are you not a little of a Fayettiste yourself?' 'Ah yes,' she said, 'with all my soul; I would give my life for that sect.' . . . One day I was speaking to her of her angelic gentleness. 'It is true,' she said, 'God made me gentle. But it is not like your gentleness, I have no pretentions so high.' . . . It is not to boast, dear Friend, that I tell you all this, although it furnishes good cause for pride, but I take sweet comfort to say over to myself with you all that recalls how tender and happy she was. . . . The doctor said, 'I have never seen in the course of a long practise, anything like or anything approaching her adorable character or this strange delirium. No, I have never seen anything to give me an idea that human perfection could go so far.' . . . *Adieu, mon cher ami.*

"LA FAYETTE"

The whole letter is so tender, so intimate, so fraught with the deepest and most precious of sorrow, that one hesitates, though it has long been published in French, and also in English, to unfold it to chance readers.

Her body was buried in the Picpus Cemetery, once a barren field, where the bodies of her sister, mother and grandmother had been thrown into a pit with thirteen hundred others, and transformed by her and her sister into a consecrated burial ground.

CHAPTER XXXIV

THE RESTORATION

IT MIGHT well be thought, and no doubt for a time La Fayette thought so, too, that the great interests of life were past and that he, now fifty years old, would remain superintending the work upon his farm, a mere memory among an alien generation. His persistent refusal to approve the imperial despotism angered Napoleon. How could the man to whom all France bowed down in adulation, ancient royalists and ancient Jacobins jostling one another for his notice, relish such language as this that La Fayette wrote him when he was First Consul, but even then with imperial bees buzzing in his bonnet: "It is impossible that you, General, the first man in a category, for which to seek comparison and find your place one must range through all the centuries,—it is impossible that it is your wish that such a revolution, so many victories, so much bloodshed, so many sorrows, so many miracles, should have, for the world and for you, no other result than arbitrary rule." But in this position La Fayette was alone, at least in protest, and there was nothing for him but retirement. He was not molested, but Napoleon with his own hand twice crossed off George La Fayette's name when the young lieutenant was recommended for a captaincy, and he attempted, so it is said, to implicate La Fayette in one of the conspiracies plotted against him. In 1812 he said: "Everybody in France has come round; all but one single man, and that's La Fayette! He has never budged a hair's breadth. He looks quiet to you; well, I tell you that he is all ready to begin over again."

One may be annoyed, irritated, disappointed, by La Fayette's devotion to his American conception of liberty inseparable from law, one may look upon that conception as a sort of dogmatic cult and believe that if he had had more elasticity of mind, a wider intellectual range, he might have contributed more to molding French polity; but fidelity is fidelity, and his conduct is very rare among men. Madame de Staël admired it. She wrote from Rome: "I shall always have hopes of the human race so long as you are alive. I send you my feeling from the top of the Capitol, and the benedictions of its memories go to you on my voice." And by an unexpected revulsion he was, as we shall see, to come again to be the first man in France.

Let us go back to just before Napoleon's first abdication. La Fayette was in Paris, for his beloved aunt, the kind and quick-witted Madame de Tessé, had died. His dominant feeling was that the enemy was invading France. He offered his services to the National Guard, and agreed to lead a battalion. His son and his son-in-law, Lasteyrie, were already enrolled in it. He thought that now was the opportunity to get rid of Napoleon, and proposed to Marshal Ternaux to compel his abdication, but the proposition was regarded as too audacious. The decision was left to the victorious allies. The Bourbons came back.

La Fayette retired once more to La Grange. While there, after a few months, came the news that Napoleon

had landed in Provence and that "his eagles were flying from steeple to steeple." Louis XVIII fled, and
Napoleon entered the Tuileries. La Fayette in a letter
to Benjamin Constant sums up the conditions on which
he would accept Napoleon: A legislature freely elected
on a wide suffrage, with control over taxes and over
the treasury, making the laws and commanding the
military forces, and debating in public; guarantees of
personal liberty, complete liberty of the press, trial by
jury, and no exceptional tribunal. He did not believe
that Napoleon would accede to these articles; nevertheless, at the particular instance of Joseph Bonaparte,
he went to Paris. Joseph, who had long been friendly,
was anxious to win his support, and said that his name
was first on a proposed list of peers. This honor La
Fayette declined but stood for the legislature, was
elected and became one of the vice-presidents of the
chamber (May 8, 1815).

Nearly a whole generation of men had passed since
La Fayette had been in the thick of political life; most
of the chief factors and almost all the lesser men were
new, and for them he was now little more than a name.
It was a new political world into which he now stepped.
At the opening session of the legislature, he met the
Emperor again, for the first time in twelve years, few
words passed between them, "but as neither would
lower his eyes, each read what the other was thinking." Then followed Waterloo (June eighteenth) and
the Emperor's flight to Paris (June twentieth). He
was reported to have said: "I need complete power, I
must be dictator." At the report, La Fayette became
a boy again. He mounted the tribune: "Now," he
cried, "is the moment for us to rally round the old
tricolor flag, the flag of eighty-nine, of liberty, equal-

La Grange, La Fayette's Library is in the left tower, one flight up

From *France and New England*

Bust of La Fayette at Richmond, Virginia

Executed by Houdon

ity and public order; that is the only flag for us to defend against foreign invasion and domestic usurpation." And he proposed resolutions that declared the Chamber in permanent session and any attempt to dissolve it an act of high treason. Perhaps he hoped that he could not only rid France of Napoleon but also dictate to the Bourbons a free constitution. Excitement was high, and wild dreams may have passed through his head. The ministers and Lucien Bonaparte entered the hall with a message from the Emperor. One of the deputies asked of them whether the country was in a position to resist the enemy, and whether Napoleon was not an insuperable obstacle to negotiations for peace, and then turning to Lucien, cried: "Tell your brother that he can save France by abdicating." Lucien defended the Emperor and said: "Our safety depends on our union, you can not abandon the Emperor to his enemies, without ruining the state, without failing in your oaths and staining the national honor for ever." At this La Fayette jumped up: "What! do you dare accuse us of failing in our duty toward our honor, toward Napoleon! Have you forgotten all we have done for him? Have you forgotten that the bones of our children, of our brothers, bear witness the world over to our faithfulness, in the deserts of Africa, on the borders of the Guadalquiver and the Tagus, on the banks of the Vistula, and in the icy fields of Moscovy? Ten long years three millions of Frenchmen have perished for a man, who now wishes to fight again against Europe. We have done enough for him! Our duty now is to save the country."

Twenty deputies supported him. A committee of five, including La Fayette, was appointed to meet a committee of peers. Napoleon, on being told of their action, had said: "What right has the Chamber to ask me to abdicate? It exceeds its jurisdiction. It is my right, my duty to dissolve it." The road forked, one branch led to a dictatorship, the other to abdication. At the committee meeting La Fayette made a motion to go to the Emperor and tell him that abdication was necessary. But the others refused. The Emperor hesitated. "You could see in him," Benjamin Constant said, "a vague indifference to his future." La Fayette sent word by a minister that, if Napoleon did not abdicate, he would propose his deposal. Needs must; and, as La Fayette bears witness, "he accepted the rôle that necessity imposed upon him in a grand manner." Once more Louis XVIII was restored, the white flag was hoisted over the Tuileries, and Napoleon exiled to St. Helena.

After the tumult and shouting of the Revolution and of Napoleon's prodigious career, the current of French politics looks to us, after a hundred years, somewhat vapid, commonplace and dull. It was not so for contemporaries. Louis XVIII seems to have been reasonable and moderate, but the triumphant reactionaries that surrounded him were too strong to be resisted. Nobody dreamed of restoring the régime that existed before eighty-nine, but short of that the party in power was all for punishment, privilege and ancient ways. One's instinctive belief is that La Fayette's part in the final abdication of Napoleon was merely that of a dramatic supernumerary, brought to the front of the stage by the muse of history for theatrical effect, but Barras, a master politician, looking back at these events, says that La Fayette preserved France from Napoleon's dictatorship, and

Napoleon himself in his will says: "The two unfortunate results of the invasions of France, when she had still so many resources, are to be attributed to the treason of Marmont, Augereau, Talleyrand and La Fayette."

La Fayette went back to his cattle and sheep, his orchards and his crops, and lived for several years in peace with his children and grandchildren. Then again, in 1818, he was elected a deputy. He had not become a mere name, or if a name, one to conjure by; Madame de Staël's daughter, the Duchesse de Broglie, says that his election, "shook all France and nearly shook Europe." For the sovereigns of the Holy Alliance entertained the same opinions of La Fayette that they had held when he was in the prison at Olmütz, and Metternich was keeping his ferret eyes on all possible causes of political discomfort.

Once back in political life La Fayette was as much concerned as ever by the high-handed spirit of reaction. Feeling ran high. In the Chamber taunts and insults were so violent that many thought they presaged civil war. During the heated debates over tyrannical legislation, La Fayette proclaimed that the charter, as the new Constitution was called, was a contract, and that if the Crown violated it, the nation was freed from obedience. He was not an orator, but as a witness says: "There was something noble and imposing in his manners, the accent of the old régime which made a curious contrast with his revolutionary thoughts and words." Again and again he repeated his challenge, again and again he reiterated that "this counter-revolution had given rise to a new order of duties." These were no idle words; he believed that the persistent violation of the charter had

opened the door to "the sacred right of insurrection."
The leading deputies of the left, with him at their
head, met secretly and associated with a society known
as the *charbonnerie,* a name borrowed from the Italian
conspirators, the *carbonari.* Dissatisfaction had
spread all over France, and secret clubs and plots were
thick as blackberries. The plan was for a new
Assemblée constituante to draw up a new constitution,
with La Fayette as provisional president. As the Duc
de Broglie, husband of Madame de Staël's daughter,
says: "He was always ready to engage in any enterprise, on the first summons from a chance passer-by,
like a cavalier of old, who fought for the beauty of
fighting, for the joy in danger, or the wish to gratify
a friend." There was danger enough to give joy to
many cavaliers. This conspiracy was high treason.
Death was round the corner. His friends begged him
to be prudent. "I have lived a long time," he
answered; "it seems to me that to mount the scaffold,
a victim of the cause of liberty, would be a worthy end
to my career." And he did enjoy running into danger
for the goddess he worshiped. It is said that he was
eminently suited for such a rôle: "His bearing of
grand seigneur, dignified and cold, masked a fiery
spirit, the courage of a covenanter, and such complete
freedom from a wish to dominate that he aroused no
jealousy."

The time was ripe. Over ten thousand members, it
is said, were enrolled in the conspiring societies,
picked men, old officers under the Empire, students,
professors, including such men as Victor Cousin, the
philosopher, and Augustin Thierry, the historian.
There were to be risings in various places, especially
in fortresses where the garrison was to be won over,

and then a march on Paris and the overthrow of the government. Only the revolt at Belfort, on the borders of Alsace, concerns us. The night of December twenty-ninth-thirtieth was fixed upon. La Fayette had left Paris and gone to La Grange. December twenty-fourth was the day of his wife's death, and every year he went there to consecrate the anniversary to her memory. The main door of her chamber he had had walled up, but he could enter by a side door which he kept locked. The committee at the head of the conspiracy urged him to hasten to the place agreed upon, but he would not leave until he had passed the sacred day in solemn sorrow and purifying memories. That done, he and George, and an old retainer who insisted upon sharing in the adventure, drove toward Belfort. The ringleaders in the plot were there, dining, and toasting the coming victory. The private soldiers of the garrison, for the most part, and the petty officers were in the secret, but the higher officers, appointed by the Crown, were not. The soldiers in the conspiracy had orders to load their guns and pack their knapsacks with necessaries. One sergeant, who had been away, received the order, but had not been told what it was all about. Seeing that the men of his company were ready to march, he went and reported so to his captain. The captain asked what he meant; the sergeant could not explain. Suspicion was aroused, the gates of the town closed. Two conspirators managed to get out and hurrying off met La Fayette's carriage. He turned his horses on a road that led southward and drove to a friend's house at Gray, as if he were coming on a visit. Some twenty men were arrested.

About the same time other vain attempts at revolt

were made. There were courts-martial and prosecutions; a number of officers were tried and shot. La Fayette stood up in the Chamber of Representatives in the King's presence, and looking straight at the King dared them to try him: "During the course of a career," he said, "wholly devoted to the cause of freedom, I have continually deserved to be a mark for the ill-will of its adversaries, whether they wished to pervert it or attack it, and whether in the interest of despotism, of aristocracy, or of anarchy. I do not complain, therefore, though I might have the right to find the word *proof,* which the King's attorney-general employed with reference to me, as a little over hasty, and I join my friends to demand, as forcibly as we can, the greatest publicity, here in this chamber, in the sight of the whole nation. Then, we shall be able, my accusers and I, *whatever rank they may occupy,* to say to one another, without compliments, those things which for thirty-three long years we have had against one another." The reason of his audacity lay in his knowledge of the King's complicity in the plot of the Marquis de Favras to murder himself and Bailly.

The challenge was not accepted. The government contented itself with defeating him at the next election. But what shall we say of the *via media?* Did not La Fayette, in this instance, suffer the "sacred duty of insurrection" to crowd out too readily and take the wall of the equally sacred duty of obeying the Constitution? There was this distinction, the charter was not a constitution emanating from the people but granted by the sovereign; or it may be that he had the human weakness of thinking that it was for an honorable man like himself, who would act solely in the interest of the public good, to decide when to overthrow a constitution, and not for *canaille* like the Jacobins, self-seekers, miscreants, suborned and bribed by aristocrats and foreign potentates.

CHAPTER XXXV

WE HAVE now reached the year 1824, La Fayette is sixty-six years old. Lady Morgan saw him in 1816. She says that he did not show a wrinkle, that his tall figure was straight and kept all its vigor, except for a limp caused by an old accident to one of his legs, and that with his grace and dignity, with his activity on his farm and his elegance in the drawing-room, you would never have guessed his past career. In 1829 she saw him again, and says that "he was younger, healthier, more on the alert, than ever. His heart-whole cordiality, his affectionate welcome, his animated manner and benignant smile exhibited the same consistency in feeling and in friendship as he had shewn in political principle." Probably he was very much the same at sixty-six. Monsieur de Ségur said to Lady Morgan on her second visit, "La Fayette is the only person in France whose health and opinions are unchangeable. So at least they have been since I remember him arriving from the paternal mansion in Auvergne some sixty years ago." Another visitor, the Duc de Broglie, the husband of Madame de Staël's daughter, reports: "One likes M. de La Fayette for himself, and that is easy enough; but one gains nothing by being a real friend. . . . The only distinction he makes, is between those who repeat to him what he has already said and those that do not. He is a prince surrounded by people who flatter him and despoil him. All his fine fortune has been dissipated in the hands of adventurers and spies.''

I take it that even when one admires a man very much, there is usually something to learn about him from adverse criticism, although we know that La Fayette did not dissipate his fortune on adventurers and spies, but that part went in the causes he advocated, and part was confiscated. He seems to have paid too much heed to persons about him of no great capacity. Broglie says so; Mirabeau said so long before, *"Vous en croyez de petits hommes."* But, the reason that he liked to hear what he had already said, was not because he had said it, but because it agreed with what he thought. A lover is never tired of hearing the praises of what he loves:

To one, of one, still such and ever so.

''I have always loved liberty,'' he said, ''with the enthusiasm of a religious man, with the passion of a lover, and with the con.iction of a geometrician.'' And, it is indeed extraordinary that a man should feel, during all the years from twenty to seventy, that liberty resided in certain definite political forms; but then fidelity of any kind for fifty years is extremely unusual. For this Talleyrand and such considered him a simpleton.

However, I will supplement the Duc de Broglie's opinion by that of his far more distinguished mother-in-law: ''If M. de La Fayette committed errors with regard to the French Revolution they were due to his admiration for American institutions and for the hero-citizen Washington; if he had had the good fortune to be born in the United States, his conduct would have been that of Washington, the same disinterestedness, the same enthusiasm, the same persistency of opinion, characterize both of these generous friends of humanity. If General Washington had been, like the Marquis de La Fayette, head of the National Guard of Paris, perhaps he, too, would not have been able to triumph over circumstances; perhaps he, too, would have come to grief before the difficulty of being faithful to his oath to the King and of also establishing the nation's liberty. . . . M. de La Fayette should be regarded as a true republican. None of the vanities of his class have ever entered his head. Power, that produces so great an effect in France, has had no ascendency over him; the desire to please in a salon has never modified his speech. He has sacrificed all his fortune to his opinions with the most generous indifference. In the prison at Olmütz, as on the pinnacle of renown, he was equally steadfast in his attachment to the same principles. He is a man whose way of looking and of behaving is absolutely direct. Whoever has observed him may be perfectly sure beforehand of what he will do on every occasion. His political outlook is like that of the Americans of the United States, even his face is more English than French. The hatred directed against M. de La Fayette has never embittered his character, his spirit is perfectly serene. Nothing has ever altered his opinions; and his trust in the triumph of liberty is like that of a religious man in an immortal life. Such sentiments, so unlike the selfish calculations of most men who have played a rôle in France, may seem pitiable to sane persons; he is a simpleton, they think, to prefer his country to himself, not to change his party when that party is defeated, to regard the human race, not as cards to be played for his own profit, but as the sacred object of absolute devotion! If it is in that fashion that one incurs the reproach of being a simpleton, would that our clever men would ever incur it! It is a strange phenomenon indeed that a character like that of La Fayette should be developed in the highest rank of French gentlemen; and we can not bring an accusation against him, nor judge him impartially, without recognizing that he is such as I have painted him. . . . Since M. de La Fayette left for America, forty years ago, no man can cite a deed or word of his that has not been on the same straight line, and no personal interest has ever affected his conduct.''

Such he seemed in 1816 to a woman of genius, and such he was, I think, in 1824, when it was his fortune, at the age of sixty-seven to receive an outburst of affection, praise and veneration such as perhaps no nation has ever offered to a stranger in blood. In France La Fayette had critics and enemies, who hated and belittled him; in England the Tory *Quarterly* said that he was a self-complacent coxcomb; in America he was honored as the last of the great heroes of a glorious age. He had often thought of paying a visit to his adopted country, and Washington had urged him to go, but the Revolution, his imprisonment, the poor health of his wife, poverty, politics, had prevented. Now, he was at leisure and Congress gave him a formal invitation:

"It has been resolved, since General La Fayette has expressed an intention of visiting this country, that the President be charged to communicate to him the assurance of the affectionate and grateful attachment which the government and people of the United States preserve for him; and moreover that in testimony of national respect, the President shall hold at his disposition a ship belonging to the state and shall invite the General to take passage on it as soon as he shall have manifested the intention of going to the United States."

The President, Mr. Monroe, accordingly put a frigate at La Fayette's disposition. The frigate La Fayette declined, but he accepted the invitation, and sailed from Havre with his son George. The ship, after a month's voyage, sailed through the narrows, passing Fort La Fayette, and anchored off Staten Island on August 15, 1824, and the next day General La Fayette, attended by beflagged river steamers, made his entry into New York as "the Guest of the Nation." The Battery, Castle Garden, Bowling Green, were crowded with thirty thousand persons gathered to welcome him. La Fayette (it is said) had asked on board ship if he should be able to get a hack to take him to a hotel. It was not necessary. The La Fayette guards, decorated with ribbons, stamped with his portrait and the words, "Welcome La Fayette," led the procession from the Battery to the City Hall; La Fayette followed in a barouche drawn by four white horses. The Mayor delivered an address on behalf of the city:

"In the name of the municipal authorities of this city I come to offer you sincere congratulations at the moment when you arrive in a country which regards you as one of the most honorable and most beloved founders of its liberty and its happiness. Your companions in arms, of whom a few still exist, have not forgotten, their descendants never will forget, the brave young Frenchman, who devoted his youth, his talents, his fortune to their cause, who shed his blood to make them free and happy; they will remember with a profound emotion, as long as they shall be worthy of the good things they enjoy, all you did to procure those good things for them. . . . A half-century has elapsed since those great events, and in that space of time your name has become as inseparably bound to that of liberty, as dear to its friends, on the old continent as it was in the New World."

From New York he drove to Boston, in a four-horse carriage. The coachman called out to one of the horses, "Behave pretty, Charley, behave pretty, you are going to carry the greatest man in the world." Everywhere the people turned out to cheer him, escorts of militia attended the stops, bells were rung, cannon fired, there were rejoicings and junketings. His route lay through Fairfield, New Haven, New London and Providence. When they came to a toll gate and offered to pay, the gate-keeper shouted: "Go ahead, the road is free. General La Fayette travels to-day, and no man shall pay toll." At Boston, the mayor rivaled his brother of New York: "This is no movement of a turbulent multitude, but the transport of a great people who yield to a great moral and intellectual impulse." At Harvard College he was harangued by Edward Everett: "Hail! Friend of our fathers, Welcome to our shores! Enjoy a triumph, not bestowed on conquerors or kings: enjoy the assurance that here, throughout America, there is not one heart that does

not beat for joy and gratitude on hearing your name."
He visited Bunker Hill, and proceeded northward,
through Salem, Ipswich, and Newburyport to Portsmouth.

An affectionate letter from Jefferson overtook him:

"Really I am afraid that they will kill you with
kindness, so many fine receptions I think must bring
fatigue and use up your strength. . . . I see that you
are to visit York-Town, my spirit will be on there with
you; but I am too enfeebled by old age to make the
journey; I do not walk outside of my garden. . . . I
imagine that you will go to Charleston and Savannah.
What place is there that will not ask to take possession
of you? Our village of Charlotteville insists upon receiving you, and would have claimed you as its guest, if
in the neighborhood of Monticello you could be anybody's guest but mine. . . . Come, then, my dear
friend, whenever it is convenient for you; make your
headquarters here. . . . God bless you and keep you;
may He permit me to see you again and to embrace
you!"

From New Hampshire, La Fayette traveled back
through Massachusetts, stopping at Lexington, Wor-
cester, and on to Hartford, and back to New York. All
the way was like the trail of a comet; a line of coaches,
escorts of horsemen, torches by night, bonfires on hill-
tops, speeches, handshakings, cheers. Heinrich Heine
was traveling at this very time in the Harz Mountains
and the miners told him that down in the deep mines
they could hear the Americans crying, "Hurrah!
La Fayette!"

On September fifth, he wrote home: "During a
tour of six hundred miles, we have experienced all that

can flatter or touch the human heart. In the midst of this continuous stream of emotions we experience a great pleasure when the name of La Grange appears on a triumphal arch or in a banquet hall. I am counting on Levasseur [his secretary], and on George, to give you the details of all these fairy scenes. I have found more old soldiers of the Revolution than I had expected, and it has been sweet to see what memories I had left in their hearts. . . . I have the satisfaction of thinking that my presence has effected many reconciliations between the political parties; men, who have not spoken to one another for more than twenty years, have made arrangements together and have invited one another to entertainments in our honor, and revive together common memories of the Revolution. I acquit myself as little badly as possible under the obligations, often unexpected, of answering to discourses in the middle of a multitude of hearers, who luckily are kindly disposed and find my accent hardly perceptible, and my English excellent. It would not be so in the streets of London; but here everything gets by, thanks to kindliness."

"(Sept. 13) I am touched to the quick by marks of affection, and when I see deputations from all points in the United States, from cities and villages come to invite me, after all that traveling, to pass an hour with them, when I see men and women come two hundred miles to shake my hand for a moment, should I not feel ashamed not to write answers to all the addresses, or do no more than barely greet people that come to see me, or to be unable to say whether I shall pass such and such a spot, especially when I am aware of all the expenses and inconveniences they have incurred in order to welcome me? I do the best I can. . . . Everything is enchanting, but I feel that I shall enjoy our beloved family circle more than ever."

He was in great fettle and accepted the welcome with boyish pleasure. He dressed in Nankeen trousers, swansdown waistcoat and a blue broadcloth coat with gilt buttons. One of his formulas was: "Are you married or single?" "Married, Sir." "Ah! Happy fellow!" or, "Single, Sir." "Ah! Lucky Dog!" And he practised his humor, or perhaps was merely reminiscent of Valley Forge: "I like your quail, and your partridge is a very delicate bird, but I can not say that I like your turkey buzzard."

At New York a fête was given him in Castle Garden. The *Evening Post* reported: "We hazard nothing in saying it was the most magnificent fête given under cover in the world. . . . It was a festival that realizes all that we read of in the Persian tales or Arabian Nights, which dazzled the eye and bewildered the imagination."

After a trip up the Hudson, he went to Philadelphia. The inhabitants rose up like one man. Four great coaches, each carrying forty veterans of the Revolutionary War, conducted him under thirty arches, to Independence Hall. There he spoke his thanks: ". . . But these memories and a crowd of others are mingled with deep regret for the loss of those great and good men whom we mourn. It is to their upholding, to your respect for their memory, to the friendship that bound me to them, that I must attribute a great part of the honors that I have received here and elsewhere, honors so much above my personal deserts."

From there he went to Baltimore. At Fort McHenry just outside the town, Washington's old tent had been pitched to receive him. He wrote home:

"Oct. 10, 1824. Here we are at Baltimore; we have been received under the most touching circumstances; we all wept, embracing old comrades under General Washington's tent. . . . The ministers of different denominations paid me a visit: the good Quakers told me that religious scruples had prevented them from signing an address in which military success was referred to. . . . All the pleasures of my journey will not prevent my enjoying, more than ever, that of going back to the farm at La Grange to see my dear daughters and my dear sons. You can guess that at these brilliant fêtes and charming balls, I always regret not to be able to bring my granddaughters to them."

At Baltimore another letter from Jefferson reached him, full of expectations of his coming visit to Monticello: "What a history have we to run over from the evening that yourself, Mounier, Barnave, and other patriots settled, in my house in Paris, the outlines of the constitution you wished! And to trace it through all the disastrous chapters of Robespierre, Barras, Bonaparte, and the Bourbons! These things, however, are for our meeting."

La Fayette then went to Washington, to Mount Vernon to do reverence to the "tomb of the greatest and best of men." On, then, to Yorktown, to Norfolk, Richmond and on to Monticello. "Invitations and deputations continue to arrive from all over this vast continent. . . . They bring to our roadside all the little population that can hold itself up on two feet, while mothers, carrying babies in their arms, walk by the side of white-haired soldiers of the revolution. This has a more serious significance for this sensible people than our fashion of throwing flowers or handing out compliments. Our trip has contributed to

tighten the union between the states and to soften
political parties, by bringing them all together in
common hospitality toward a ghost from the other
world. This hospitality is very great, beyond all that
I could have allowed myself to hope for; there has not
been, over a course of fifteen hundred miles, during
two months and a half, one hour of interruption or of
slackening in the testimonies that have been lavished
upon us.''

Then came the visit to Thomas Jefferson, at that
time eighty-one years old, ''enjoying all the vigor of
mind and soul,'' and after that to James Madison at
Montpellier. Again at Washington, where President
Monroe had made ready to receive him in the White
House; but the city wished him to remain the *Guest of
the People.* On December tenth, the House of Representatives was prepared for the great occasion, the
galleries were crowded: the Senate was present, also
the foreign legations, except the French Minister. La
Fayette was announced and everybody rose to their
feet. Then the Speaker, Henry Clay, made his address.

''. . . Although but few of the members who com-
pose this body shared with you, in the war of the
revolution, all have knowledge from impartial history,
or from faithful tradition, of the perils, the sufferings
and sacrifices which you have voluntarily encountered,
and the signal services in America and in Europe which
you performed for an infant, a distant and alien people,
and all feel and own the very great extent of the
obligations under which you have placed this country.
But the relations in which you have ever stood to the
United States, interesting and important as they have
been, do not constitute the only motive of the respect

and admiration which the House entertains for you. Your consistency of character, your uniform devotion to regulated liberty, in all the vicissitudes of a long and arduous life, also commands its highest admiration. During all the recent convulsions of Europe, amidst, as after, the dispersion of every political storm, the people of the United States have ever beheld you true to your old principles, firm and erect, cheering and animating with your well known voice the votaries of liberty, its faithful and fearless champion ready to shed the last drop of that blood which you so freely and nobly spilled in the same holy cause."

La Fayette rose in reply: ". . . Sir, my obligations to the United States far surpass the services that I was able to render to them. They date from the time when I had the happiness to be adopted by America as one of her young soldiers, like a well beloved son. During near a half-century I have continued to receive constant proofs of their affection and confidence; and at present, Sir, thanks to the precious invitation that I have received from Congress, I find myself welcomed by a succession of touching receptions one hour of which would more than compensate for the labors and sufferings of a whole life.

"The approbation bestowed by the American people and their representatives upon my conduct during the vicissitudes of the European revolution, is the greatest recompense that I could receive. In truth, I can stand firm and erect, when in their name, Mr. President, you solemnly declare that on every occasion I have remained faithful to those principles of liberty, equality and of true social order, to which I consecrated my youth and which till my death will be for me a sacred duty."

Words were not all. A resolution was passed by Congress:

"Article I. The Senate and House of Representatives, in Congress assembled, decree that in consideration of the services and sacrifices of General La Fayette, during the war of the Revolution, the Secretary of the Treasury is hereby authorized to pay him the sum of two hundred thousand dollars, taken from funds which have not been otherwise appropriated:

"Article II. That there is allotted to General La Fayette, for him and his heirs, a township, to be designated by the President out of lands belonging to the United States and not yet granted."

So, on he went upon his triumphant tour through North and South Carolina to New Orleans and up the Mississippi River to Ohio. In Charleston he saw the gallant Huger who had tried to rescue him, and he wished him to accept a portion of Congress' gift: "You shared my prison, now share my wealth," but Huger would not.

All glories end. The leave-takings—with Jefferson, Madison, Monroe and others—were affecting. On December 8, 1825, he sailed for France on the frigate *Brandywine,* so named in honor of the little stream where he fought his first battle and received his honorable wound. The President, John Quincy Adams, made the farewell address: "The old generation is gone," he said, "a second, a third have come to replace them, and their children's children, according as they have advanced in life, have learned from their fathers never to bless the memory of their ancestors without at the same time blessing the name of the man who came from afar to conquer or fall with them."

CHAPTER XXXVI

THE REVOLUTION OF 1830

IN 1828 La Fayette was again sitting in the Chamber of Deputies. Charles X, last of the royal brothers, had succeeded Louis XVIII; he was a convinced believer in the old régime. He disliked intensely the charter which circumscribed his royal authority, and proposed, if he could, to push it out of his way. A moderate Ministry was defeated in the summer session of 1829, and the chamber was prorogued (July thirty-first). La Fayette went on a visit to Chavaniac, where George was then living. The distinguished old man,—he was now nearly seventy-two years old,—his reputation heightened by news of his reception in America, had become a symbol of the ideas of eighty-nine, a rallying point for all liberals, all opponents of the counter-revolution that the King and his counselors were setting their hands to. In his native province he was admired and beloved. He was fêted at Clermont-Ferrand, he was fêted at Issoire and at Brioude. From there to Chavaniac, the distance of a few miles, a cavalcade escorted him; men came from the villages roundabout, from Langeac and Paulhaguet, to swell the procession. After his visit to Chavaniac, he went to le Puy, where he arrived on August eleventh. Here he heard disquieting news. The *Moniteur* announced that the

King had appointed a new ministry, a number of gentlemen, who were, or were popularly believed to be, in favor of absolute rule, with the Prince de Polignac, son of Marie Antoinette's old favorite, at their head. This was hoisting the standard of counter-revolution; and the country seethed with indignation. More than ever La Fayette was become the sign and beacon of liberty. From le Puy, welcomed and saluted all the way, he went to Grenoble; at the gates of the city the townsfolk met him, and the Mayor presented him with a silver coronet interlaced with sprigs of oak. Here, again, was a banquet, and in his answer to the toast, he referred to the political situation:

"Gentlemen: Your excellent young men, your deputations, your entire population almost has come out to meet me, not that these honors were deserved by a private citizen among so many other servants of the people's cause; but because, as you have just said, you wished in the present circumstances to give a solemn manifestation of your perseverance in the sentiments of liberty and equality that we have to defend."

From Grenoble he went, very much as in America, acclaimed and fêted from village to village, and so to Vienne. One hundred and fifty young men on horseback, followed by a great part of the population, came out to escort him. The next day at the frontiers of the department a deputation from the city of Lyons came forth to meet him. There the Mayor made a speech. In his answer La Fayette said: "To-day, Gentlemen, I find myself here among you at a time that I should call critical, if I had not seen everywhere along my route and in this mighty city, the calm, even contemptuous, firmness of a great people that knows its rights, that is conscious of its strength, and will be faithful to its duties." And the following day, September sixth, his birthday was celebrated by an excursion on the river, attended by a multitude of little boats all gay with flags and streamers, ending with the inevitable banquet. Here he again challenged the counter-revolutionary government: "I am proud and happy, Gentlemen, that my passage through this great patriotic city has served as an occasion to manifest its constant hatred of oppression, its love of true liberty, its determination to resist all the efforts of the incorrigible supporters of the counter-revolution." Here cheers interrupted him for several minutes. He continued in the same strain and ended, "The French nation knows its rights, it will know how to defend them." From Lyons, having declined the invitations of other cities, he returned to La Grange; there he learned that the mayor of Vizille, the town where in 1789 Mounier had first demanded a double representation for the Tiers État, had been deposed for what he had said in his address of welcome to La Fayette.

The chambers met on March 2, 1830. The deputies stated, in their reply to the address from the throne, that that harmony did not exist, that should exist between the policy of the government and the wishes of the people, and manifested their intention to resist. The government dissolved the chambers (May sixteenth). It was obvious that a crisis was approaching; the King stood firm, "The nation is against me," he said, "but I have duties toward God." La Fayette records that somebody said to him: "The whole trouble comes from the King; he will go to the limit; I don't know where that will lead us. Of all possible solutions I do not see one good one." La Fayette thought to himself, "That may be so for doctrinaires;

but for more resolute patriots I see a solution, if the people will back us."

In the new elections the liberals won; both La Fayette and his son were returned, and were waiting to attend the opening of the new session set for August third, when the report reached La Grange that the government had published counter-revolutionary ordinances. This was true; the King had suspended the liberty of the press, dissolved the new chambers, and changed the electoral law. The Constitution had been overthrown. The next day (July twenty-eighth) La Fayette was in Paris. Revolution was afoot. The government had stopped the radical newspapers, broken their presses, and turned the printers out on the street. The liberals did not sit with their hands in their pockets. Barricades were thrown up; an association of students chose La Fayette for their chief and made ready for insurrection; rioters effaced the royal emblems from public buildings. Cries echoed through the streets: *Vive la liberté! A bas les Bour bons!* Troops were stationed all about. La Fayette and thirty other deputies met; they declared the chamber not dissolved, and concerted means of resistance. Other deputies came in and doubled their numbers. The tricolor was hoisted. That same day there was fighting in the streets. From windows and housetops patriots hurled down all movable things on the soldiers below. La Fayette asserted that the deputies must name a provisional government, stating that "by the wish of the people, and with his approval, his name had been placed at the head of the rebellion." Rumor said that a republic had been proclaimed and La Fayette appointed president. Events moved fast. La Fayette was nominated commandant of the National Guard; Guizot said that the safety of Paris depended on his acceptance. He accepted: "My conduct at seventy-three shall be what it was at thirty-two."

Not only his conduct but his popularity with the crowd was what it had been forty years before. While the deputies were in conference some one rushed in crying: "There is great agitation outside, La Fayette's name is called everywhere, he must show himself to the people." He issued an order of the day:

"Dear Fellow Citizens, brave Comrades!

"The people of Paris once again call me to take command of their forces. I have accepted with devotion and joy . . . their behavior in these days of trial makes me prouder than ever to be at their head. Freedom shall triumph, or we will all perish together.

"*Vive la liberté! Vive la Patrie!*

"LA FAYETTE."

Defenses were thrown up in the adjacent streets, he says: "*Nous sommes admirablement barricadés.*" There was severe fighting; according to La Fayette, 163 soldiers were killed, 578 wounded, and of the citizens 788 killed, 4,500 wounded. The soldiers were beaten. Their officers withdrew them to Saint Cloud. La Fayette wrote: "The people of Paris have covered themselves with glory, and when I say *the people* I mean those usually termed the lowest classes of society, this time they have been the first; the courage, the intelligence, the devotion of the Parisians have been admirable." The poor King remarked: "Here I am in the position that my brother was in 1792." He sent to say that he would withdraw the counter-revolutionary ordinances. La Fayette declared: "Reconciliation is impossible, the royal family has ceased to reign."

Some republicans went to La Fayette: "General," they said, "if there is a monarchy the Duc d'Orléans will be king; if there is a republic, you will be president. Will you take the responsibility of a republic?" M. Charléty (in Lavisse) says: "Ce vieillard indécis est encore le maître de l'heure." (This undecided old man is still master of the hour.) La Fayette's indecision lay in the uncertainty as to what ought be done; he remembered the Jacobin Clubs, the Reign of Terror, and the differences between the French people, always at the mercy of the emotional population of Paris, and the comparatively sluggish American people, who, following the teachings of Washington, had instituted a successful republican government. He concluded that the French people, as Washington, Jefferson, Morris and other sagacious men of counsel and action had said, were not ready for a republic. And, be it remembered, if he was undecided, self-interest was never laid in the balances of indecision. "What we need," he said, "is a popular throne surrounded by purely republican institutions." The upshot was the acceptance of the Duc d'Orléans as Lieutenant-General of the Kingdom. Notification was given, and an Orleanist procession marched down the street; the Duc d'Orléans, with a great tricolor ribbon and a pocketful of pledges, entered the Hôtel de Ville. In the crowd, some applauded, some cried, "No more Bourbons!" La Fayette met him at the foot of the stairs, took him by the hand, and, though those present, being of many minds, showed little enthusiasm and some harsh remarks were heard, led him to the

window, put a tricolor flag in his hand, and embraced
him. The crowd outside shouted: *"Vive La Fayette!
Vive le Duc d'Orléans!"* Chateaubriand said that La
Fayette's republican kiss had made a king. As in the
earlier days of revolution, some have blamed him, some
have praised. Barère, the old member of the Committee of Public Safety, says in *Memoirs* that did not
appear until after his death: "In the popular revolution of 1830 La Fayette showed himself to be a great
citizen in the midst of public danger and the fires of
civil war. He never deserved so well of the country."
The *vieillard indécis* had indeed risen, like a phœnix,
from long oblivion to be what he had always wished
to be—*le modérateur* (Brissot's word) *le conciliateur*
(Suard's word)—of his country, this old La Fayette
*"qui deux fois en 1790 et en 1830 a tenu le sort de la
France en ses mains"* (who, twice, in 1790 and in
1830, held the fate of France in his hands).

Let us leave him at this. His reputation in Europe
was greater than ever. Metternich said to a French
general: "Your July days have crushed the foolish
dictatorship of the old King, and you will soon be
obliged to attack the majesty of M. de La Fayette."
But Metternich did not understand the fidelity of La
Fayette's character. Besides, La Fayette was old, and
the Duc d'Orléans, now Louis Philippe, Roi des
Français, entertaining some such apprehensions as
those of Metternich, took steps to remove him from
command of the National Guard. He still continued
to sit in the Chamber of Deputies, still continued to be
a rallying point for troubled patriots, and even for
riotous republicans, but his work was done.

On February 1, 1834, he caught cold while attend-
ing the burial of a friend's body in the cemetery of

Père Lachaise, and took to his bed. His last manifestation of his dominant passion was a letter written to the president of an Abolition Society in Glasgow, applauding action taken by the British Parliament for the emancipation of slaves. In the early morning of the twentieth, he seemed to come out of a stupor, and his son noticed that he put his hand to his chest fumbling. George understood, and put in his father's hand a medallion of his wife that he always wore on a string round his neck. It contained her picture and a lock of her hair. La Fayette lifted it to his lips and fell back into the stupor. So he died. Cloquet, the surgeon who attended him and wrote *Recollections of the Private Life of General La Fayette,* says that "all the distinguished residents in Paris, including the members of both legislative chambers, the academies, the civil and military administration, the national guard, refugees, foreigners, etc., assembled together to attend his interment." Barère, on the other hand, says that the government hedged the funeral procession about with soldiers, and let nobody come near. His body was taken to the Picpus Cemetery and laid in a grave beside that of his wife, and American earth from Bunker Hill was reverently laid upon it.

CHAPTER XXXVII

EPILOGUE

A FOREIGNER, a man of genius, happened to be in Paris soon after the revolution of July, 1830. He was a correspondent for a German newspaper, and on January 19, 1832, wrote a long account of La Fayette and of the esteem in which he was held by the French people. As he was an admirer of La Fayette, and believed in liberty and the high causes that La Fayette cherished, and perhaps prided himself on his own sympathy with high causes, for he says in one of his *Lieder,*

> *Denn ich selber bin ein solcher*
> *Ritter von dem heilgen Geist,*
> For I myself am likewise such
> A knight of the Holy Ghost,

I will quote at length what Heinrich Heine says:

"La Fayette is, next to Robespierre, the purest character in the French Revolution, and next to Napoleon he is their most popular hero. Napoleon and La Fayette are the two names in France that now bloom the fairest. Verily, their fame is of a different kind; La Fayette fought for peace more than for victory, and Napoleon fought more for the crown of laurel than for that of oak leaves. Verily, it would

411

be laughable to measure the greatness of the two heroes with the same measure, or to put one of them on the other's pedestal. It would be laughable to put La Fayette's statue on the Colonne Vendôme, on that column cast with the cannon captured in so many battles, which, Barbier sings, no French mother can bear to look upon. On this iron column stands Napoleon, the man of iron, here as in life planting his foot on his glory of cannon, and in dreadful isolation reaching to the clouds.

"La Fayette built a better column than that of the Place Vendôme, and a better monument than of metal or marble. What marble is so pure as old La Fayette's heart, what metal so steadfast as his honor? Verily, he was always pointing one way, but pointing one way like the needle of the compass that is always directed toward the north, and never once swerves to the south or the east. In that fashion La Fayette has repeated every day for forty years the same thing, and unceasingly points to North America. It was he that opened the Revolution with the Declaration of Rights; and to this very hour he persists in this Declaration, outside of which lies no salvation—the one way pointing man with his one way heaven of liberty! Verily, he is no genius, as Napoleon was, in whose head the eagles of inspiration built their nests, while in his breast the serpents of intrigue curled up, but he never let himself be browbeaten by the eagles nor tempted by the serpents. When a lad prudent as a graybeard, when a graybeard fiery as a lad, a protector of the people against the cunning of the great, a protector of the great against the fury of the people, pitying and defending, never arrogant, never despondent, equally strong and gentle, in such guise La Fayette has always been the same. And so in his one-sidedness and his steadfastness he remains always standing in the same place, since the time of Marie Antoinette to this very hour.

"It is indeed true, nevertheless, that the dead Napoleon is still more beloved by the French than is the living La Fayette. Probably from the very fact that he is dead; at least that is what I like best in Napoleon, for if he were alive I should feel obliged to fight for him. Outside of France no one has any idea how the French people are attached to Napoleon. For the French, *Napoleon* is a magical word that electrifies and overpowers them. A thousand cannon sleep in that name, as in the column of the Place Vendôme, and the Tuileries will tremble when those cannon wake up. You see his likeness everywhere, in prints and plaster, in metal and wood. On every boulevard, at every cross-street there are speakers that praise him, street minstrels that sing his deeds. Yesterday evening as I was going home I came upon a dark lonely alley; a child was there, not more than three years old, by a tallow candle stuck in the ground, who was chanting a song of the great Emperor's glory. As I tossed a penny into its outspread handkerchief, something glided up to me and also begged for a penny. It was an old soldier, who also might have sung a song on the great Emperor's glory, for that glory had cost him both legs. The poor cripple did not ask alms in God's name, but with most credulous fervour, 'In Napoleon's name give me a penny.' So his name serves for the strongest adjuration; Napoleon is their God, their cult, their religion. On the other hand La Fayette is honored more as a man than as a guardian angel. He, too, lives in pictures and poems, but less heroically.

His *bonhomie* affects even children, and they understand his greatness better perhaps than grown people do. Here again I can tell a little beggar's anecdote which marks how La Fayette's glory differs from that of Napoleon. A little while ago I was standing at a street corner in front of the Pantheon, and as usual looking at this noble building I was lost in a train of thought, when a little Auvergnat begged me for a penny, and I gave him a ten-cent bit, in order to be rid of him at once. But he came up closer to me trustfully with the words: 'Do you know about General La Fayette?' And as I answered yes to this strange question, a proud pleasure shone out in the pretty boy's dirty baby face, and with droll seriousness he said: 'He comes from my country.' He had confidence that a man who gave him ten cents must also be an admirer of La Fayette, and so he deemed me worthy to have him present himself to me as La Fayette's fellow countryman.''

It may seem extravagant in Heine to compare La Fayette with Napoleon. But Armand Carrel, ''one of the most generous and loyal men that have honored journalism,'' wrote: ''La Fayette and Napoleon, the two most renowned Frenchmen of this century, have died in these days when that France, that they set free and made glorious, stoops under the weight of misfortune. We say nothing of the official mourning for La Fayette as we say nothing of the restoration of the statue of Napoleon on the imperial column. France has other thoughts; she has ceremonies and memorials more worthy of her heroes, of her great citizens.''

It would be idle to quote, as I might, scores or hundreds of passages from those who spoke his eulogy or from those that blamed him. Almost all judge from a preestablished opinion of the best form of political government for France, or from personal motives. Undoubtedly he had his faults. He was overfond of the applause of the multitude—and yet he might answer that, as he would not use illegal force, popular following was the only instrument with which he could cast down what should be cast down and build up what should be built up. He lacked decision at certain times—not in going to America, not at Barren Hill, not when he cashiered ten officers and one hundred and eighty men of the National Guard for failure to do their duty, not when he suppressed the riot in the Champ-de-Mars, not when he came to Paris and denounced the Jacobin Club. And, even now, is it easy to tell the best course to have followed in the swirls and rapids of the Revolution, under the despotism of Napoleon, or during the uncertainties of 1830? He heeded too much the approbation of unimportant men, inexperienced in statecraft; perhaps he trusted them, and it hardly lay in the mouth of Mirabeau or of Talleyrand, to criticize him for not trusting such as they. He was not a man of genius, all agree to this; but he possessed a character compounded of courage, truth, loyalty, love of country, love of liberty and love of fame, that in the history of nations is of rarer occurrence than genius. France may not hold him among her great men, but in America, it is likely that his reputation will last as long as our history. The eulogies of famous Americans we may take for granted. I will rather cite the estimates of two or three of his countrymen, and first, two eminent historians. Thiers says: "La Fayette did not possess passion or genius to that degree that always ends in the abuse of power. His spirit was equable, his intelligence quick and comprehensive, his disinterestedness invariable; he was above all fitted to the rôle that circumstances had assigned him, of compelling observance of the law. Adored by his troops, though he had not captivated them by victory, full of resources in the midst of the fury of the crowd, he maintained order with indefatigable vigilance. Factions that had found him incorruptible, accused him of incapacity because they could not accuse his character." Guizot says: "I never knew a character more generous, more kindly to all, more attached to justice for all, more ready to risk all for his faith and his cause. His kindness, a little indiscriminate toward individuals, was none the less true and deep toward humanity in general. His courage and devotion were ready, ardent and serious under a sometimes careless exterior, and of a metal as good as it was gracious. He was constant, all his life, in his feelings and opinions, and he had days of vigorous resolution that would do honor to the stoutest friends of order."

I now proceed to a friend's judgment. Odilon Barrot, a lawyer and statesman of a younger generation, when he died in 1873 left this appreciation in a posthumous memoir: "This great citizen died on May 30, 1834. Perhaps he was too much my friend for me to be able to speak of him with complete impartiality. Even to-day, after so many years have glided by, after so many vicissitudes, I can not recall our relations to one another without deep emotion. I never met in any man more greatness of soul joined to so much kindness and simplicity; never a more complete faith in the rights of the people, joined to the most absolute devotion and the most heroic courage . . . and if one can address a reproach to this noble nature, it is the exaggeration of his good qualities. General La Fayette found it hard to suspect others of the evil from which he was free, and therefore bestowed his confidence too readily, and it was often abused. Carried away by the need of devoting himself, he was too much inclined to prefer enterprises in which he exposed his life to the patient and persevering efforts of legal struggle. When he said that 'the happiest day of his life would be when he should mount the scaffold in witness of his political faith,' he did not exaggerate, he merely expressed a sentiment natural to him. It was because liberty was religion to him. And if he had the faith of the martyrs, he had also their sublime resignation. No life in our modern times has displayed a nobler or more perfect unity.''

The summing up by Odilon Barrot I believe to be just, nevertheless I prefer to take leave of my subject with the estimate of a very subtle master in the art of tracing truth through the labyrinth of human actions and of human motives. Sainte-Beuve says: ''Taking him all in all, one may consider La Fayette, from the very beginning in 1789, as the most forward, the most intrepid and the most honest assaillant in the assault upon the old régime. There was always something of the knight in him, of the gallant foe, when he dashed at the breach in 1789, sword in hand, and when he reappeared as the general standard-bearer of the revolution of 1830. A very keen-sighted writer, M. Saint-Marc Girardin, praising La Fayette . . . conjectured that, had he lived in the middle ages, he would have founded by the power of a fixed moral idea, some religious order. I think that La Fayette, in the middle ages, would have been what he was in our day, a knight, always pursuing, after his own fashion, as if in quest of the Holy Grail, the triumph of the rights of man, or a crusader bound for the Holy Sepulchre, the right hand of the enterprise, the first aide-de-camp, under a Peter the Hermit, that is under the voice of God, in one of the great crusades.''

If one were to follow Socrates' speculations that the soul hereafter might repair to the abode where the souls of heroes dwell, and converse with them, my wish would be to behold La Fayette's feelings when, fourscore and three years after his bodily death, he looked down from his celestial habitation and saw France in danger, sorely pressed by foreign enemies, and a general in an American uniform standing by his grave in the cemetery of Picpus and heard him say: ''La Fayette, we are here.''

THE END

APPENDIX

APPENDIX

Authorities

GENERAL BIOGRAPHY

Mémoires, correspondances et manuscrits du général La Fayette, publiés par sa famille (1837-1838), 6 volumes.

This collection of documents, letters, etc., is the main source of our information concerning La Fayette's life. Of course, it presents facts from his point of view.

Le Général La Fayette 1757-1834, by Étienne Charavay (1898).

Charavay was an Archiviste-Paleographe and collected all the important reference to La Fayette's life. It is more of a book of sources than a biography.

La Jeunesse de la Fayette, by A. Bardoux (1892).

Les Dernières Années de La Fayette, by A. Bardoux (1893).

These contain little not to be found in the *Mémoires.*

There are several slight volumes by Henri Doniol.

Mémoires pour servir à la vie du général La Fayette et à l'histoire de l'Assemblée constituante, by Regnault-Warin (1824).

The author is rather a violent anti-Jacobin.

Various biographies have been written by Americans: by Ebenezer Mack (1841), by P. C. Headley (1865), by Bayard Tuckerman (1889), by George Morgan (1919). Bayard Tuckerman's was written before a great deal of important material became available.

CAMPAIGNING IN AMERICA

The Marquis de La Fayette in the American Revolution, by
Charlemagne Tower (1895).

This is a very complete account.

*Histoire de la Participation de la France à l'établissement des
États-Unis d'Amérique*, by Henri Doniol (1886-1892), 5
quarto volumes.

This elaborate work supplied Tower with the French
material in his book.

The Writings of George Washington, by Jared Sparks (1838).

Furnishes the correspondence between Washington and
La Fayette, etc.

South Carolina Historical and Genealogical Magazine,
Volumes VIII and IX; letters to Henry Laurens.

DURING THE FRENCH REVOLUTION

La Fayette comes into every book on this subject. If you
know the author's politics—that he is a conservative, liberal,
socialist or anarchist—you can easily infer his opinion on La
Fayette. Histories are legion. Carlyle is thought not to have
known very much concerning his subject. Taine is anti-
Jacobin. Aulard is pro-Jacobin, but a little troubled since
the Russian revolution and solicitous to draw distinctions
and explain how right-minded the Jacobins really were.
Lavisse is conscientious in pursuit of facts. Louis Madelin is
fair-minded. Bainville is a royalist. Biographers, too, are
usually biased; admirers of Mirabeau, Marat, Danton, Robespierre, and so on, are in consequence unjust to La Fayette.
For Mirabeau, see *Correspondance entre le comte de Mirabeau
et le comte de La Marck*, 1789-1791; for Marat's robbery of
the Ashmolean museum, see *Jean Paul Marat, his career in
England, etc.*, F. L. Phipson; for Danton's venality see Louis
Madelin; for Talleyrand's venality see *State Papers and
Publick Documents of the United States*, Vol. III, pp. 473-
479 etc.

Most memoirs of the time mention La Fayette; Bailly, Barère, Barras, Bouillé, Broglie, Mathieu Dumas, Dumouriez, Ségur, Madame de La Tour du Pin and a host of others, as well as the Americans, Gouverneur Morris, Thomas Jefferson and so on. See Charavay pp. 608-612 and *Bibliographie de l'Histoire de Paris pendant la Révolution française*, by Maurice Tourneux (1890-1894).

PRIVATE LIFE

Vie de Madame de La Fayette, by Madame de Lasteyrie (1868).

Vie de Madame la duchesse d'Ayen, by Madame de La Fayette (1868).

Anne-Paule-Dominique de Noailles, marquise de Montagu, by A. Callet (1869).

Souvenirs sur la vie privée du général La Fayette (Recollections of the Private Life of General La Fayette), by Jules Cloquet, M. D.

Cloquet was a surgeon who attended La Fayette and knew him intimately. The book was written at the request of an American and first published in English in a New York newspaper. The French version was published in 1836.

La France (1817), *France in 1829-1830*, by Lady Morgan (1830).

PRISON LIFE

Correspondance inédite de La Fayette, 1793-1801, by Jules Thomas (1903).

Here are La Fayette's letters in prison and in exile together with a not very illuminating psychological study.

Justus Erich Bollmann, by Fredrich Kapp (1880).

Statement of the attempted rescue of General La Fayette from "Olmutz" (189-). By friends and family of Colonel Francis Kinloch Huger.

La Fayette in Oesterreich, by Max Büdinger (1878).

VISIT TO THE UNITED STATES 1824-1825

La Fayette en Amérique en 1824 et 1825, by A. Levasseur (1829).

Lettres d'un cultivateur Américain etc., by Saint John de Crèvecoeur (1787) Volume III, French edition, p. 314-386.

Recollections of General La Fayette etc., by A. A. Parker (1879).

France and New England, by State Street Trust Company (1925).

Figures of the Past, by Josiah Quincy (1926).

Our Country Fifty Years Ago, etc., by Mrs. M. J. R. Lamb (1887).

An Account of General La Fayette's Visit to Virginia, etc., by Robert D. Ward (1881).

REVOLUTION OF 1830

La Fayette et la Révolution de 1830 etc., by B. Sarrans jeune (1834).

There are some collections of La Fayette's letters, and many random letters, that concern his private relations with American friends; those letters that I have seen merely corroborate my opinion of his character.

INDEX

INDEX

Adams, John, 51, 69, 135, 142
Adams, John Quincy, 402
Adelaide, Princess, 200
André, Major, 119
Arnold, Benedict, 118, 119, 120, 121, 123
Artois, Comte d' (Charles X), 149, 157, 160, 162, 177, 184, 230, 405, 407
Ayen, Duc d'
  his character, 8
  letter from La Fayette from London, 21
  letter from La Fayette from Pennsylvania, December 16, 1777, 49
  letter from La Fayette from Bristol, September 11, 1778, 93-94, 302
Ayen, Duchesse d'
  her character, 8-9
  visits Chavaniac, 270
  her death, 333

Bailly, 169, 177, 178, 181, 199, 251, 260, 261, 263, 272
Bardoux, 108
Barère, 410
Barnave, 169, 190, 254, 256
Barras, 351, 352, 356, 358, 384
Barren Hill, 70-73
Barrot, Odilon, 416-417
Bastille, 174, 175, 180
Beauharnais, 252
Beaumarchais, 19
Belloc, Hilaire, 110, 317
Bollmann, 286, 336-341

Bonaparte,
  see Napoleon,
Bonaparte, Joseph, 382
Bonaparte, Lucien, 383
Bouillé, Marquis de, 10, 202, 206-207, 218, 231, 232, 244, 245, 247, 250, 253
Brissot, 144, 145, 146, 210-211, 215, 225, 287, 301, 321, 328
Broglie, Comte de, 14, 17, 18
Broglie, Duc de, 386, 390, 391
Broglie, Duchesse de, 385
Brunswick, Duke of, 301
Bureaux de Pusy, 315, 346, 357

Calonne, 152, 153, 155, 156, 158
Canada,
  expedition, 57-67
  second proposed expedition, 96-97
Carlyle, 179
Carnot, 352
Carrel, Armand, 414
Cayenne,
  plantation at, 141, 142, 144
Champ-de-Mars,
  affair of July 17, 1791, 259-263
Charles X,
  see Artois, Comte d'
Chastelar, Marquis de, 312, 349
Chastellux, 120, 140
Chateaubriand, 183, 409
Chavaniac, 1
  La Fayette's visit there in 1791, 267
  La Fayette's visit there in 1829, 403

Chenier, André, 279
Choiseul, Duc de, 106
Clay, Henry, 400
Clinton, Sir Henry, 69, 70, 124
Cloquet, 410
Cochran, Doctor, 102
Condorcet, Marquis de, 109, 212
Condorcet, the philosopher, 140, 165, 280
Conway, General, 52, 57, 60, 64, 65
Conway's Cabal, 52
Cooper, Samuel, 101
Cordeliers, 185, 257, 259, 260
Cornwallis, Lord,
  at Brandywine, 39, 40
  in Virginia, 123-125
  at Yorktown, 126-132
Couthon, 244, 316

Danton, 165, 185, 233, 248, 253, 258, 264, 272, 280, 293, 303, 315, 316
Deane, Silas, 18, 19, 20, 21, 23, 25, 69
Deffand, Madame du, 25, 106
Desmoulins, Camille, 173, 191, 226, 258, 263, 264, 280, 293
Duer, Mr., 60
Dumouriez, 278, 279, 282, 288, 305
Duquesnoy, 211, 212

Elisabeth, Princess, 199, 251
Espinchal, Comte d', 108, 166, 168
Estaing, Comte d', 81, 82, 85, 86, 87, 88, 89, 91
Everett, Edward, 395

Favras, Marquis de, 230, 388
Fersen, Count, 251-252
Feuillants, 264
Fouché, 304
Foulon, murder of, 182-183
Francis II, Emperor, 281, 344, 345, 349, 350

Franklin, Benjamin, 20, 69, 101, 106, 134
French Alliance, 68
Frestel, 330, 331, 343

Gates, General, 52
Gibbs, Philip, 110
Gimat, 40
Gironde, political party, 276, 277, 278, 280, 281, 285, 286, 288, 314, 327
Gloucester, Duke of, 14-15
Grammont, Madame de, 343, 361
Grasse, Admiral de, 126, 127, 128, 129
Graves, Admiral, 129
Greene, Nathanael, General, 43, 83, 84, 116, 121, 123
Guizot, 407, 416

Hamilton, Alexander, 130, 363
Hancock, John, 34
Heine, Heinrich, 396, 411-414
Hénin, Madame de, 317, 325
Houdon, 125
Howe, Admiral, 87
Howe, Sir William, 38, 40, 71
Huger, Major, 30, 31
Huger, Young, 339-341

Isnard, 276

Jacobins, 236, 245, 264, 276, 278, 280, 301, 303, 306, 307, 313, 314, 326
Jacobin Club, 236, 237, 258, 264, 289-293, 296, 299
Jefferson, Thomas, 151, 154, 166, 169, 189, 243, 396, 399, 400
July 14, 1789, 174-175
July 17, 1791, 259-263, 264
June 20, 1791, 250-255

Kalb, Baron de, 17, 18, 27, 30, 43
Knyphausen, 39

La Fayette, Marquis de,
baptism, 1
birth, 2
autobiographical letter, 2-8
his father, 3
youth, 9-10
marriage, 10
meets Duke of Gloucester, 14
meets Baron de Kalb, 18
meets Silas Deane, 18
preparation for America, 21
at London, 21
letter to Duc d'Ayen, 21
to Bordeaux, 26
difficulties at starting, 26-27
sails for America, 28
voyage, 29
letter to wife, May 30, 1777, 29
at Charleston, 31
letter to wife, July 17, 1777, 32
received by Congress, 33
meets Washington, 35
Brandywine, 39
letter to wife, September, 12, 1777, 39
skirmish with Hessians, 47
letter to G. W., November 26, 1777, 47
appointed to active command, 48-49
expedition to Canada, 57
letter to G. W., February 9, 1778, 59
letter to G. W., February 19, 1778, 60
letter to G. W., February 23, 1778, 61
letter to Laurens, February 23, 1778, 62
letter to Laurens, March 12, 1778, 64
letter to Laurens, March 20, 1778, 67

La Fayette, Marquis de—con't.
reconnaissance, at Barren Hill, 70-73
letter to G. W., June 26, 1778, 75
at battle of Monmouth, 76-80
letter to G. W., June 26, 1778, 77
letter to G. W., same date, 78
letter to G. W., same date, 79
letter to Comte d' Estaing, 82
Newport Expedition, 81-91
quarrel with Sullivan, 88-89
ride to Boston, 90-91
letter to Laurens, 92
challenges Lord Carlisle, 98
leave of absence, 100
illness, 102
voyage to France, January, 1779, 103
arrival in Paris, 105
celebrity, 107
false scandals, 107
labors with government, 112
returned to United States, April, 1780, 115
Virginia campaign, 116-125
Yorktown, 126-133
welcomed in Paris, January, 1782, 133
republicanism, 135-136
visit to America, 1784, 136
Protestants, 138
negroes, 141
Assembly of Notables, 147
letter to G. W., 155
letter to G. W., August 3, 1787, 161
letter to G. W., October 9, 1787, 162
in Auvergne, 166
States-General, 169
Declaration of Rights, 172
Commandant of National Guard, 178

La Fayette, Marquis de—*con't.*
murder of Foulon, 182
clash with Danton, 186
mob to Versailles, October 5, 1789, 193
Versailles, October 5-6, 195-200
Duc d' Orleans, 202
Mounier, 206
Bouillé, 206
Mirabeau, 209-219
via Media, 213
dealings with King, 228
between Scylla and Charybdis, 228-237
Fête of Federation, July 14, 1790, 238-240
mutiny at Nancy, 243-245
riot at Vincennes, 246
conspiracy in Tuileries, 246
King attempts to go to Saint-Cloud, 247
resignation recalled, 249
flight to Varennes, June 20, 1791, 250
affair of Champ-de-Mars, July 17, 1791, 259
resignation as Commandant of National Guard, 265
waning popularity, 266
holiday at Chavaniac, 267
General on Belgian frontier, 273
dispute with Dumouriez, 282-283
dispute with Roland, 286-287
letter to Assembly, of June 16, 1792, 289
anger of Jacobins, 293
riot of June 20, 1792, 294
visits Assembly in person, June 28, 1792, 296
King refuses to cooperate, 297
further plan to get King to Compiègne, 298
further refusal, 299

La Fayette, Marquis de—*con't.*
motion to impeach La Fayette lost, 301
attempt to rouse Sedan, etc., for King, 304
unsuccessful attempts to induce army to move, 305
flight to Liège, 305
arrest by Austrians, 312
prisoner, 312
Magdebourg, 322
Olmütz, 334
attempt to escape, 336
joined by wife and daughters, 346
release, 354
life in Holstein, 363
interest in La Grange, 366
thoughts turn toward America, 367
Bonaparte in power, 371
La Fayette's return to France, 371
relations with Bonaparte, 372-374
death of his wife, 376
letter to Maubourg about wife, 376
share in Napoleon's abdication, 377
plots under Louis XVIII, 386
defies the King, 388
visit to America, 394-402
triumphal tour in southern France, 1829, 403-405
revolution of 1830, 406
La Fayette Commandant of National Guard, 407
street fighting, 407
acceptance of Duc d' Orléans as King, 409
end of career, 409
death, 410

La Fayette, Marquis de—*con't.*
  Heine on Napoleon and La Fayette, 411-414
  Armand Carrel's opinion, 414
  Thiers, 415-416
  Guizot, 416
  Odilon Barrot, 416-417
  Sainte-Beuve, 417-418
La Fayette, Anastasie, 320, 331, 363, 375, 380
La Fayette, George Washington, 343, 347, 372, 375, 376, 403, 410
La Fayette, Madame de, 8, 9
  letter to, May 30, 1777, 29
  letter to, July 17, 1777, 32
  letter to, September 12, 1777, 39
  letter to, October 1, 1777, 42-43
  letter to, October 29, 1777, 43
  letter to, January 6, 1778, 54
  letter to, February 3, 1778, 58
  letter to, September 13, 1778, 95
  letter to, August 24, 1781, 127, 144, 145, 222, 268-270, 280, 310
  arrest at Chavaniac, 320
  at Brioude, 329
  taken to Paris, 331
  execution of mother, sister and grandmother, 333
  her release, 343
  goes to Vienna, 344
  to Olmütz, 345
  joins La Fayette, 346
  illness in prison, 348
  release, 354
  sees Larevellière, 363
  sees Sieyès, 366
  sees Bonaparte, 371
  death, 376-379
Lameth, Alexandre, 190, 205, 306, 313
La Rochefoucauld, Duc de, 165, 170, 296, 298, 313, 323

Lasteyrie, Madame de (Virginie La Fayette), 143, 268, 344, 345-348, 350, 354, 375
La Tour-Maubourg, 313, 322, 326, 341, 346, 357, 362, 368, 377
Launay, de, Governor, 174, 175
Laurens, Henry, 41, 62, 63, 64-66, 67, 68, 73, 74, 97, 99, 100, 101
Laurens, son to Henry, 74, 96
Lee, Charles, General, 74, 76, 77, 78, 79, 80
Lefebvre, Maréchal, 359
Louis XV, 148
Louis XVI, 101, 105, 136, 148, 169, 170, 171, 172, 176, 180, 181, 191, 195, 198, 228, 229, 230, 239, 240, 247, 248, 250, 252, 255, 265, 288, 294, 295, 297, 298, 299, 302
Louis XVIII, 12, 148-149, 217, 230, 382, 384, 385
Louis Philippe, 408, 409
Lovell, 33, 34
Lückner, General, 274, 296, 299, 300

Madison, James,
  on La Fayette, 136-137, 154, 400
Maillard, 193
Malesherbes, 143, 144
Marat, 233, 244, 245, 254, 261-263, 264, 328
Marie Antoinette, 105, 134, 135, 148, 192, 193, 194, 197-199, 217, 229, 251, 255, 272, 297, 299
Maurepas, Marquis de, 24, 105, 130, 131
Mesmer, 145
Metternich, 409
Mirabeau, 165, 169, 171, 176, 202, 203, 204, 209-219, 224, 241-242, 247, 249, 391

Monmouth, battle of, 74-80

Monroe, James, 334, 343, 394, 400

Monsieur,
see Louis XVIII

Montagne, political party, 285, 286, 288, 327

Montagu, Madame de, 271, 361, 365

Morgan, Lady, 390

Morris, Gouverneur, 168, 182, 183, 202, 215, 216, 219, 224, 266, 277, 286, 301, 306, 354

Mouchy, Maréchal de, 10, 332

Mounier, 190, 205, 206

Nancy, mutiny at, 243-245

Napoleon, 257, 306, 309, 351, 352, 353, 356, 358, 368, 371, 372, 373, 374, 375, 380, 381, 382, 383, 384, 412-414

Narbonne, Comte de, 274, 277, 336

National Guard, 178, 239

Necker, 169, 173

Newport, expedition against, 81-92

Noailles, Adrienne,
see Madame de La Fayette,

Noailles, Louise,
see Vicomtesse de Noailles,

Noailles, Vicomte de, 8, 11, 16, 19, 20, 176, 187

Noailles, Vicomtesse de, 8
her death, 330

Notables, Assembly of, 147-163

October 5-6, 1789, 187-200

Orléans, Duc de (Philippe Égalité), 184, 185, 197, 202-205

Orléans, Duc de,
see, Louis Philippe,

Parish, 344, 354-355

Pétion, 272, 273, 295, 297, 298

Phillips, General, 3, 122, 123

Polignac, Prince de, 404

Rabaut, Paul, 143

Rabaut, the son, 143

Richmond, city of, 122

Robespierre, 223, 256, 263, 280, 293, 299, 314, 328, 333

Rochambeau, Comte de, 114, 116, 117, 118, 120, 126, 131, 255, 274, 284

Roland, 278, 286, 287, 288, 321

Roland, Madame, 260, 264, 278, 328

Rouget de Lisle, 281, 301

Saint-Simon, General, 127, 128

Sainte-Beuve, 417-418

Ségur, Comte de, 16, 19, 20, 23, 235, 390

Sieyès, Abbé, 236, 280

Simiane, Madame de, 108, 109, 361

Sparks, Jared, 24

Staël, Madame de, 215, 336, 351, 357, 358, 381, 391

Stark, General, 57

States-General (États-Généraux), 164-175

Steuben, Baron, 121

Sullivan, General, 39, 81, 82, 83, 85, 86, 87, 88, 89

Talleyrand, 240, 356, 359, 360, 373

Tessé, Madame de, 110, 140, 360, 363

Thiers, Adolphe, 415

Tour du Pin, Madame de La
quoted, 110, 146, 181, 196, 374

Valley Forge, 52, 67, 68

Vercingetorix, 1

Vergennes, Comte de, 15, 16, 68, 96, 105, 112, 113, 114, 125

Vergniaud, 275, 278, 328

Vigée-Lebrun, Madame, 109, 148

Vioménil, Baron de, 130

Virginia campaign, 116-125

Voltaire, 140

Washington, George, 35, 36, 116, 118, 119, 124, 127, 128, 129, 137, 139, 141-142, 155-156, 161, 162, 166, 168, 180, 225, 226, 265, 266, 335, 362

letter to Benjamin Harrison, 37

letter to President of Congress, 46

letter to La Fayette (Valley Forge), 53

letter to La Fayette, March 10, 1778, 66

Washington, George—*con't.*

letter to President of Congress, May 19, 1778, 73

letter to La Fayette, 78

at battle of Monmouth, 80

letter to La Fayette, 82

letter to La Fayette, 83

shadow of suspicion concerning expedition to Canada, 97

Wayne, General, 123, 124, 129

Yorktown, 126-134